S0-AKB-223

CLICKS AND MORTAR

Passion-Driven Growth in an Internet-Driven World

DAVID S. POTTRUCK
TERRY PEARCE

FOREWORD BY LEW PLATT

JOSSEY-BASS
A Wiley Company
San Francisco

Published by

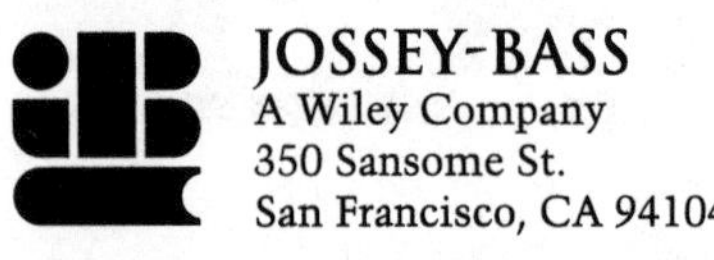

JOSSEY-BASS
A Wiley Company
350 Sansome St.
San Francisco, CA 94104

www.josseybass.com

Library of Congress Cataloging-in-Publication Data

Pottruck, David S., 1948-
Clicks and mortar : passion-driven growth in an Internet-driven world / David S. Pottruck, Terry Pearce ; foreword by Lew Platt.— 2nd ed.
p. cm. — (The Jossey-Bass business & management series)
Includes bibliographical references and index.
ISBN 0-7879-5688-0 (alk. paper)
1. Business enterprises—Computer networks. 2. Information technology—Management. 3. Internet. I. Pearce, Terry, 1941- II. Pearce, Terry. III. Title. IV. Series.
HD30.37 .P68 2001
658'.0546—dc21

SECOND EDITION
PB Printing 10 9 8 7 6 5 4 3 2 1

The Jossey-Bass
Business & Management Series

CONTENTS

For
Stephanie and Craig
&
Ainsley and Abigail

FOREWORD

When Dave and Terry first asked me to write this Foreword, I was in week one of being the official "former CEO" of Hewlett-Packard. For three consecutive days, I had gone to an office of relative calm; I was beginning to feel as though the remaining four months of daily activity at the company would stretch into an eternity of reflection and pencil tapping. Looking back, I concluded that I was fated to read this book, because as soon as I agreed, the phone began to ring as though the four months would be only four minutes. I immediately wondered why I had consented to take on such an important role with regard to a publication I really hadn't reviewed.

I soon found out.

Clicks and Mortar: Passion-Driven Growth in an Internet-Driven World discusses the most important business transformation I have encountered in thirty-three years of experience. The Internet and its companion technologies are changing the very boundaries of a company . . . they are causing us to literally redefine what it means to *be* a company. The revolution affects every area of commerce: financial models, leadership, measurement, and marketing. The network is changing the relationship of a company with all the actors: suppliers, stockholders, employees, and—most of all—customers. I had worked with these realizations every day for nearly ten years. Dave and Terry have captured the essence of these changes and given us a primer on how established companies in established businesses can move into the new millennium successfully.

This is a comprehensive book, yet it is written in a style that presents vitally important ideas in easy-to-understand language. There are two voices in the narrative, one of a considered and practiced consultant and teacher, and the other of a proven, successful operator of a major American corporation. The combination allows us to understand the concepts mentally, and then to appreciate them emotionally and practically through real-life examples. We don't have to wonder whether the ideas work; they are already working at one of the most successful financial services companies in the world, The Charles Schwab Corporation. The authors have not only worked at the Internet's transformation of business, they have codified it for others to critique and apply as they choose.

Clicks and Mortar looks at the three most significant aspects of this business transformation in what I consider to be their order of importance. First is the building and sustaining of a culture based on strong values. Bill Hewlett and Dave Packard believed in this idea so strongly that they wrote down our values and practiced them every day. Those values became the foundation of a culture now known as "The HP Way." I'm convinced that sustaining that culture was the single most important enabler of Hewlett-Packard's ability to change so easily and so frequently throughout our sixty-year history.

It is unusual, in today's world, to find a book with such an emphasis on character as the way to build passion. Yet I know that strong values allow everything else to change, and they unleash passion because people care about them, want to be associated with them. In *Clicks and Mortar,* we see how to build and sustain such a values-based culture through story, ritual, and image.

The Internet makes everyone who is interested aware of anything they want to know. That fact puts tremendous responsibility on the leadership of a company as well as the company itself. Integrity has new meaning when your customers and employees can see everything you do. In the second section of the book, Dave and Terry explain what this means in terms of day-to-day personal conduct and day-to-day business decision making. The change required from pre-Internet times is profound.

Then, in the third section, the authors look at some fundamental business practices and give us some guidance in adapting traditional business concepts to the Internet world. They chose the practices of measurement, marketing, and the management of technology as the disciplines that would be the most important in the next decades. I agree with them. Measurement will change dramatically because we are so much more aware of relationships—of how everything affects everything else. Marketing will move from mass merchandising back to one-to-one relationship building. As for the management of technology, it is hard not to agree that we will either shape it or it will shape us. It presents marvelous opportunities and perhaps equally daunting dangers. Dave and Terry discuss both possibilities.

There are several ideas in *Clicks and Mortar* that I will shamelessly use in my transition at Hewlett-Packard and in my later work. Here are just a few:

- In the same way that a strong culture holds a leader's feet to the fire, the Internet holds a brand to the fire. What you purport to be . . . you had better be. Otherwise, you will be discovered as a fraud and be punished for it.
- A truly visionary company survives its founders. Bill Hewlett and Dave Packard knew this early, and started to build, in the fabric of the company, the values and practices necessary to make it possible for others to lead. That idea is inherent in this book.
- Building culture on purpose is more difficult than "letting it happen." It may be a surprise, but in the long run, established companies could have a distinct advantage over start-ups that don't pay attention to values. Start-ups might have the edge in technology, but established companies might have an edge in what really matters.

Finally, there is an idea in the bridge passage between Chapters Eight and Nine that I believed in long before Dave and Terry asked me to write this Foreword. Their synopsis reminded me of its importance. "Passion is built . . . by making good promises, making good on those promises, and by giving people a chance to collectively and individually respond to their impulse to serve, to make a difference for others."

This was a good idea before the Internet world. In the Internet world, it is an operational imperative.

My daughter, Hillary, is, right now, helping to set up "cyber-cafés" in Africa. What is a cyber-café? It is a place where people who otherwise could not have access to ideas beyond their small communities will have access to all ideas, from all parts of the world. People can come in off of the street, get on the Net, and converse with anyone they wish, access any information they want. Will this have an impact on that society? Of course—in the same way that information technology had an impact on the Iron Curtain. In a real way, people will find the truth on the Internet and the truth will, over time, set them free. In the meantime, there might be a struggle or two.

In the last chapter of this book, I get a chance to join a dialogue about the future and these same topics with Dave, Terry, and seven of my most distinguished colleagues. But before you read that last chapter, you have a treat in store. Enjoy.

December 1999
Palo Alto, California

Lew Platt
Former Chairman and CEO,
Hewlett-Packard

PREFACE TO THE PAPERBACK EDITION

Clicks and Mortar was first published in April of 2000. We did most of the writing in 1999, a year when "dot-coms" were swarmed over by venture capitalists and later by stock traders cashing in on the first wave of the Internet. The World Wide Web made many things possible for the first time. Barriers to entry came down in a variety of businesses. Amazon.com and eBay were the predominant models for "pure-play" virtual businesses, minimizing the need for physical facilities, doing business solely over the Internet. Cisco, Intel, and others made their mark by providing the hardware and services that would supply the "backbone" of the network. Other companies pioneered the virtual business-to-business model, providing software and services via the Web to others who served the ultimate consumer. Still others proposed to provide a variety of valuable information to consumers for free and developed business models that showed future revenue sources from site advertisers and referrals. There was a frenzy to find the next application and a frenzy to invest.

At the same time, many established businesses—particularly those that had been in the traditional "bricks and mortar" environment of stores, branches, offices, and warehouses—didn't know if or how to respond to this wonderful new international and fundamentally free network.

This environment of hype, excitement, and confusion was the crucible for our writing.

In response to this context, many companies concluded that "clicks and bricks"—a combination of Web and physical presence—was the correct model. Companies such as Gateway Computer and large financial services houses such as Merrill Lynch and PaineWebber added the missing component, offering their customers multiple ways to access their products and services through stores or offices and on-line.

But the critical component of success in this environment is not multi-channel access, although such an offering is necessary. Rather it is the passion of the people who operate the business. This is the "mortar" that holds a company together, regardless of the modes of delivery. This is the central theme of *Clicks and Mortar*. . . . Its timing could not have been better.

Early in the summer of 2000, we were invited to a dinner meeting of several dot-com CEOs and venture capitalists at a home in Silicon Valley. The stocks of most of the companies represented that evening had suffered substantial market corrections. The subject of discussion was "values, value, or valuation: which is the most important?" The somewhat somber group concluded that while valuation (market capitalization based on expectation of future earnings) seemed critical and value (the value proposition for clients) was essential to raise more capital, in the long run, it is *values* themselves (the principles expressed in the company mission) and the drive of the entrepreneurial founders to inspire employees to build something substantial and meaningful, that are the sustainers of business success.

The Internet has had two major impacts on the world of business. First, it has emerged as a new channel for buying, selling, and other discourse, a channel that is not impeded by the boundaries of geography or politics. In this function, the Internet is a very effective electronic way to create relationships. Second, it has multiplied the power of individual employees and customers, allowing them to hold a business responsible, to hold its integrity to the fire every single day. Accordingly, it has created new and greater demands on business leaders.

Our original premise is proving to be at least substantially accurate as this transformation continues; therefore, we have changed very little of the text in the first edition. However, in presenting the material, we now clarify two distinctions that are made in that edition. In Chapter One, we comment on the four functions of culture and suggest the first one as a foundation that doesn't change as everything else is changing. We now speak about that idea in these terms: *people hate change, but they love progress.* The difference between the two is a sense of purpose—a shared purpose—provided by a culture that is intentionally built.

In Chapter Four, we suggest that character is dependent on appearances and perceptions as much as reality. We now explain this idea by suggesting that while leaders experience themselves from their *intention,* others experience the leader from their *interpretation* of his words and actions. Therefore, while a leader may intend to inspire, his position, physical characteristics, demeanor, or actions may be threatening rather than inspiring to some. Each leader, as an individual, is responsible not only for his intention but also for being aware of the possible interpretation of others—and adapting.

Some of the participants in the last chapter of the book ("Dialogue on the Future") have changed titles and roles. Since the chapter has not been modified, it reflects their affiliations and positions at the time of that discussion.

One of our primary motives for writing *Clicks and Mortar* was to provide the seed for training executives and managers to be successful during this reformation. We would both like to express our gratitude to Christy Tonge and the design and implementation team at BlessingWhite for their unmitigated success in creating and delivering a program of quality and impact that is beyond even our expectations. The comments from the initial sessions suggest that the "movie" this team has fashioned is, in fact, more powerful than the book.

We hope *Clicks and Mortar* will prove to be a valuable and lasting contribution to your life as well.

January 2001 DP
San Francisco, California TP

PREFACE

It turns out that the Buddhists are right: nothing is permanent and everything is interdependent. Indeed, change and interconnectedness were the two central business themes of the last two decades of the twentieth century. As more countries became part of the great world of the Internet, as more and more people around the world gained the power to change things, change naturally accelerated. The network creates a need for itself to grow. The Internet has spawned entire *new* industries and has had major impact on all companies that supply knowledge and technology for its expansion.

The Internet has also had a profound influence on *established* businesses, businesses that are still engaged in the same fundamental arena as before but that have faced the challenge of adapting to the environment created by a worldwide technology network. Five workers sharing an e-mail system is a productivity enhancement; a hundred million people, many of them your customers, on-line to your central systems is a whole new way of life. The Internet seems to be part of an external environment that is dictating not only what leaders must do but also the pace at which they must do it. Many leaders, regardless of the organization, are beginning to feel uncomfortable about moving into the future at "warp speed"—and without total control of the ship.

Increasing speed of change, decreasing control of the throttle . . . not a dynamic that lends itself to old theories. The speed and seeming chaos raise a myriad of questions both inside of work and outside. The questions we address in *Clicks and Mortar: Passion-Driven Growth in an Internet-Driven World* boil down to this: How do we marry technology and people to create an inspiring place to work? What does it take to continue to grow a company in today's environment? Our central premise is the proposition that the spirit and passion of people are the ingredients essential to organizational success in such a world.

WHY CLICKS AND MORTAR?

"Clicks" represent the Internet, where the world of information is a click away. But we are not driven or inspired by mere digital purity, by the virtually unlimited information available on the Internet and the World Wide Web. We are inspired by our passion for providing meaning from it, by creating something from the chaos that makes a difference to others. Passion has always driven growth, and passion is even more important in today's world. For it is passion and conviction that hold people and their companies and customers together in the Internet world. The passion that created the business, the passion that drives employees and that creates loyal customers—that is the "Mortar."

Start-up companies seem to automatically inspire passion and conviction in the "garage to penthouse" dreams of their founders. But how do they maintain it? And how do existing companies find and inspire this passion and conviction in people, some of whom might be used to working in a more static and reliable environment? How do these companies use passion to drive change and growth? These questions—and our answers—arise in part from our experience of working together at one of the world's fastest-growing and most innovative financial services companies.

WHY US?

We've seen and been part of the remarkable shift in the business environment brought by the clicks of the computer; we know, firsthand, that passion is the all-important mortar of the Internet world. With our combined backgrounds, we bring a unique perspective to the topic. Our collective experience is academic, consultative, and operational. Between the two of us, we've studied, taught, advised, and actually had to apply the principles that we speak of here in a wide variety of circumstances.

When we met late in 1992, Dave had become president of The Charles Schwab Corporation and president and CEO of its chief subsidiary, Charles Schwab & Co., Inc. Terry was a university teacher and communication consultant who coached executives in authenticity and inspiration. We were destined to spend the next few years in partnership, as Dave grew to become co-CEO with Charles "Chuck" Schwab of the entire corporation, and Terry built his practice and authored *Leading Out Loud*, a highly acclaimed book on leadership communication. Having spent a few years with his hands on the levers of a small part of IBM, Terry understands the real issues of trying to make the numbers work without doing the work yourself. But his primary emphasis for the last twenty years has been the application of leadership *by others*, as a consultant, writer, coach, and university teacher. His is a conceptual perspective that is largely unmarked by battle scars. His practice and teaching responsibilities provide great opportunities to read theory and to see principles at work in different organizations and with different leaders.

Conversely, Dave has put all of the concepts to the test. Although he's also had a background as an adjunct university teacher, he's found his greatest success in operations, in actual leadership. He's spoken to audiences of employees and year after year searched for ways to keep them inspired, sometimes even when executive decisions are being broadly questioned. He's coached other executives in the firm, occasionally reaching the dreadful conclusion that one of them just couldn't grow fast enough to keep up and would have to be replaced. He's participated in many big decisions to launch products, funded multimillion-dollar projects, expanded into new businesses, and occasionally made "bet the future" commitments.

Together, we have explored the very tough issues of growing and transforming a business at a time of unprecedented change in the industry. Our shared experience makes us especially suited to explore the questions of the future for a number of reasons.

First, no business is more of a pure bellwether for the new economy—where information is power and rapid change its currency—than financial investment services. Thanks to electronic information and transactions, there is precious little time to enjoy competitive advantage in the actual products Schwab offers, so the only true differentiation is in the way in which the company serves customers and the speed with which we innovate on their behalf. Buying a hundred shares of IBM will have the same impact on a portfolio pretty much wherever a customer does the transaction. But the *way* in which that service is delivered—the total experience that the customer has in the process of the transaction, how the customer trusts the company he or she deals with, the company's ability to introduce innovations ahead of competitors—these things differentiate one firm from others.

Second, because Schwab and the industry depend on technology, people, and the interaction between the two, growing profitably requires leadership that generates the loyalty of people both inside and outside the company. It takes passionate leadership to establish the right environment for employee and customer relationships to develop and grow strong in an atmosphere of mutual trust, respect, and excitement.

Because of its significance in the world of business and our depth of involvement there, many of the examples we present are from recent experiences at Schwab. But this is not the Schwab story. Much as we hope that story will be written someday—by the founder and spiritual leader of the company, Charles Schwab—this book reaches far beyond Schwab on a number of levels. We have looked to other successes and failures in the analysis and in the conclusions that we draw and the recommendations that we make. Further, while much of our work has been about business issues, an equal amount has been "thought partnering" about our own growth—the issues we face in our lives as human beings and how we move through them to greater levels of happiness and effectiveness. We have spent many hours talking about the things that matter the most to us: our families, our relationships outside of work, our spiritual practices and disciplines, our mental and emotional progress. It is in the integration of business and life that we have found the ingredients of passion and conviction, the mortar that holds it all together. The objective and the subjective, the clear and the deep, these have come together to give the information in the book a much richer context than simply growth of market share and revenue.

In the process of writing this book, we used our strengths and experiences, collectively. Because Terry's strength is in language and Dave's in operations, we have written the section openings and the bridges from one chapter to the next in Terry's voice, and the chapters themselves in Dave's. But we cannot separate the ideas so easily. Our relationship continues to be one of real synergy . . . often we can't remember who said what first. We just know it is mostly Terry's responsibility to write and Dave's responsibility to act. With that understanding, we think the mixture of voices is more interesting to read.

Like all authors, we struggle with the "pronoun problem," with using a shorthand that acknowledges women and men equally. The solution we are most comfortable with is that of alternating between "he" and "she." If it startles our early grammar teachers, so be it; breaking the old pattern seems worth the risk. It is, after all, just a small part of the changes ahead.

WHAT'S HERE?

In our experience, there are three essentials—building culture, practicing a particular brand of leadership, and using a handful of management disciplines—to igniting the fire that is necessary to generate the loyalty and commitment, the energy and the courage, that are necessary to integrate the Internet and to continue to build a great company. This book is about such organizational transformation. It is also, by necessity, a primer of personal change, of learning the difference between managing for compliance and control and leading for passion and commitment.

We examine the topic in three main sections, each of which is introduced in Terry's voice. Part One, "Culture at the Core: Creating a Passionate Corporate Culture in the Internet Age," explores the corporate culture as the primary driver of growth. In Chapter One we describe how such a culture is created on purpose, using the vision and values of a company as the foundation. In Chapter Two we illustrate how a meaningful culture is sustained through story, image, and ritual, in order to constantly realign people around what they care about and set them free to contribute their very best to the ideals of the company. Chapter Three discusses the inevitable role of diversity in forming and sustaining a postmodern company culture, and how the very best leaders leverage it to inspire everyone in the firm.

Part Two, "Leadership Practices: Inspiring Passion-Driven Growth," deals with the new leadership required in such a passion-driven culture, discussing how personal leadership can balance the inherent objectivity of technology to form an atmosphere where risk and failure are part of the growth process and communication part of the nourishment. Chapter Four is about the leader as role model, and points out how the leader's personal integrity is critical to success in this world of expanding information and decreasing privacy. Chapter Five details the requirements of leadership communication, what differentiates it from "other" communication as a vehicle to inspire contribution. Chapter Six addresses the importance of innovation itself, how leadership can actually create a field where breakthrough thinking is possible from nearly everyone in the firm.

Part Three, "Management Practices: Bringing Passion to the Internet World," picks from the array of management practices those we believe are most critical and most affected by the pace of competition in an Internet world. We discuss how traditional business functions such as advertising, marketing, branding, budgeting, recruiting, and performance appraisals—often considered to be bureaucratic, analytical, and boring—can be used to create new levels of inspired commitment. In Chapter Seven we distinguish between measuring the business and measuring the people who run the business, and then describe how to establish metrics for both that become dynamic and enabling rather than passive and stifling. In Chapter Eight we discuss the important tasks of managing technology and partnering with technologists. We look at how a company can maintain the enthusiasm and engagement of a technical staff in this Internet world of talent deficits. Chapter Nine is about marketing in the world of the Web, when people have more information than ever, more choices than they can manage, and an attention span that is growing shorter. Chapter Ten speaks to the customer experience itself, how the importance of personal relationship grows as the number of impersonal contacts with the company increases. Each of the first ten chapters ends in Terry's voice, with thoughts on the implication of the chapter's content and a look ahead to the next chapter or part. Beyond this overview, Terry also includes specific pointers about actually applying the principles discussed.

Finally, we look ahead through our eyes and those of eight distinguished business and academic leaders, and give a synopsis of our private on-line chat room discussion about the critical factors for commercial growth in the future, as the Internet and its follow-ons increase their impact on our lives.

We were asked at the outset of the project to define the essence of this book, the most important message for readers. In summary, it is this. The book is what we know about growing as a leader, in every dimension, and expressing that leadership in the context of a leading business operating in a networked world. It includes the ways we have learned to increase competence and trustworthiness, and it also includes ways of increasing revenue and income. If we've met our goals, you will finish reading *Clicks and Mortar* armed with new tools to grow a business, some insight into what it will take to grow yourself at the same time, and a strong sense that the two are inseparable.

December 1999
San Francisco, California

Dave Pottruck
Terry Pearce

ACKNOWLEDGMENTS

Writing this book was both a project and a process. It required not only inspiration, but an immense amount of sheer hard work in testing ideas, sorting research, and attending to details of the actual production. We have enjoyed the best of partners throughout, both professionally and personally.

A small group provided immense support by managing demanding schedules to allow us to stay reasonably productive. These included Colleen Bagan-McGill, Miki Grandin, Paulette Dorsey, Tony Berry, Rita Becker, and Daniela Morgan. Yet another cadre of colleagues supplied valuable counsel about content, including Michael Alexander, Jeff Benton, Bob Duste, Kirsten Garen, Gerald Graves, Jackie Hipps, Jeff Lyons, Michael McGrath, Phil Nicolaou, Brad Peterson, and Mark Phillips. All of them gave the time and effort to read preliminary drafts and offer wonderful suggestions. Roberta Cairney not only participated with this group, she also collaborated with Linda Stoick, Brian Belardo, and Gale Gebstadt to make the complicated details of contracts, legal, regulatory compliance, and publishing arrangements seem easy. Evelyn Dilsaver continued to monitor manuscripts and provide great counsel throughout the process, and Emily Scott Pottruck read every word of every chapter, making a host of substantive contributions to the content.

Eight executives participated in forming the final chapter of the book; their dialogue was instructive and thought-provoking. It was also time-consuming, and they were gracious and precise with their comments. Our thanks to Steve Ballmer, Leonard Berry, Tom Gerrity, Bill Harris, Lew Platt, Condoleezza Rice, Eric Schmidt, and Ann Winblad. Lew Platt also generously wrote the Foreword, a contribution that was a true gift, particularly given the continuing demands of his own transition at Hewlett-Packard.

We owe special thanks to Ken Askew, who made initial sense out of reams of material and provided a preliminary "cut" of some of the chapters; Mary-Claire Blakeman, whose imaginative mind gave birth to the title of the book; and Paula Nichols, who checked facts, tracked down references, and gained permissions with tidelike persistence.

It's hard to imagine better publishing partners than Jossey-Bass executive Cedric Crocker, senior editor Susan Williams, and developmental editor-extraordinaire Jan Hunter. They pressed at just the right times; Cedric and Susan keeping us true to the themes and on time, while Jan tirelessly provided direction that made the book far broader in reach than it would otherwise have been. More than focusing merely on clarity and precision, she kept pressing for depth; a dimension important to us both. Our sincere thanks also go to Cheryl Greenway, Judith Hibbard, Karen McChrystal, Hilary Powers, Kathe Sweeney, and Jeff Wyneken, integral to our production team at Jossey-Bass.

In truth, the inspiration for the book came primarily from the employees at The Charles Schwab Corporation, who provide the model for most of the ideas with their day-to-day work and their loyalty and dedication to their mission. Our thanks to them.

And of course, each of us was individually supported in the process by people close to us.

As Dave says:

> The book is a culmination of many influences, and I've been blessed by having inspiring men and women in my life as role models. Of course, Dad and Mom are first, but right behind is Chuck Schwab, who taught me that the idea of "doing well while doing good" was not

a fantasy. His steadfast faith in the principle of "customer-first" is a model for our industry and for our entire business community. Chuck's confidence in what I could become, and in fact what our entire enterprise could become, is what has made this whole journey possible.

Larry Stupski was a challenging boss, and one of the most talented businessmen I've ever met. From him, I learned the value of analysis, the importance of detail and the power of tenacity and faith.

There are others who had long and lasting impact on my business acumen and my character, including Ed Fels, Joe Plumeri, Ed Valencia, Larry Lauchle, Don Frey, and Joe Martone. I hope I can influence others with even a fraction of their effectiveness.

Clearly the best coaches I've had around the ideas in *Clicks and Mortar* are the members of the planning committee at Schwab: John Coghlan, Linnet Deily, Lon Gorman, Dan Leemon, Dawn Lepore, Beth Sawi, and Steve Scheid. No one could ask to work with a more talented and forthright group of people. Their incredible performance and honest feedback continue to help me learn how to lead more effectively.

My wife, Emily, is not only a good editor, she is simply the best listener I have ever met, and her patience is beyond reason. She somehow manages to provide unparalleled support for me while making her own substantial contributions to the world. In like manner, my kids, Steph and Craig, allow me to recognize that life is not just about work. Parenting is mostly about practicing humanity, and they have made me a better dad and a better friend to others in the process.

Now to Terry:

Writing is hard for me, and I'm rather self-absorbed when I'm in the process. I suspect that attitude made it very difficult for people to be around me for the year or so that this project took. If so, they were gracious enough not to tell me, and I have emerged with some friendships intact. My thanks to Sharon Landes and Jeff Rosenthal for masterfully teaching my university class, and to my confidant and business partner, Kim Soskin. A more understanding friend does not walk the earth.

Thanks too, to Mina Solemani, an extraordinary model of love and courage, and to Isa Foulk and Sandra Hopkins for unrelenting positive reinforcement.

I also owe a great deal to Lonnie Barbach, an insightful and thoughtful coach; to Gary Fiedel for keeping me practical and on course; and to Mark and Bonita Thompson, for staying "way out there" in the world, and reminding me of the possible reach of good ideas and adventurous spirits.

Jim McNeil, Darlene Anaman-Perry, Paul Burns, and Leni Miller provide my spiritual underpinning. I am fortunate to have them in my life. And Karen Chang is an irrepressible spirit and brilliant business mind who helped me beyond what she could possibly know.

Family does it all. To Jeff and Alissa, Joel and Jennifer, and my daughter Jodi, my thanks for understanding and support. To Hayden Mackenzie, and to Abigail and Ainsley—the most recent additions to the Pearce group—big hugs.

And finally, our thanks to one another, for a partnership that clearly brings out the best in both of us. We have inspired each other's finest work and helped each other grow in ways we could not have achieved alone. Throughout this odyssey of seven years, our collaboration has expanded; more important, our friendship has deepened. We hope the book reflects that friendship as much as anything else.

San Francisco, California DP
TP

ABOUT THE AUTHORS

David S. Pottruck is president, co-CEO, and a member of the Board of Directors of The Charles Schwab Corporation. Dave oversees all the company's businesses and strategic development worldwide. He joined Schwab in 1984.

As co-CEO with Chuck Schwab, Dave led the firm's expansion beyond discount brokerage into its position as one of the foremost distributors of mutual funds in the United States. He oversaw the move into Internet investing in 1996. In 1998, Schwab became widely recognized as the world leader in on-line investing and the model for traditional firms to reinvent themselves by thoroughly integrating their Internet and physical distribution systems. Dave was named CEO of the Year by Morningstar in 1999 and was designated "the year 2000's most influential executive of the mutual funds industry" by *Smart Money Magazine*.

Before joining Schwab, Dave was senior vice president of consumer marketing and advertising for Shearson/American Express. His prior experience was with Citibank. He graduated from the University of Pennsylvania with a B.A. and received his M.B.A. with honors from Wharton.

His contributions to the fields of marketing and management include publishing several articles and teaching at the graduate level at several universities, including State University of New York and the Haas School of Business at the University of California, Berkeley.

Dave serves on the Board of Directors of Intel, McKesson HBOC Corporation, Preview Travel, Inc., the NASD, and the U.S. Ski and Snowboard Team Foundation. He is a trustee of the University of Pennsylvania. He served as a congressional and presidential appointee of the Advisory Commission on Electronic Commerce.

Dave is past co-chair of the San Francisco AIDS Foundation (SFAF) Leadership Dinner, and the recipient of the SFAF 1994 Leadership Award. He is a past president of the Board of Trustees of the Seven Hills School.

A native of New York, Dave lives in San Francisco, California, with his wife, Emily. He is the father of two grown children.

Terry Pearce is founder of Leadership Communication, a San Francisco Bay Area–based company that offers one-to-one coaching and leadership communication programs to corporate, political, and community leaders. The content and method of his coaching are radical departures from conventional wisdom, and are designed to move people to commitment rather than mere compliance, inspiring new levels of contribution and innovation.

Terry is grounded in business, having been a manager and executive with IBM for seventeen years. His business clients include executives at Fortune 500 companies as well as senior public officials and elected leaders. He has spearheaded communication projects that won both the Golden Quill award from the International Association of Business Communicators and the Compass award from the American Association of Public Relations.

His book *Leading Out Loud* was honored by "Executive Summaries" as one of the thirty best business books of 1995, and as "one of the best books on speaking ever written." Terry developed and teaches a highly rated course in leadership and communication at both the Haas Graduate School of Business at the University of California at Berkeley and at the London Business School. His video presentation on authentic speaking is featured in Stanford University's catalogue of Executive Briefings. He is a frequent speaker on the subjects of leadership, communication, and the intentional building of corporate culture.

Terry is a former director of the Healthy Cities Project, Institute for the Study of Social Change, University of California at Berkeley; and a former director of the Partnership for a Drug-Free California. In the mid-1980s, Terry frequently traveled to the then Soviet Union, pioneering U.S. business activities. He is the co-founder of Partners, a company that continues to facilitate joint ventures in Russia.

Terry earned his B.S. in business administration, Magna Cum Laude, from Linfield College, Oregon, and his Certificate, IBM Advanced Financial Management, from Harvard Business Faculty in La Hulpe, Belgium.

He has three grown children and lives in Novato, California.

PART ONE

CULTURE AT THE CORE

Creating a Passionate Corporate Culture in the Internet Age

We all live inside a culture. It is the water we swim in; we don't often see it because it is given. Culture is the sum of our beliefs, what we accept as right and wrong, and all the expressions of those beliefs. A nation's culture speaks to us through its many languages: its poetry, its prose, its art, through the actions that it takes and the alliances it builds—and, perhaps not so obviously, through its forms of government and commerce. A company's culture has the same indicators.

Dave and I believe that in this business world driven by the Internet, which requires rapid and continuous innovation to compete, corporate culture is the central competitive advantage. It is for this reason that we address the fundamental aspects of culture—what it is, why it is important, and how it is built and sustained—in the first part of this book. Culture is the underlayment, the foundation.

As a consultant and teacher, I define *corporate culture* as "a set of values, a shared purpose, a common language, and all the actions that make the values real." I further define *values* as the "nonnegotiable tenets against which we measure the worthiness of our choices." Accordingly, the values inherent in a culture are the basis for creating meaning for those who live and work in it.

Please notice that values do not always *dictate* our behavior, but they do form the basis for our judgment of the worthiness of that behavior. This may seem like an academic distinction, and if we were merely observing culture, it would be exactly that. But when we begin to build culture rather than observe it, this distinction between the actual and the ideal forms the primary measuring stick for our success. Building culture is deliberate and difficult. It is not, as some of the business press would have us believe, done merely by wearing casual dress and having beer and pizza parties on Friday nights. It is, at its heart, a thoughtful and lasting endeavor that starts with defining what is most important to us at the core.

So why do such hard work? Why would we want to build a culture, anyway? The answers to these questions lie in the new reality of business.

As recently as the 1970s, culture was a very squishy thing to most corporate executives in the United States. It was only after we began to get our business brains beaten out by Japanese companies that favored consensus and participation that we paid any attention at all to the intangible, sometimes difficult to measure, softer elements that inspired workers to produce more and better goods and services. Quality was the initial driver. American executives, perhaps a bit grudgingly, bought into the idea that if workers had more say in the process of manufacturing, then they would take more pride in their work, using their own ideas to produce a better quality, more consistent product. The shift in thinking marked a major change—or, more realistically, the beginnings of one.

The 1970s were the portent of the new reality. Although the more forward-looking companies adopted some of the quality practices of the best Japanese companies, few found that a full-blown cultural shift was possible. Retrospection shows us that fundamental differences in our national culture prevented us from adopting what the Japanese were so very good at. Our national culture is based on personal initiative and entrepreneurism, traits that result in individual opportunity rather than collective security. Accordingly, the rise of U.S. companies in the 1980s and 1990s was laced with layoffs, restructuring, and a general tearing of the fabric of the contract between the collective workforce and the companies that employed that workforce. The effects of that period linger today most markedly in the relationships between workers and management in the heavy manufacturing industries, but they are increasingly manifested in the attitudes of new applicants to the jobs available in the new economy.

Concurrently, and in some cases because of this restructuring, knowledge and its means of dissemination—the computer—became more important than merchandise. The growing global market in information has driven advancements in technology so powerful that the traditional barriers of time, distance, and form are now transcended by universal, ubiquitous connectivity and international protocols for information transfer and translation. Technological doors have opened wide to a new global, electronic economy. But the new economy is not built simply on fast distribution of information. This new economy is built upon a central premise of continuous change. In other words, we the people have to *create new information:* ideas that have not been thought of before. Thus the new economy rewards constant improvement and innovation, and these are derived from the minds and imaginations of people. To compete, we have to innovate faster than the next guy—who is trying to do the same thing. And of course, the next guy is no longer just in the office building across the street or across town, but could be anywhere, in any garage or carriage-house, in just about any country in the world.

These two phenomena, the end of long-term employment and the growing need for innovation and imagination, have now met—perhaps more accurately, they have clashed. Innovation requires people's passion to contribute; this passion is fed by a certain loyalty to a compelling cause or purpose that will be advanced by your ideas. This, at a time when loyalty to a company is judged to be a thing of the past. On average, each American worker will now work for eleven different companies in a lifetime. In fact, in *The 500-Year Delta,* authors Jim Taylor and Watts Wacker—both bona fide futurists—suggest that loyalty takes the fun out of work. "Work can be fun," they suggest, if we can only "shed the notion that any loyalty is to be given or received in a business relationship, realize that you are a freelancer moving from deal to deal even when you are in someone else's employ, and understand that there is only one person you are working for: yourself. You're the boss . . . this is freedom."[1]

In the scenario Taylor and Wacker describe, which is becoming more and more popular with business theorists, independent people move in parallel play, never really connecting with one another around the business as a whole, but rather connecting like bumper cars in a giant amusement park called the workplace. These players move in and out of groups to accomplish specific tasks and then move on. A business is merely a holding tank for accomplishment of objectives.

Ironically, it is also true that there has never been more need for loyalty in a company. The competitive advantage based on product innovation is fleeting at best. What used to be called *models* (and changed annually) are now called *versions* that change daily. Information and modular manufacturing technology have cut cycle times in even the most physical and complex of products. Chrysler, for example, has built the world's first cars designed entirely over a network—the 1998 Intrepid and Concord—and built them in record time. It was all done with computers in different locations, talking to each other in the language of binary code. So today, even solid objects—like those new Chryslers—essentially are *ideas* that computers can replicate and transmit anywhere, almost instantly, and at negligible cost.

But how does this relate to culture? This kind of production and application of knowledge require that people work well together, sharing knowledge and a sense of urgency. Businesses need commitment, not merely compliance. Everyone has to participate, to be engaged. Ownership is not just a financial concept, it needs to be a psychic reality as well. To generate the kind of effort and results that are needed in today's environment, employees need to "own" the business; the business has to represent that compelling cause or purpose that inspires full participation.

So in a world in which there is little loyalty, loyalty itself becomes a competitive advantage. One of the central questions of business is how to generate that environment of commitment. How do we build a culture that encourages commitment? How do we sustain that culture over time and through change—and still encourage change within the culture? How do we best strengthen a culture amid diversity? Dave has telling insights to these questions, for nowhere is the need for commitment and answers to those questions more acutely felt than in the financial services business. When transactions and information are the product, there's no real competitive advantage inherent in the actual product itself. And when the Internet can deliver transactions and information without the apparent need for people, the advantage has to be created out of the relationship to the customers, the customers' experience of what it is like to do business with the people of one company versus the people of other companies. To distinguish one business from others, the people in the company have to be personally dedicated to the culture of the company. Their dedication needs to be such that they will automatically take the actions that make the company's culture live.

How do you build that into the company as it grows beyond a few core people? Barry Posner and W. H. Smith of the University of Santa Clara found a direct correlation between commitment to the goals of an organization and individuals' knowledge of personal and organizational values. "People who had the greatest clarity about both personal and organizational values had the highest degree of commitment to the organization."[2] Values, the cornerstones of culture, form the basis for passion and commitment.

Steve Jobs knew this when he formed Apple Computer. He talked about the remarkable loyalty of Apple workers when the company was in its infancy. Did he emphasize the stock options? Hardly.

"What Apple has really been to me is an opportunity to express some deep feeling about wanting to contribute meaning. I really believe that people have a desire to put something back, to give something in a greater way. . . . In a sense, that's part of the joy of Apple Computer . . . [The company is] sort of a framework . . . where, if it's done right, people really can put something back."[3]

With this as a starting point, in Part One, we see how collective beliefs, expressed through values, language, and action, are central to inspiring loyalty, passion, and therefore growth in the age of the

Internet. In Chapters One and Two, we look at the corporate culture and see how it is built and sustained, how it really works, both in Schwab and in a number of other organizations. In Chapter Three, we look at diversity, a concept and reality that have become integral to building and sustaining a culture. We discuss diversity in depth for, despite its importance, diversity remains one of the most misunderstood aspects of culture in this new environment.

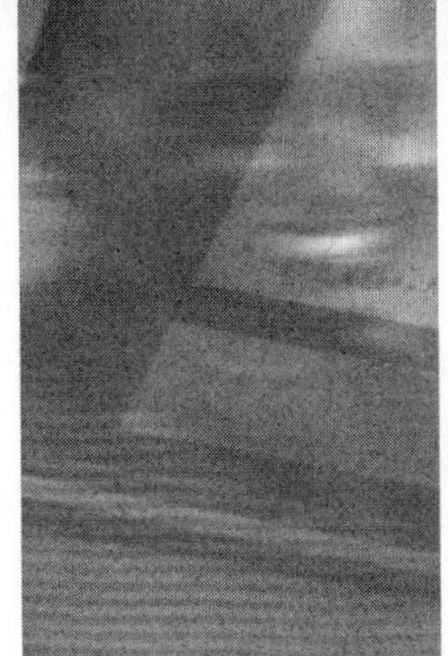

ONE

BUILDING A CULTURE FOR GROWTH

Steve Jobs wanted to make the computer easy to use. He was and is a visionary, and saw himself and his charges as "changing the world." That vision sustained Apple Computer for a long time. Reportedly, it was due to the vision that former Pepsi president John Sculley took over at Apple. Jobs's idea of the nature of the business as a vehicle to contribute showed an unusually meaningful view for the times, and it paid off for him and for Apple—at least for a while. What happened?

Jobs clearly said the right words. He defined Apple's culture as "other-directed" (changing the world), but the company was just as clearly focused inward. The company's strategy and actions reflected its real values: to keep others out, to build a bastion of Apple-based users. Oddly, about the same time, IBM was making a similar blunder regarding the mainframe computer. IBM's declared values were also impressive, calling for "the best customer service in the world," but the company ignored the customers' clear desire for a distributed environment supported by personal computers. Apple and IBM started to believe that they could control a major portion of the world of computing. They both shifted their focus from the customer to themselves, trying to partition that world to serve their own needs. Therein lies the mistake of perspective: they forgot to take their own values seriously when they developed these business strategies. It was a turn away from what had inspired their respective worlds.

The Apple case is perhaps more understandable, because even in those times, when the PC was just being born, the cultural values of start-ups could be summarized as "work hard, work long, go public, and get rich." This is a very successful formula for the first few years of a business, and it prevails today. Most Internet start-ups and even second-stage companies view themselves as equity factories. They all compete with the same formula for the same competencies, the same people, that we want at Schwab. This, at a time when the unemployment rate for technical people in Silicon Valley is estimated as minus 3 percent.[1] There are more jobs than qualified applicants.

The labor shortage gets compounded for firms like ours when we add the other major components of our company, the broker, the customer service representative, and the myriad of financial services experts that are required to administer our business as we expand. These competencies are very much in demand by every major financial service company in the world. Most brokerages, mutual fund companies, and banks pay high commissions and offer tremendous incentives to the best in these fields. What is the role of culture in this Internet world of competition for human capital? What kind of cultural foundation attracts the people we need? It took me awhile to learn the answers to these questions. Indeed, it took me awhile to *ask* those questions.

My introduction to Schwab was also my introduction to culture and what it could do for a company to sustain it over the long haul. Until I joined the company in 1984, my work experience was really focused on my own learning and my own career growth. I had worked for some great companies where the internal rules clearly encouraged individual accomplishment and internal competition for the top jobs. The cultures of these companies were expressions of the more traditional rules of business: make money, pay homage to the hierarchy, and promote yourself with hard work and exposure so that you could race your peers up the corporate ladder. These rules had worked for a long time and across a wide range of companies.

I soon found that life was different at this little discount brokerage on the West Coast. Charles "Chuck" Schwab had certainly started the firm to make money. But he believed that could be done by actually serving others, giving market access to people who wanted to manage their own accounts. He knew if he provided value to customers and paid attention to good business principles, profit would follow. He was determined "to provide customers with the most useful and ethical brokerage services in America." Talk to Chuck for an hour and you will hear all about the things we should be doing for customers. You'll probably never even hear the word "profit." Chuck's vision reflects his personal values—fairness, empathy, responsiveness, service—and these have become the bedrock for how he expected everyone in his company to behave. I personally have never seen Chuck behave any other way. Hearing him, people respond with a resounding, "Me too!"

ANCHORING THE CULTURE WITH SERVICE AND CUSTOMER EXPERIENCE

"A chance to serve others," "A chance to make a difference," "A chance to leave a personal legacy that is meaningful"—these are some of the comments that are repeated and repeated in our employee opinion surveys. These statements reinforce the rational models of Maslow and Rogers on human development. We need food and shelter, we want love and acceptance, we want to find and express our individual gifts, and ultimately, we want to leave the earth with the knowledge that others are better off for our having been here. Aside from the academic verification of these giants of psychology, direct experience tells us that helping others and *knowing* that we are helping others is a great joy in life. At Schwab, it is actively encouraged.

Let me tell you a brief story to make the point. In 1998, at one of our Midwestern branches, the phone rang late on a Thursday evening. The representative answered the phone to hear what sounded like an elderly lady telling her that she needed to check a particular trust account to make sure that it was funded. It seemed that her husband was dying, and it was important to make sure that the loose ends had been sewn up.

The representative checked the account, and found that although it was open, the balance was not nearly what the customer had expected it to be. The lady told our representative that her husband had intended to fund the account with some stock in a large communication company. Having worked for the company in New York, he had accumulated the shares before he retired, which was before the company was merged with another, larger company. She was sure that he had kept the original stock certificates, but he was in a coma, and she didn't know what the shares looked like.

Our rep realized that the tax implications could be substantial. She called the company in New York, and found that, indeed, certificates had been issued to the customer's husband. She then called back and described the certificates to the woman, asked a few more questions about the family, and with the lady's permission, phoned the couple's adult children and told them the problem. The children instituted a full-scale search for the certificates.

Late Friday, one of the children arrived at the branch with some certificates that they had found in a box. They turned out to be only copies of the originals, but now at least the family knew what they were looking for. Our representative gave them her home phone. Saturday morning, they called to say they had found the originals in the back of the family's grandfather clock. The rep took the necessary paperwork to their house and completed the transfer of assets into the account.

The gentleman died early Sunday morning.

The representative's involvement and attention made a six-figure difference to the family. As a result of the extraordinary service, they transferred several million dollars to other Schwab accounts. But the significance to the representative, and to everyone who hears this story, was not the added revenue to the company. The significance was the effect of her action on this family; she felt enormous personal satisfaction—as did the rest of us, vicariously.

Telling this story and others like it is an integral part of what we do to sustain the culture, as you will see in the next chapter. Will people always serve for no compensation? No, except for the very rich and the saints. But given a level of compensation that seems fair, that gives people a chance for financial security, most of us will opt to serve others for a living. We often refer to it as "doing well while doing good," and it is the linchpin of our company. It connects our employees with our customers and benefits both groups immensely.

If serving is the foundation of a culture that attracts people, then, as other companies have shown, keeping the focus on serving is critical to success in culture building. There are multiple opportunities for distraction, including the lure of market share or—as we are currently seeing in much of the high-tech world—a focus on a particular competitor or even a personality. But beating a competitor or cornering a market does not create inspiration, nor do such dreams create real long-term success.

This book describes a number of aspects of growing a business in the new Internet environment. Above all else, and regardless of the technology, the driving force is the customer experience: our desire and ability to create it, and the customers' satisfaction with it. Serving, serving, serving. It is the heartbeat of a company that works.

NEW CULTURE IN OLD INDUSTRIES

In contrast, the financial services industry was modeled on banks and old-world brokerage houses with the prevailing attitude that customers *needed them*, which indeed they did. Until the last two decades, access to financial markets was limited to the wealthy, the well-connected, and the institutions that enjoyed virtual monopoly through regulation. As a customer-focused company, Schwab plowed new ground for the retail investment business. Rather than model ourselves after the traditions of this industry, we have modeled ourselves after great retailers—Wal-Mart, Home Depot, and the Gap—companies that have thrived by being responsive to customers' needs.

As I'll discuss in Chapter Nine, at Schwab we practice specific habits to assure that we are hearing what the customers need and then providing what they need in the most efficient way possible. For now, the central point is that *service* is the value that inspires, it is at the heart of people's willingness to commit, and in today's world, its practice is difficult to maintain as the focus of a company. When the desire to serve is applied to something as important as a family's financial future, it can inspire us and it can inspire our customers. As we have seen, it can also inspire competitors—and in fact, an entire industry.

DETERMINE AND DECLARE VALUES: THE DNA

In 1997, I had a chance to listen to Lew Platt, then president and CEO of Hewlett-Packard, as he explained his diagram of a corporate universe. The drawing showed values—which he described as the "why"—as the sun, an unchanging, unmoving core, with everything revolving around it. In close orbit—like Mercury—was the corporate vision, which he described as the "what." One orbit out were procedures, processes, and practices, which he called the "how." The further out the orbit, the more subject it was to change, Platt said.[2] Procedures, processes, and practices change all the time. A vision may need updating every ten years or so. But the values stay put. The gravity of values keeps everything else in order.

I wish I had seen this model a few years earlier, because when I arrived at Schwab, the values and vision that remain the heart of culture had not yet been committed to writing. That didn't happen until 1991. By then, we had three thousand employees and the company had grown big enough that Chuck was no longer able to call everyone by name. I thought it was time to write the values down on paper. Clearly, I was being infected with the culture of the company. I was beginning to see it as at least a part of our competitive advantage, and I knew how important it was for everyone in the company to feel the same way.

Chuck seemed surprised. "Why write them down? Everybody knows them." I said, "Yes Chuck, all the people you talk to know them.

The other hundreds we're hiring who've never met you don't. We're too big. You can't assume they know what you and this company are and are not."

Until then, it hadn't dawned on us that the firm had gotten big enough that we needed to communicate the fundamentals of the culture explicitly. In a way, it was like the drafting of the Declaration of Independence. It put in writing what we understood to be the truths of our company, truths that we had been operating with for a number of years, but that could now stand as a beacon to guide our actions not just as a company but as individuals within that company. It was a major step—the beginning of the formal culture-building process at Schwab. (See Appendix A for other significant events in Schwab history.)

Chuck concurred, and the values found a home on paper. The entire Executive Management Team worked on the project. We gave Chuck our thoughts, and he huddled himself away and emerged with the values of "fairness, empathy, teamwork, and responsiveness, constantly striving to be worthy of our customers' trust." For years, not a word of the vision or the values changed, and every employee knew them by heart. We kept growing larger and larger.

By 1994, I was president of the corporation, and we had started an annual opinion survey of our employees. We had grown to over five thousand and were feeling a little out of touch with the way people saw the company from the inside. The results of the survey were surprising—and not that pleasant. Many of our employees (more than 30 percent) expressed concern or ignorance about three critical elements: the direction of the company, trust in senior management, and their own career possibilities.

The top ten officers of the company debriefed the survey and we quickly found ourselves mired in denial. Some of us blamed others, some of us didn't believe the survey results, and others just commented sarcastically that we had hired the wrong five thousand people. But in the end, we realized that once again, as the company had grown, we had failed to communicate effectively. So we set out to etch the vision and values we believed to be our cultural DNA into the mind and heart of every Schwab employee. To make this process tangible and effective, we also needed to articulate the strategic priorities that would bring us to where we wanted to be.

At this point, Terry had been working with me for more than three years; he was fully embraced by the management team as the right person to take the lead in the communication process. I glibly told him that I would take my laptop to my home in Lake Tahoe over the Easter weekend and clarify the vision and define the strategic priorities. I thought all we needed was a clear and motivating document. So I spent the weekend swapping drafts back and forth with Terry, my wife, Emily, and a couple of my other most trusted colleagues. I figured if it resonated for them I had a winner.

But I had defined the problem badly. As I learned, the *process* was to prove far more important than the paper. The challenge was not document creation, it was commitment generation. To achieve that objective, a process of much broader inclusion was essential.

In truth, it took ten months, the input of eighty executives, and a million-dollar communication project to realize what we wanted—the commitment of the entire company to continue to grow the company in new directions by living the rules of the Schwab culture. Virtually every executive had an opportunity to have extensive input into the process. We traced the history of the firm, created a rich context so that newcomers could understand our heritage, revisited the original purpose of the company, reviewed our long-range goals, and finally, at a ritual in a hotel ballroom in San Francisco in August 1995, all eighty senior officers of the company raised glasses of champagne and then signed their names to the written versions of the vision, values, and strategic priorities. (See Appendix B for the text.) We had changed only three words in the vision, shifting "investors" to "customers," "brokerage" to "financial services," and "America" to "world." Our values remained the same. Our strategic priorities were clearly defined, more specific than anything we had set to paper before but reflecting many of the things we were already doing, so they resonated with familiarity and credibility. We committed to a shared goal of serving 10 million investors and having $1 trillion in custody within ten years, multiplying our 1995 totals by a factor of five.

We took our expanded vision, values, and strategic priorities on the road, talking to all seven thousand Schwab employees in face-to-face meetings. Everyone traveled to one of seven central locations, where Chuck and I met them and discussed the fundamentals of our own commitment, the goals for our joint effort, and the values that we used to measure our actions. We asked for their engagement, for their thorough review of these critical elements, and we asked them to consider two questions:

- Do the values of the company fit with your own personal values?
- How does what you do day to day contribute to the achievement of one or more of the strategic priorities?

This may seem like a lot of effort and a lot of time away from the "work" of the business over three changed words, a one-page statement of vision, and ten strategic priorities. But the process was one of culture building and reinforcement. It affirmed our values, created a common language, and recommitted us to actions that would make the values real in the world of serving customers.

In each of the seven venues, Chuck and I engaged in about ninety minutes of "Town Hall" questions and answers. Some of our colleagues raised heartfelt issues like compensation, career progression, or job security that everyone was thinking about but few wanted to risk bringing up. We discovered that communication about these issues can take a back seat in the rush of double-digit growth. But as soon as one of these issues surfaced, we would congratulate the questioner, asking everyone to give him or her some rousing applause as a way of reinforcing a cultural norm. The questions became more real; few wanted to hold back concerns that had been on their minds for some time. New employees, particularly, were impressed with the candor and access in these sessions.

That's culture building, and that's inspiring. Top management can tell employees they are important forever, but employees believe them only when leaders actually demonstrate that importance with openness. I've stopped counting the number of employees and recruits who have candidly expressed that their reason for being here or wanting to be here is our full-bodied dedication to living our values.

I consider the 1995 process of revisiting the values and vision and defining the strategic priorities for the next decade as a major turning point, a major foundation for growth, for the company. Although only a few words in our vision statement changed, they were the *right* few words, and in the process all the other words were called into question, scrutinized, and embraced once again. In the end we had succeeded in defining our corporate genetic code. These values, applied correctly, act like DNA, through which each cell—regardless of its own specialized job—knows the master plan for the whole body. They are critical for the individual and the organization.

THE FOUR IMPACTS OF CULTURE

As we learned over time, and have constantly reinforced, culture fills four important needs:

- It grounds people in something unchanging.
- It builds a basis of alignment.
- It serves as a virtual filter for people and practices.
- It exports values to customers.

These needs, like the DNA, speak to the individual and the organization.

A Sense of Stability

A strong culture grounds people in something unchanging. Since 1900, technology has moved us from the stagecoach to the space shuttle, from the telegraph to the Internet. In only seventy years, the world saw the rise and fall of Marxism, one of the most influential political systems in history. In only the past ten years, we have seen the map of the world and the cultural landscape that the map represents go through painful upheaval. Old cultures and cults have reemerged to assert their special place on the world scene.

Socially, just in the United States, and just since the 1960s, we have moved from Snoopy to Snoop Doggie Dog, from *Ozzie and Harriet* to *Beavis and Butt-Head,* from occasional concerts in the park to MTV, 24/7.

Some see such rapid change as negative, yet this social shift has also been accompanied by the end of the Cold War, the rapid expansion of democratic values worldwide, and progress in medicine and other life sciences that have put us on the brink of some magnificent breakthroughs in the treatment and prevention of disease. We are no longer bounded physically by Earth, and rapid and global communication has moved us well into a new era of expanded—perhaps unlimited—personal knowledge and personal ability to respond to life. While this century may not have been the Age of Enlightenment, it has certainly been the Age of Change.

In such an environment, people long for the unchanging security of the values of truth, integrity, and ethical behavior. A healthy culture can offer that kind of stability, and it draws people to it like a magnet. Many of our best business scholars, including Peter Drucker, have commented on the growing need for community and the possibilities for creating that community in a business organization.[3] After all, this is where people are spending more and more of their time. What better place for them to find their community, their "common unity"?

This need for community explains the phenomenon of *logowear*—employees' actually wearing shirts, caps, jackets and other apparel that shows the company logo. It is a sign of belonging, a symbol to the outside world that you are part of something bigger than yourself. Wearing a company shirt is the equivalent of flying the flag. If the culture of the company is one that is admired in the community, then the incentive to be identified with it is even stronger. Such is the case with great companies.

IBM probably created the first corporate culture widely recognized in American business. There is a legend that the founder, Tom Watson Sr., personally checked up on his managers to make sure they were living the values of the company, even when they were at home. The traditional IBM salesman was often teased about his sincere tie, conservative suit, and wing-tipped shoes. But these "IBMers" took pride in setting the standard for their industry if not the entire world of business with their principles of "excellence, the finest customer service in the world, and respect for the individual." Likewise, Nordstrom, Hewlett-Packard, and other great American companies have flourished with their focus and dedication to their own values.

For those who share their company's sense of values, purpose becomes infectious. Within the unchanging values of the culture, employees learn to expect and even welcome the unexpected. Culture gives them a firm footing. Only when people know the values of the culture can they reply when the company asks, "Want to come along?"

A Basis for Alignment

If the answer to "Want to come along?" is yes, then you can take that as a pledge of willingness to align with others around those values and common vision. That alignment is a very powerful force: everyone facing in one direction, understanding what the company is trying to do, and moving with conviction toward it. Many organizations have to watch their people going in different directions, dissipating and even canceling team energy. We see this particularly in mergers, when the cultures of two companies come together. The fit is never perfect, and energy is dissipated while alignment takes place, if indeed it ever does.

In our industry, the merger of Citibank and Travelers was a very big deal, but I don't believe that either CEO, Sandy Weill or John Reed, fully appreciated the benefits or difficulty in building common culture. In an interview with *Business Week*, both men said as much. Reed, in particular, was thoughtful about the issue: "The business promise is greater than we expected . . . [and] the human part of making it happen has been more difficult than I might have imagined."[4]

Certainly, the idea of synergy was terrific, and it may well be that in a few years, the operation will be smooth and seamless. At Schwab, we learned the difficulty on a much smaller scale when our company was acquired by Bank of America in the 1980s. Clearly, there were advantages in terms of capital for expansion, but the cultural differences were severe. Beyond question, Schwab would not have thrived in that banking environment, and the millions of customers and thousands of employees who benefited from Schwab's culture would have missed a great opportunity. In retrospect, we were fortunate to have been able to buy ourselves back, and realign around a core set of principles.

This kind of cultural binding is an organizing principle that forms lasting bonds with those who are aligned with you. It's incredibly powerful and worth almost any amount of effort to create. This sense of alignment is especially important now, when the pace of change actually prevents us from seeing a clear picture of the future. At Schwab we often use the phrase "we're heading west" to suggest that we have a clear *direction.* But we are also communicating that our *destination* is not so clear. This lack of clarity can be unsettling. Confidence in our culture is the central factor in keeping us aligned even as we rush forward toward a distant horizon.

A Filter for People and Practices

Culture is a de facto recruiting, staffing, and procedures tool, naturally winnowing out people and behaviors that don't support our values and our mission. Since we have a very clear set of values to guide behavior, and since people believe in those values, the chances are pretty high that they'll do the right thing in any given situation. It's a good thing, too, for we simply can't write policy manuals fast enough to guide all the behaviors we need. Besides, who could have foreseen the instance of the elderly lady with the urgent need to locate missing stock certificates, and then written a procedure to deal with it? Nordstrom's procedures manual gives a short, effective cultural statement that provides part of the base: "Use your best judgment at all times."

This one incantation is evidence of the strength of the corporate culture and the trust the company has in its power to guide employees to do the right thing.

Just as a culture guides those who are in alignment, it opens the exit door for people who don't share the values. For example, Schwab is team oriented and rejects self-servers very quickly. You can bet that someone who is asked to contribute to a solution and responds, "Sorry, no time—I'm not measured on that," won't last long. In the final analysis, *we are all* measured on our team skills.

An Exporter of Values

A strong culture exports values to customers. Harley-Davidson builds a distinctive motorcycle. It's not an engineering masterpiece, but it does make a strong statement about style and philosophy. Where Harley-Davidson truly stands out is more in the spirit it shares with its customer than in its paint and iron. Harley riders don't buy a bike as much as they buy into a *company*, a marque. Even Mercedes owners won't drive all weekend to attend a factory rally and meet the people who assembled their vehicles. But Harley owners enthusiastically do—showing an ironic power that this marque (which champions maverick independence above all else) has to compel its rebel riders to gather and share common values. For them, who the company *is* truly becomes more important than what the company *makes*. In fact, Harley-Davidson now makes more money from logowear than it does from motorcycles.[5] That's a remarkable—and invaluable—market commentary. Belonging to the family seems to be more important than using the product.

How do you do it? Build around a distinctive idea, a value that is uncommon. Chuck Schwab certainly did this, and still does. Once I rode an elevator with him to a senior management gathering in a hotel, and a fellow passenger noticed his badge and asked some quick advice between floors. Chuck would not let him go—quizzing him on his needs and circumstances—and as I tried to drag him off the elevator to attend the meeting, I caught a glimpse of the passionate fire that sparked his remarkable company. Everything flowed from an intense sense of identity: his plan, his engagement with people, his purpose—they were just under the surface, and now focused like a laser on the fellow in the elevator.

CULTURE–EVERY DAY AND THROUGH THE NETWORK

Culture, unfortunately, is only a concept until it is actually lived. The next chapter is about breathing life into that concept from day to day. I can give you a preview: it is hard work. There are lots of symbols of the culture around . . . signs on the wall, sayings in the annual reports. But the only way to know if it really works is by watching and listening. In that regard, the Internet has provided a wonderful tool to hold companies accountable for consistency between rhetoric and reality. Dilbert (the cynic) is present every day, on-line and in print, and every day, employees have the capability to instantly communicate with everyone else in the company about their perception of what is really happening. They can chat, complain, and encourage like never before. In short, the days are gone when a few company executives could get away with platitudes about culture. Now, to inspire, the action that follows the rhetoric has to be consistent. If it isn't, the new communication tools will be used to alert everyone that the emperor has no clothes. The same tools can also enable stronger affirmation than was ever possible. Once we learned of it and began retelling the incident of the funded trust, it spread throughout the company in a matter of hours—with positive results. A negative incident can spread just as rapidly, or more so—and with deleterious effect.

We've known for a long time that company culture was eventually reflected in performance. The speed and reach of the Internet magnifies the possibilities, both negative and positive. It gives us the possibility of including the widest possible range of employees in events that were once reserved for select audiences.

One of the most powerful expressions of the culture came from a man that I admire a great deal, and it happened under what would be considered rough circumstances. I had to decide to pass over one of my dearest friends in the company and appoint someone else as president. Tom Seip would've made a fine president, but we felt at the time that there was a better choice. I asked Tom to take another assignment, one that was exciting and certainly important, but it was not the presidency of the company.

The affirming lesson from that experience was watching Tom stand up before our senior management team a few weeks after being passed over for the biggest promotion of his career and talk from his heart. The cultural DNA showed through, loud and clear. Here's what he said, pretty much in its entirety:

> I would not for one moment want you to believe that I didn't want the job. I did. I was at first angry, and of course it was a fairly significant blow to my self-esteem. And to the degree my identity is linked to my job, the answer to the question "Who am I?" in this case comes back very quickly, "You are not the president." And so now what?
>
> For me, there was the issue of how all of you would perceive me. That was the biggest hurdle. In a sense, I felt I had somehow let you all down, and that this was one glaring sign of it that I could never recover from. That idea was nearly unbearable. There was a part of me that just wanted to disappear.
>
> But I didn't.
>
> The decision not to retire was easy. But deciding to stay here or go elsewhere was not easy. It was, however, a chance to grow a little. Growth means change and adventure, and of course, the phrase "growing pains" was not coined without cause. . . . growth is usually painful, and absolutely essential to life. And those ideas about growth were predominant in my thinking about staying or leaving Schwab. Here is just some of my thinking.
>
> First: I needed to not just understand, but really experience, the value of commitment and loyalty to the mission of the company and to all of you, and to see how far that commitment went beyond my own particular disappointment.

Now that might sound like B.S. but it isn't, at least not for me. I really believe at our level in the organization, we should be expected to carry the mission of the company inside of us . . . at a gut level. . . . In fact, it should be part of the requirement to be an officer of the company.

Along with that responsibility comes the requirement to recruit peers who can compete with us, people who can be better than we are. I have always preached this and practiced it. But of course, this means that we have to face the inevitability that our subordinates will become our peers, and our peers will become our bosses. But there is a payoff. It also means that we can take pride in those people rising to be our peers in the organization. This is just part of the biology of a good organization, and I think it is part of the DNA of a good leader.

But I had to really go through some questions and answer them truthfully. Here's what I asked myself:

Do you believe in the mission of the company?

Answer: of course.

How does the fact that you didn't get this job affect your commitment to the mission of the company?

Answer: not at all.

Is there any place else, other than starting your own company, where you could express that commitment?

Answer: probably not.

Do you believe in the strategy?

Answer: I helped fashion it.

Is there any group of people that you would rather be with, leading and following, with all the foibles and all the successes? Can you imagine having the kind of long-standing and committed relationships in another environment?

Answer: of course not.

Do you respect the new person you are going to be working for?

The answer is "absolutely."

So then, for me, the only reason to leave would be petulance . . . because I didn't get to play the position I wanted to play. And then I asked, "How am I going to explain this to Jake, my twelve-year-old son, that I quit the team because I didn't get to be starting center forward? I had no answer to that . . . and I couldn't find one.

> To have to answer the question years from now . . . to my son or to anyone else . . . when someone asked me why I left Schwab . . . to answer that it was because my ego was injured . . . that was totally unacceptable to me.
>
> So I decided that I wanted to stay. But there was a final set of questions. The moral issue about whether or not it was right to continue taking a paycheck from the shareholders. Someone asked, "Are you really here or are you 'in transition'?" And we all know what he meant. Was I excited? Did I have the energy? Or would I just be going through the motions?
>
> Well, his question started me thinking, and in the final analysis the decision was pretty easy. The hard part was coming to grips with growing up as a leader, to decide not to retreat but to go forward to the next challenge and continue to build on what we have here that is so very, very special.
>
> So I'm still playing, better than ever, I hope, in the right industry, where we can actually provide something that people need, in the right company, where we are truly serving, not selling, and with the right group of people . . . all of you and the thousands who are not here. As Chuck said . . . it's nice to go to work every day feeling like you are doing something important . . . fundamentally to help people . . . and doing it with people you care about.
>
> Truthfully, it doesn't get a whole lot better.

Tom was right—it doesn't get a whole lot better than that. I don't know if I've been more proud of anyone. My own emotional reaction was mirrored in the rest of room, and thanks to the Net, in the rest of the company. Everything he expressed pointed to the success of our culture. Obviously we'd recruited a highly principled, thoughtful, and dedicated man. He was part of our team ethic, and he put the higher good—including the customer and shareholder, as well as management—ahead of himself.

Tom retired from Schwab about a year after this event, and is enjoying a well-earned rest. But I'm still grateful for his remarks that afternoon, which reaffirmed his belief and dedication to the values he so ably reinforced. Tom Seip that afternoon was a living, breathing poster boy for the power of culture, done right.

And done right, it means this: Everything else can fall away; the industry and products and circumstances may change; but an abiding culture can serve as the custodian of dreams for your company team, and for the customers on whose faith you build your house of business. It is an unchanging constant in the midst of a tornado of change, and it is something people want badly. It allows us to offer a choice to those who work here and for those we want to work here . . . to live and work with others who want to make a lasting contribution, who are guided by their values, and who will toil together toward something larger than themselves. Steve Jobs did catch that part of the key idea. The company, at its best, can be a vehicle for everyone to make a difference.

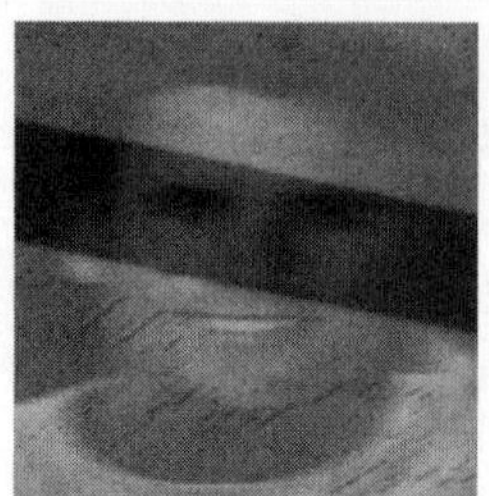

FROM BUILDING CULTURE TO SUSTAINING CULTURE

Culture is the bond, the understanding that holds the organization together, even as individuals in the company express themselves differently. While the process of vision-development that Dave described was important, and in fact vital, the real linchpin of success was the commitment of middle management and their employees, commitment not merely as a matter of good business, but as a matter of personal passion. When they listened to the vision and values, most of them heard something that they wanted to be part of; it fit for them. Had that not been the case, then the culture that was espoused by the "leaders" would have been nothing more than a wall plaque. No amount of repetition, by itself, could make others take it to heart.

This is a critical point. We speak of "national" and "company" cultures, but cultures are formed among any group of people who work together. Some are explicit but most are implicit, understood but not spoken, residing in the language and habits of interaction between the people. So in every organization within a company, the central culture lives or it doesn't, primarily on the basis of the manager and his commitment. In every company, every manager has the power to support the culture or to start a counterculture. Actually, each manager does one or the other, consciously or unconsciously.

Accordingly, each manager actually influences the whole. Countercultures are started consciously by those who see reality differently, who have different values, and who want to move the organization toward a purpose that is important to them. These can be beneficial additions or they can be destructive.

Realistically, if you are in the middle management of a company, there are some things you can't do. If your company has a clear and consciously supported culture of fierce internal competition, then you will have real difficulty changing it to a culture of team play. Or, if your company values only the bottom line, then you may have trouble insisting on a richer customer experience or a primary emphasis on quality.

It will take an epiphany on the part of the official leaders of the organization to change values that dramatically. But if top management is ambivalent, or if the managers simply haven't thought about the power of culture to form commitment in a company, then you can make a real difference.

Within such a vacuum, you can set up the kind of organizational values that you want within your own sphere of influence, communicate those values to your organization in a language that inspires others to want to be a part of it, and then produce measurable results. You can create the culture of your own organization, regardless of its size, in the same manner that Dave described:

- Write down the values.
- Develop a compelling vision, a statement of your aspiration for your organization.
- Communicate your thoughts and feelings to your entire group.
- Ask for the group's comments and additions.
- Ask the members of the group to relate their own job to the vision and values. What are they contributing and how are they contributing it?

When you have taken these steps, you will find that your own job and the jobs of those around you will be filled with anticipation that was not there before. The energy that comes with it can be remarkable. And it's important to acknowledge that building the culture and making it known are merely the starting points.

Remember, Dave said that culture fulfills four needs—it grounds people in something unchanging, builds a basis of alignment, serves as a filter for people and practices, and exports values to customers—and is made up of values, a common language, and actions. The discussions in Chapter One have taken us through those four needs and the values and language part of culture building. In the next chapter, we look at sustaining that culture and the hard work doing so entails.

Culture can't be sustained only with words, but it can be destroyed with actions that seem to run counter to the values. Like our nation, a company is at first an amalgam of unrelated people. Then as it adopts principles such as freedom and equality and puts those principles into language (as Jefferson and the Continental Congress did in the Declaration of Independence), it begins to draw to it people of like mind and heart. Immigrants are required to learn the stories and swear an oath to uphold the values in order to be admitted to the culture. Finally, a nation solidifies the culture with its collective actions toward a common vision. And, in times of crisis, stories and reminders of our history and common vision help to support us. One could argue, for example, that President Kennedy's challenge to put a man on the moon was designed to help unify the country toward a common purpose. Further back in time, Henry Wadsworth Longfellow wrote the poem "Paul Revere's Ride," not to set history straight (indeed, he exercised poetic license with some details), but as his attempt to unify a country divided by slavery, to help people remember the sentiments of the Revolutionaries and what had held the fledgling country together.

Over time, our cultural underpinnings are sustained through story, image, and ritual. The United States thrives on the heroics of its Minutemen, its sons and daughters of war, its astronauts, its flag. The ritual holidays, even elections—these support and sustain what we all believe.

Any organization sustains its culture in like manner, but unlike Paul Revere, we spread the word in a hurry—everywhere. New technology makes it possible for everyone to find out just about everything. Worldwide company cultures are common now, they exist because of the ease of communication and contact provided by our new tools. Accordingly, sustaining culture takes much more attention than it did in the last century. Beyond the abstractions of language, there must be consistent action and then active myth building: the values must be reinforced with story, image, and ritual, new recruits must learn the stories and metaphorically swear an oath. These are all aspects of sustaining the culture, as Dave discusses in Chapter Two.

TWO

SUSTAINING CULTURE DAY TO DAY

I wish I could take credit for creating the culture that allowed Tom Seip to make that speech. Chuck did that as he started the company and held fast to his values through the years. My job is to sustain the culture as best I can. I know for sure that culture is nothing, and I mean nothing, without daily reinforcement. As Terry suggested, in this time of rapid and easy communication, culture cannot be sustained in a business without a great deal of attention to detail and a great deal of faith in its importance. It takes concentrated effort. In this chapter, we want to look at some of the ways culture gets re-created daily in the minds and hearts of everyone in the company. In preparation, it might be useful to revisit some of the impediments that get in the way of sustaining any culture.

BARRIERS TO CULTURE BUILDING

I don't suggest that you dwell on these—rather that you become aware of them and look out for them, daily. They aren't obvious, they don't appear like brick walls on your path. Rather these barriers appear in people's attitudes and actions. From a tendency to lump all businesses together to assumptions about how people work, the barriers can chip away at culture.

The habitual response of learned behavior is a major and insidious barrier in a growth company that recruits people from everywhere. At Schwab, between increased needs and turnover, one in four people is new to the company each year. And each one brings learned business behavior along. Unfortunately, in the world of financial services, that learned behavior is frequently not consistent with customer focus, teamwork, and trustworthiness, the very values that we feel create our competitive advantage. The problem is compounded by the fact that many companies, if not *most* companies—and individuals—will mouth these same words but actually operate in the old dog-eat-dog paradigm. That habitual response is encouraged by a set of beliefs that operate without conscious thought. These beliefs are fundamentally the result of unexamined questions.

Are All Businesses the Same?

There is in the general population a belief that business *as a whole* has a consistent culture. Many people feel that although norms will vary slightly from company to company, the culture learned in one company is roughly the same as the culture in all companies. Metaphors reflect the atmosphere that is assumed to mark the world of the capitalist, and they are largely aggressive and warlike. "Dog-eat-dog," "climbing the corporate ladder," or—the favorite of Sun Microsystems CEO Scott McNeely—"eat lunch or be lunch." Such metaphors are fed by the media of generalization. Dilbert's popularity comes from a common experience of people in companies that operate more or less the same way. To deviate from an atmosphere depicted by these metaphors, leaders have to create an atmosphere that consciously defeats the stereotype every single day.

Does Building Culture Waste Precious Time?

With results measured quarter to quarter and competitive pressures demanding ever-faster decisions, any practice that sounds like it will slow things down feels antithetical to business success. Any principle that requires an attention to process, such as culture building, can seem useless. Building and reinforcing culture takes time, lots of it, and it can seem like a waste or a luxury in a world with a premium on speed.

But, as we saw in 1995, ignoring cultural construction breeds discontent and actually slows progress. Investing time in alignment is like tuning an engine; it creates efficiency that will not only pay off in results, it will make the whole journey smoother and more fulfilling.

Is Teamwork Natural?

The presumption that people are naturally going to work together as a team is in fact a barrier in disguise. My experience suggests that the natural state of affairs in American business is *entropy.* Chaos is more likely than teamwork. In fact, cultures that appear to cooperate naturally actually have centuries of practice, usually because of necessity.

Japan is a great example, primarily because the national style of cooperation was a model for business in the postwar era, but that nation has 120 million people living in a space roughly the size of Montana and 98 percent of the country is very mountainous. Their culture learned to cooperate simply so everyone could eat. Conversely, the American culture, with its manifest destiny and rugged individualism, is short on team skills. That's why we often see a certain level of latent chaos at American corporations—and we see a lot of the standard organizational response to control it—more bureaucracy, more rules.

All these attitudes and beliefs are barriers to sustaining a culture that focuses on the customer, rewards teamwork, and encourages individual contribution.

As a "new" financial services company, we have worked on these barriers. And in doing so, we've come across different barriers that may seem at first to be unique to our field, but do indeed extend beyond it and have roots in the new economy. Our struggle provides at least part of our competitive advantage. I'll have to make some gross generalizations to make the point, but let me explain.

MIXING DIVERSE TALENTS

Schwab's business heritage comes from three very different bloodlines—financial services, retail, and technology—a mix that presents its own set of challenges and needs its own organizational model.

We were born from the financial services business: our competitors were banks and brokerage companies, most of which focused inward and strictly adhered to a "hierarchy and title" power structure. The holy grail of banking has traditionally been to become a vice president; frequently, a title and an office are enough to gain respectability in the organization.

Our second bloodline is the retail business. Unlike most banks, we focus outward, toward the customer, and our idols are great retailers like Home Depot, the Gap, and Wal-Mart. While these companies still use a hierarchy, they find their success not in offices but in front of the customer. The source of power is customer satisfaction and innovative marketing techniques. They are run by retailers and merchants.

Our most recent bloodline is the technologist. The conventions of technology are so different and so important that I'll devote considerable discussion to them in Chapter Eight. To put it briefly—unlike banks and retailers, technology companies work as teams. Titles are irrelevant. Success is defined by technical expertise and contribution to the project. While technologists can be customer-focused, their main concern is for the completion of the project and its contribution to the leading edge of technology. Their loyalty is not to the hierarchy but to their teammates and to the principles of the project itself.

Clearly, these are generalizations. Not all bankers are focused only on their title and the size of their office, not all retailers are merchants, and not all technologists are interested only in how slick the application turns out. But by generalizing, I've hoped to give a feel for the difficulty of molding these three dramatically different norms into a single culture.

It is a challenge in which the Internet is proving to be an invaluable resource.

INTERCONNECTED ON THE WEB

The World Wide Web makes obvious what we have known intuitively: that the Japanese experience is becoming our own. Whatever our organizational structure, everything is actually networked, everything we do affects everything else. A most interesting theory of mathematics was articulated earlier this century and branded as the "butterfly effect." Often cited facetiously as an extreme example of interdependence, the theory held that if a butterfly flapped its wings in the Amazon basin, it would affect the weather in Chicago two weeks later. In the 1970s the butterfly effect was good for a laugh—but today it seems not just intuitively obvious, but experientially true. In our business, seemingly disconnected events rapidly join as part of chain reactions to affect markets all over the world. A trader can raise a finger in New York and dramatically change the financial position of someone he doesn't know in Singapore a split second later.

The Web is merely a symbolic depiction of that interdependence, and of course that symbol makes the universal impact of our action or messages obvious. The Web also allows and encourages a free flow of information, so it is impossible for one person to operate in a vacuum. It makes information available to everyone, and is, therefore, the single most important tool for collaboration that has ever been invented. No longer can a single individual operate independently by hoarding and monopolizing information.

These two aspects of the Internet—the free flow of information and its symbol of interconnectedness—make conscious teamwork eminently possible. Organizations that are aligned behind common purpose will find it a powerful tool. Those still operating with rules of independence and control will find it a formidable obstacle.

But just as a hammer can't build a house, the Internet can't create a team. Appropriately enough, the word *culture* has the same derivation as the word *cultivation.* Constant tilling of the cultural soil is exactly what is required to sustain growth. The time and effort spent sustaining culture is uncomfortable for many general managers, who see their primary responsibility as quantifying and measuring performance. But I deeply believe that this time is as strategically important as anything else management can do. Sustaining culture means turning the abstractions of values into a common reality. This is critical, because abstractions, by their very nature, are open to the interpretation of each person's experience. The words *responsive, fair, empathetic, trustworthy, striving,* and *teamwork* are all interpreted in a context of individual knowledge. Let me give you an example.

BUILDING A COMMON EXPERIENCE OF TEAMWORK

In the American culture, many but not all people have had some experience as part of a team. It's also true that everyone's experience is different, so to espouse "teamwork" as a value could, in our case, generate twenty thousand different ideas, one for each person in our company. Today, I like the definition of Peter Senge, systems guru and author: "A team is a group of people who need each other to take effective action."[1] I like the element of interconnectedness in this definition. We really never know how big the team is until a crisis occurs. When a computer system goes down here at Schwab, it is painfully obvious to the people in our call centers and branches that the folks in information technology are part of their team. When the elevators stop, it is clear that people who work in what some would consider the "mundane" department of facilities are part of the team. Day to day, our service to each and every customer, the playing of our newest advertisement on television, right down to the serving of meals in our cafeteria—these are all the result of teamwork, and in most cases, we do not personally know our teammates. Understanding interdependence can build deeper understanding and immense appreciation for all of our fellow employees.

Learning About Team Play

Like many of you, I didn't always know about interdependence. I learned it only a few years ago. My lesson began when my boss told me I was "too persuasive."

"What do you mean?" I wanted to know. "I'm head of marketing. We're growing at twenty-five percent a year. I like to think some of that success is because I lead. Isn't persuasion part and parcel of leadership?"

"Yes and no," he said. And my boss, Larry Stupski, then president of the company, was right. British statesman Benjamin Disraeli put it this way: "There go my people. I must follow them. Am I not their leader?"[2] Instead, I was bulldozing, pushing my peers with powerful arguments for why they should follow my ideas—and I was good at it.

It took awhile for Larry's message to sink in, and I think that's because I was raised in the classic American culture that rewards individuals who take charge and win. This "John Wayne management" came naturally to me. Physically I'm a big man; I was a football linebacker and a heavyweight wrestler in college. Also I'm enthusiastic by nature, and unless I watch it I can be overwhelming. I can use this energy and physical presence to get my way, and that's how it often went as I came up through the organization, first at Citicorp and then at Schwab.

But when Larry first made the observation, I was managing senior vice presidents. That is, I was herding cats—big ones, with no interest in being herded. I adjusted to their power by exerting more of my own. It took two years from the time Larry made his observation about my "too persuasive" style for me to learn my weakness and make a change. If I hadn't changed it would've sunk me. Fortunately, a major decision point made it possible for me to learn what he meant.

Sharing Decision Making

We had decided to build call centers, enormous information and switchboard facilities where customers could call to effect transactions over the phone. We studied the whole country to figure out where the first one should go. I was one of five on the management committee, and my staff came up with the recommendation to put it in Indianapolis. Another executive thought it should be in Sacramento.

When the management committee met to hear the case, I argued hard and convincingly for Indianapolis. The executive partial to Sacramento pushed back as hard as she could. I eventually won the day, but it was a painful experience and no one felt very good at the end. It was divisive to the team, because people felt that they had to get behind her or get behind me. My own staff celebrated because we had "won." It reminds me now of a quote attributed to a negotiator on the 1998 team that put together the Northern Ireland peace initiative: "*Where there is division, victory is not a solution.*"

During the Indianapolis decision, I was in constant conflict with Larry. He was president of the parent corporation, and I was president of the largest operating subsidiary. He and I both worked closely with Chuck Schwab, who is the ultimate team player. Larry and I had developed a sense of competition that caused a win-lose environment, and that played out in everything I did. I resisted his counsel. But shortly after this episode, Chuck called Larry and me into his office and said, "Look, I need both of you guys on my team. Stop competing. Dave—Larry is going to run the company, your role is to grow it. Larry, you've got to give Dave some freedom to create new revenue opportunities." And then again: "I need both of you."

Chuck didn't take sides. He defined our relationship as an organizational issue. I saw the practicality of making a commitment to Larry and Chuck to put forth an effort to be a team player, but I also came to realize that if I was going to create a better environment of collaboration with my peers and visibly support Larry's leadership, I would have to change. I would have to discard that internal voice that said, "*Sure, I'm a team player. As long as I'm captain.*" I worked at it, and through reflection, will, and discipline I feel I've made great strides. (Work like this is never done.) Larry changed, too—after a heart attack at age forty-seven when he reevaluated the worth of everything in his life. His transformation from a Type A driven businessperson to a more reflective executive was remarkable.

Two years later, the location of the second call center arose. The other executive still believed we should select Sacramento, while I was partial to Denver. This time, however, instead of spending all of my mental energy preparing my arguments for Denver, I listened to her rationale for Sacramento. What I heard was that Sacramento really wasn't a bad idea, it was actually a very *good* idea. While I still thought Denver was better, my attitude was different and I had listened so much better, my demeanor was totally different. As it turned out, at day's end everyone said, "Let's go with Denver," including the pro-Sacramento executive—not that she felt Denver was the best possible location, but it was the best *decision* because the team made it. Everyone felt heard, felt comfortable, and felt passionate about going forward with a decision that we could all get behind.

What made this decision work? Simply this: I didn't handle it personally or emotionally. I was beginning to trust the judgment of other people to do the right thing for the company. I had learned the meaning, and danger, of being "too persuasive," and the value of really leading a team from the middle rather than the front. In essence, by insinuating that I always knew best, I had been defeating any concept of team. Disrespect caused me to say, "Here are all the reasons we should do this." That attitude excludes discussion, backs people into corners, and stifles the kind of teamwork inherent in Senge's definition. We do indeed all need each other to take effective action. By this point, I had learned to present the facts as I saw them, with my biases, and allow the group to make the decision together. As I continued to mature as a leader, I began to talk even less, to ask better questions, and to give full credit to the team as a whole—where it is deserved. Now, of course, I find myself in the shoes of my boss years before, only hoping to help people grow as he helped me.

Everyone has their own idea of what *teamwork* means. It is up to the leadership to bring common definition and to sustain that over time.

This is but one example and one aspect. A culture is made up of values, language, and action; it is sustained by grounding these abstract values in a common understanding in reality.

USING STORY, IMAGE, AND RITUAL FOR COMMON UNDERSTANDING

Anthropologists identify cultural sustainers as story, image, and ritual. Two of these, story and image, are the language devices that we use to reinforce values. Ritual is the action . . . it is the sum of what we do that reflects the repetitive, predictable themes of the culture. These three bring abstractions to the realm of everyday existence and provide common meaning to any organization.

Stories of Value

When Terry and I first met, he asked me to write an autobiography. He said he wanted to learn the "defining moments" of my life, to help him discover my values. Since we were both single parents, we talked about the difference between the rules we make for our kids and the principles by which they live. *Rules* are imposed values. *Principles* are values that have been made real by our own experience. We do not learn someone's principles when we hear their concepts, we learn them by listening to their experience, their story.

Anyone who has read recent management and leadership theory has been exposed to the power of story. Terry hasn't been alone in his advocacy. Howard Gardner (*Leading Minds*[3]), Noel Tichy (*Leadership Engine*[4]), Jim Kouzes and Barry Posner (*Encouraging the*

Heart[5]), Robert Cooper and Ayman Sawaf (*Executive EQ*[6]), and others devote considerable space and import to the telling of stories. I leave you in their capable hands for the theory. The important thing to me is that stories connect to the limbic brain; they connect to the emotions and can therefore inspire passion, not just consideration. It is this heart connection that I am looking for when I speak to the values of the firm, when I am working at sustaining the culture.

For example, I could have just told you that I learned the real definition and value of teamwork from reading Peter Senge, but that would be untrue. Senge's "rule" of teamwork became a "principle" of teamwork out of my own experience. My hope is that by telling the story of the call center decisions, I have made it real for you.

At Schwab, we spend a lot of time gathering stories of our values in action. At a senior management committee meeting in Carmel in 1997, we arranged a dinner around the theme of storytelling, and we captured the stories on videotape. Everyone was seated in tables of eight. Each table was to vote on the most compelling story at the table and share it with the group. These "signature stories" were videotaped to be used in orientation and other events of the company. It was at this event that we heard the following story about Schwab's value of fairness.

> After the market crash in 1987, there were a few individuals who owed the firm large sums of money. Generally, these customers had been trading on margin and got caught in the downdraft. The task of collecting these large balances fell to Jim Losi, one of the senior vice presidents. His first call was on a family in Southern California who had lost more than their net worth. All that they had left was an IRA account with Schwab and the family home overlooking the Pacific Ocean. The client knew that he owed Schwab the money, and told Jim that he couldn't pay it. Both he and his wife were in their late sixties, and neither was in very good health. Jim talked to him for a long time, and finally struck an agreement that Schwab would take the equity in the house to settle the debt. By agreement, the customer and his wife could live in the house until they no longer needed it, at

> which time it would revert to Schwab. We also agreed that they could keep the IRA account as a necessary adjunct to their retirement funds.
>
> Jim felt like he was out on a limb when he made this deal. After all, we are not in the real estate business. Nonetheless, the debt would eventually get paid, and Jim's empathy and sense of fairness would not allow him to put this couple out of their family home.

This would have been a good story of our values if it had stopped there. But there was more.

> A couple of years after the settlement, the husband of the couple died, and his wife continued to live in the house. But in 1993, there was a fire in that part of the Southern California coast, and the former client's house burned to the ground. Schwab could have taken the insurance money at that point. Appropriately, an entirely different Schwab employee assessed the situation in exactly the same way that Jim had. We helped the woman negotiate a settlement with the insurance company, rebuilt the house, and she moved back into it. She lived in it until she died in 1998, and then the debt was finally settled.

We could talk for a long time about the abstractions of fairness and empathy, but we could not possibly have the impact that this story has. We use the story now to recruit and to illustrate to new employees just how far we will go to live our values, to sustain our culture.

Every company that pays attention to its culture collects stories. Jim Casey started UPS at age fourteen and was on the board when he died at age ninety-eight. Throughout, he was a living, shining laser of vision and values. Jim Kelly, current chairman and CEO, began his career loading trucks. His predecessor, Oz Nelson, started in customer service. When loaders are promoted to drivers, and drivers to managers, they know the career path can lead far if they adhere to the principles—the values and the vision of their heroes.

Casey's values survived him, and the company still focuses on customer service: reliability, courtesy, promptness, neatness, safety, value, responsiveness, total satisfaction. Kelly now tells stories to sustain that culture. He tells, for example, of a customer who shipped a signed original lithograph of an elk to her son as a housewarming present when he completed his hand-built log cabin in Montana. She packed it poorly and in transit it was destroyed. So was she, when she heard the news. She called the UPS route manager in tears. The manager inspected the wreckage, found the artist's name and contacted him, explained the situation, and arranged for a replacement to be express-delivered to the son's door.

Stories are the living proof of the culture. They sustain it by reinforcing the abstractions in life. They give real examples to people, new and old, and they give permission to create a story of one's own that will, in turn, provide inspiration for others.

Image

It's often said that we remember about 80 percent of what we see and only 20 percent of what we hear. This is the limbic brain at work, working literally eighty thousand times faster than the cerebral cortex. While I'm sure that researchers are refining this data, it is undeniable that the world of image and visual symbol is a powerful reinforcement. Story is a moving picture in which the participants all play their roles. Other images also form powerful reinforcement to the abstractions of the culture. For the corporate culture, these images range from simple logos to all-out advertising programs, from the office furniture to the art on the walls.

Logos, Faces, and Pictures. Most companies create logos, images that have no meaning until the company imbues them with it through advertising. At that point, if the company is lucky and has done the right job, the image takes on meaning and becomes a symbol of the company's values, its brand. The Red Cross is unmistakable in its meaning, and the shiny apple with the bite out and a twig at the top is a symbol of simplicity and egalitarianism in computers.

We are fortunate at Schwab to have a very likeable and popular image in the form of our founder's face. Chuck's face has come to represent our culture to our employees and to many if not most of our customers. His story is familiar: he started the firm to give access to people who didn't have access before, established the firm as a discount transaction specialist in the face of the seemingly mysterious and untouchable world of Wall Street, then created a vehicle to make it easy for customers to access mutual funds from one source, and finally, simplified and demystified the use of the Internet. He has spoken enough, been vocal enough, been public enough that his face is the image of the firm. When Chuck shows up at company functions, he always gets an enthusiastic and heartfelt standing ovation. He is the embodiment of the culture of Schwab.

Beyond a logo or, in our case, a face, other images can be displayed that will reinforce and sustain the culture of any organization. In some cases, these images are obvious, like the art on the walls or the decor of the offices. These images have to be consistent with the values of the culture to be reinforcing of it. When there is a seeming inconsistency, it can cause eyebrows to raise, in both employees and in customers. When we think of FedEx, we see their uniforms, trucks, and airplanes, and the ever-familiar drop boxes in the neighborhood. Should any of these change, the company would develop incongruity almost immediately. What if we saw a Mercedes Benz with the FedEx logo adorning its side? What if we saw someone else's face speaking solely for Schwab? These would clearly make us wonder about a change in ownership or philosophy.

Advertising as Image-Maker. We will discuss the specifics of effective advertising in Part Three. But it's impossible to describe the image of a culture without including one aspect of this discipline, its function in accurately reflecting the culture of the company and the people in it. In a company that defines culture as important, every advertising image re-creates and reinforces the values we want our employees to share. We want them to see themselves in the pictures, if not actually, then virtually. In 1999, Schwab began to use real people in our advertising, people from within the firm as well as our customers. We did it in part to inspire our employees to see themselves as advice-givers, as professional and expert brokers who could provide even better investment counsel than their more expensive competitors.

Advertising also provides the image of where the culture will take the company in the coming years. As we write, Schwab is going through a transformation, what we call "The Re-invention of Full-Service Brokerage." A recent *Wall Street Journal* article referred to the effectiveness of the approach: "Indeed, new Schwab television ads stress personalized, intelligent customer service. They position Schwab as a competitor to full-service firms, not merely a 'transaction specialist.' In several ads, the camera zooms in on the faces of young Schwab brokers, including one recent Harvard University graduate who talks about how much he wants to contribute to the company."[7]

These ads are obviously, at least to the *Journal*, accomplishing our goals. They are describing the future in a way that is compelling to our customers and employees, and they are also a vehicle for our employees to see themselves as an integral part of that future, expressing the values of the firm in new and exciting ways.

In-House Images. We also make extensive use of video, not only as a real-time communication tool but as cultural reinforcement. In 1998, Chuck made a video with the backdrop of the American flag that was meant to communicate our vision in broader terms to an internal audience. The narrator asked Chuck what he wanted the business pundits to say about the company in two hundred years. His response was very uplifting to those who saw it. He said that this "little company on the West Coast" had started a revolution that allowed people who had never had access to financial markets to make a happier and more secure future for themselves, that we had demystified a vital part of the system for the majority of Americans. That video is a terrific combination of image and story that reinforces the culture to every one of our employees.

We think so highly of this process that we produce videos of values-supporting stories whenever we can. The story I related about the house in Southern California was so powerful that we found the son of the couple who had owed us the money, and asked him if he would explain on video what had happened. He was eager to help. In fact, we shot the video in the actual house. He spoke eloquently about the way Schwab had handled the situation. At the end of the video, with a picture of his parents in the background, he said, "There is a lot more to life than the bottom line . . . or 'business is business.' There are other things that are important, like faith, forgiveness, love, and family . . . and I think that is part of the way [Schwab] dealt with our family."

We tagged the film with the caption: *"This short film is dedicated to the Roberts family . . . and to all the individuals at Schwab who have perfected the art of being fair, empathetic and responsive."* By tying the values directly to this image, we have again reinforced the importance of our culture and encouraged all employees, new and experienced, to live those values every day.

Metaphors of the Culture. Images can be created with videos, advertisements, logos, office spaces, or for the skilled, with the voice. Terry and I are constantly looking for the right metaphorical images to describe our cultural norms. Is the company a family, a machine, an organism, or a brain? Is the next change similar to jumping a chasm, crossing a river, or climbing a mountain? These are all different images, and the choice can make a substantial difference in whether the culture is supported or degraded. At a recent management committee meeting, a particularly heated discussion about our continual need for facilities ended when one of the executives reported that her group referred to their cubicles as "veal pens." That image was a wake-up call to move more aggressively to fix the problem. For the same reason, we don't refer to employees as "the troops" or the "rank and file." Language is one way in which image is created that supports the culture; we'll discuss this more in Chapter Five.

Ritual: Culture in Action

Left to themselves, cultures will change with strong leaders who have different ideas, and with new participants who practice different values. Accordingly, particularly in a growth company, a ritual that is aimed directly at cultural reinforcement is critical to prevent erosion. While we try to screen and initiate so as to bring in people who will find our values congenial and then make sure they absorb those values on the job, occasionally we need to reaffirm our values as a group.

VisionQuest. I marked the 1995 vision and values "road show" as a turning point in our development. By 1999, because of attrition and growth, more than ten thousand of our employees had not experienced such a reinforcement. Accordingly, we once again involved the entire company in a reexamination of our vision, this time in the context of the Internet, in a world that is substantially different from the one that existed in 1995. Called *VisionQuest,* the ritual used a combination of colored and elaborate maps to depict the current state of our industry and our role in it. On a single Saturday in March, every one of our employees worldwide worked with these maps and a group of facilitators to gain a personal experience of the vision and values and of their individual role in making our combined purpose real in the world of financial services.

In the third quarter of the year, we conducted our annual employee survey. Once again, more than 90 percent said that they knew where the company was going, more than 80 percent believed that their own personal work made a difference in the company's progress. Most important, the survey also reinforced their knowledge of the strength of the values and their role in guiding our day-to-day decisions.

VisionQuest is a ritual, and a very direct one. And while we tend to think of ritual as this kind of special event, the repetitive elements of all company activities reflect the values of the culture. The timing, attendance list, and tone of meetings, for example, can support the stated culture or be in conflict with it. The organizational structure itself, the titles of those operating in the structure, and the extent to which these formal positions generate power in the company all need attention.

Market Storm as Ritual. Throughout the years, Schwab has experienced substantial spikes in volume when our capacity to answer phones and execute trades is stretched to its limits. To buffer these "blips" in volume, we have constructed extra telephone and computer facilities in buildings that house employees who are not typically helping customers directly. When the volume gets so great that customer service is in jeopardy, these people pitch in and help. In 1998 and 1999, we experienced tremendous runs of trading volume. To meet the need, we offer premium pay, bring in lots of food, and really support the extra effort that it requires. These periods, which we refer to as "Market Storm," have become rituals. It is inconvenient and often disruptive for employees to let their own normal job duties lapse, but they do it willingly and with great pride in accomplishment. Market Storm is a ritualistic affirmation of the service base of our culture. Such participation knows no hierarchical boundary.

In early 1999, one of the executives was questioning whether some highly paid vice presidents should participate in Market Storm. Clearly, we could never economically justify executives' answering phones, but they wanted to be there just as I did. It is part of the culture to drop everything and help the customer, and Market Storm participation reinforces these values. They went, were needed, and enjoyed it immensely. Their participation was worth every penny.

Taking Ritual Outside the Organization. Generally, our company culture encourages people to act on their own to express the values outside work as well. We focus on a few select rituals outside the company that will bring us together around what we believe. Right now, Schwab is organized around various enterprises, or business units.

Each year, we have kick-off meetings, generally by enterprise, as a way of celebrating the old year and setting up the year to come. These meetings are usually quite productive, and most of the time is spent in general session in a hotel ballroom.

In 1996, our Retail Enterprise decided to try something totally different. They contacted the local chapter of Habitat for Humanity and suggested that Schwab would bring more than five hundred people to bear on projects of construction and reconstruction in the East Bay on a single day. It took immense conviction on the part of the meeting organizers to get this done. There were security and insurance considerations, some feeling that many people (the bankers) wouldn't want to do it, some concern about the strenuous nature of the work. The group persevered.

It wound up being one of the most successful rituals we have ever done together. It has since been repeated by other divisions, and in 1999, the people of Schwab constructed a dozen houses in various places throughout the country. The project has provided a repeated, common experience (a ritual) that expresses the values of the company and reaffirms the importance of our culture to our business activity. What's important is not only that we did the work in the community but also that the same spirit gets reflected when there is a need for extra telephone work, or when someone from another function calls and needs help, or when someone who is not a vice president asks for cooperation. These are the times when ritual pays off.

Story, image, and ritual—these are the anthropological supports of culture. But here the parallel between companies and civilizations breaks down. Unlike a civilization, a company has no natural birth rate. We have to replenish our population with adults who have lived in other company cultures, some of them the equivalent of other civilizations. More than any other aspect, the recruitment of people who can perform in a business and yet who also share in the basic values of a particular company is an ongoing issue, because making sure the DNA matches is critical to their success and ours.

RECRUITING: EXPANDING THE POPULATION

The late Bill Gore, the founder of Gore-Tex, believed that recruiting was the number one limitation to the growth of a company with strict principles, such as his own. He should know. In 1999, Gore-Tex was ranked number seventeen in the annual *Fortune* survey of "Best Companies to Work For."[8] Gore had found that growing or replacing associates beyond 25 percent per year was impossible, given the importance of finding people who were a cultural fit with the company. The company's preference is to employ only those who come recommended from someone within the company.

I share his concern and I envy Gore's process. I also believe that in a proprietary product business like Gore-Tex it is possible to limit growth and still sustain demand for the product. But in a service business like Schwab, if customers find that we can't deliver, they will take their transactions and their money elsewhere and stay. A skier might wait a week for just the right jacket, but most investors won't wait five minutes to trade a stock or make a deposit. Satisfying every single customer who wants our service is critical to our survival. So we have to find a way to match the growth rate with a similar rate in finding and employing people who fit.

A company can't recruit well unless its communication is accurate and its procedures are finely tuned. We have to lure the people we want, screen the ones that we don't, and make offers that are compelling. Like other growth companies in this age of super-speed, we are constructing and refining this capability at the same time we are hiring a total number of people that approaches one-third of our population each year. It feels like we are trying to change the tires on a runaway car.

Internet posting and applications have made this part of the job easier. But the Web is more valuable than just an administrative tool. For a rapidly growing company, it does part of the job of the search firms or placement offices, giving direct exposure to available professionals or new college graduates even before we have developed the relationships we need with recruiters or placement officers. Additionally, recruiting by Internet gives us an automatic screen for people who are technologically savvy, and it signals those hard-to-reach technologists that we are using their tools appropriately. (I would imagine that there are technologists who would not even apply to companies who do not recruit on the Web.) So the Internet gives us a way to reach more broadly and also provides a process edge until the résumé arrives. Still, the basics of recruiting that are most vital to sustaining our culture happen either *instead* of Web connection or in addition to it. These basics have to do with Bill Gore's observations about culture-conscious companies. I think there are three principles to hiring well for passion-driven growth:

- Everybody recruits.
- Sell a life's work, not a job.
- Hire for intelligence and attitude, train for skill.

I'll examine each in turn.

Everybody Recruits

If we have done the job of instilling pride in the people who are here, they will want to fill the jobs available with their friends and family. We offer some financial and gift incentives to employees to bring in good people in certain elements of the company, just so we can get some attention on it day to day, but if the culture is working right, our employees will recruit without the incentives. Many of our best recruits have come from other service industries, and have been encouraged by employees who have noticed a certain spirit and capability. Rental car companies, banks, even restaurants have unwittingly provided some new hires to Schwab.

I personally have a "farm team" and I ask the other executives to develop one as well. Most of the people on mine don't even know they are. I've spotted them over the years, at conferences and events and through peers, and they've impressed me with insights and attitude. I make a point to get their business cards, and every six months or so, I flip through my Rolodex and give them a call. They may be happy where they are, but I keep in touch. I send them annual reports, copies of articles I think they might enjoy. Why? They may never work for me (and they may) but I never want to be in a position where I do a search from scratch. When mergers occur in the industry, the very best people find their next position through a list of relationships. I want to be included on that list. Most recently, when First Interstate was eaten by Wells Fargo Bank, we landed two of First's best executives. They, in turn, have brought others from their own following.

Now I don't want to miss a major point. I ask everyone to recruit, but it's not only to increase the number of bodies in the company. I know from personal experience that when I recruit, I get excited about what we offer all over again. Recruiting makes a person articulate what is so great about the place he works, and the very act of speaking about it renews his own spirit. Getting everyone to recruit provides new and renewed employees. This is an e-mail message I received in July 1999 from a Schwab technology employee:

> I just got off the phone with a dear friend of mine, who's looking to make a change in his job. He had just put his résumé on the Web, and was inundated with "hits" and phone calls. His skill set is very versatile, he is going to be in great demand.
>
> He was leaning toward working with a project management consulting firm, and in talking to his potential supervisor, he learned that they do lots of work with Schwab. That led him to consider "cutting out the middleman" and working for Schwab directly.
>
> He told me about his skills, but he kept coming back to the notion of how important it was to work for a company with integrity, that has a culture. He wasn't asking me if there were any job openings, he was more interested in knowing the ethos of Schwab.
>
> I told him that if those things were important to him, then there was little question that Schwab is where he wanted to be. I told him about "VisionQuest," and how much of an impact it made on me. I

> kept starting statements with, "I feel hokey saying this, but . . ." then going on to say how, for me, I can't imagine another corporate setting I'd rather be in.
>
> I recounted how my parents, who have been visiting from LA, came to visit the office, walked in the lobby, and immediately noticed the bins for the Kosovo Relief Drive. Then they saw the moving panels of the Names Project Quilt hanging. In the cafeteria, they saw the display about the Habitat for Humanity, and were just blown away. I told this all to my friend . . . continuing to feel hokey, and he was more and more impressed. I also told him that it was a tough job, that our customers were the most demanding in the world, and that we take their well-being as our own responsibility.
>
> As of today, he is looking at the opportunities here. He said, "You should be in recruiting." I told him that I am, just like everyone here.

Yet another noteworthy story that spread quickly.

Sell a Life's Work, Not a Job

This e-mail message also shows the power of talking about values that are larger than the nature of the work. Job changes are the rule, not the exception, in this environment, and according to the Bureau of Labor Statistics, despite nearly full employment, job anxiety was three times higher in 1999 than it was in the recession of 1981. This despite the fact that no more jobs are disappearing than before. The analysts conclude that while employment itself is more secure, particular jobs are not. Mergers are the order of the day. People feel insecure about the job they have, and their feeling about employment itself is less secure than it used to be.[9]

We just have to take advantage of this dynamic. A job is temporary, a life's work is not. While many believe that a life's work is reserved for artists and writers, we all know intuitively at least that a life's work is determined internally, by what we care about. It is not dependent on the particular company we work for. By instilling real purpose into a company and talking about that purpose openly, we can attract nearly everyone except the real cynics. What we can promise is a chance to contribute, a chance to make a difference rather than merely the opportunity to put in time for money. As we communicate about that difference, the issues of job security get reframed. Our intention is to remain independent, and we do not plan to lay people off. Those are not promises, but we believe we can sustain our growth to create more opportunities for individuals, and that each opportunity is another chance to contribute, perhaps on a bigger scale than before.

People want to become part of that.

Hire for Intelligence and Attitude, Train for Skill

The speed of change makes much of what people learn in school, particularly professional school, obsolete by the time they've been in the market for five years. While that fact is an argument for studying liberal arts and other foundational disciplines that create curiosity and learning skills, it is also a signal that a company can't hire only for today's job requirements. So within limits, I hire for intelligence, character, and attitude, and then train for skill. There are famous examples, like Michael Eisner, who took only ninety days to get up to speed on the entertainment business, or Peter Ueberroth, successful at careers as diverse as travel executive, CEO of the Olympic Games, and Commissioner of Baseball. The examples we hear about are at the top of their businesses, but the principles apply just as well to entry-level positions. There are associates at car-rental companies who have transferred to Schwab and been equally successful. Their attitude with customers is going to come across whether they are matching customers to the cars they need or assisting investors in balancing portfolios. Fundamentally, they care about other people, and they have enough intelligence and enough motivation to learn just about any application that allows them to express that caring.

In the introduction to Part One, Terry made reference to the Posner and Smith research that showed that people who have thought about their own values are nearly twice as committed to their organization's goals. We check, in the interview process, to make sure that applicants have at least thought about their values. If they haven't we suggest that they do before they come to work here.

Intelligence isn't enough, and experience isn't enough. I've had a lot of practice hiring for sheer intellectual horsepower and previous knowledge of the job. Mistakes are inevitable. The sad truth is, I've found in almost every case when I knew I made a mistake, I've done everything I can to make it work, but it rarely does. In a passion-driven business, when a person's heart is not in the right place, the corporate body will spit them out like a germ.

In a passion-driven company, these are the key questions:

"Does he have the intelligence to do the job?"

"Has she demonstrated good character?"

"Is his attitude one of commitment to others and to the values of the company?"

"Will she welcome change and new learning in order to continue to contribute?"

"Will others want to work with him?"

If the answers to these questions are "yes," then your recruits will be successful anywhere.

The critical aspect of working at Schwab or Gore-Tex or Hewlett-Packard is not the money, although the money is important. What makes these companies different is the meaning, it is the chance to make a difference every day. That meaning is what people thrive on, and it is what they miss when they leave.

Good recruits, renewed people . . . a continual buffer against invasion of the culture. I recently received an e-mail message from a customer service representative who wrote to me out of desperation. A seventy-four-year-old client had made a mistake trading on our Web site. The result was a $400 trading loss. Someone in our dispute department had decided the best we could do, since it was "the customer's fault," was to split the loss with the client. This is the "bad" part of the story. The "good" part of the story is that our field representative knew that we would stand for something better, so he refused to accept this decision and e-mailed the CEO! His final comment to me was "I hope this isn't career suicide." Quite the contrary, I'm delighted to see that our culture encouraged him to challenge this decision and gave him the confidence to go as far as he had to to make it right.

A culture works like the human body. Each cell has a specialized function, and performs it in enlightened self-interest. But the most amazing thing is that every single cell—no matter how humble its function—also contains the master plan for the entire body.

A passion-driven company works the same way. Whether you work in accounting or marketing or customer service or anywhere else, in an effective company you share and identify with the "DNA" of the master plan for the whole enterprise—its vision, its values, its purpose.

The building and sustaining of culture is what aligns us all, and it is culture at work when the traditional rules of business need to give way to the higher authority of "the right thing to do." It is an outcome that is worthy of our time and effort.

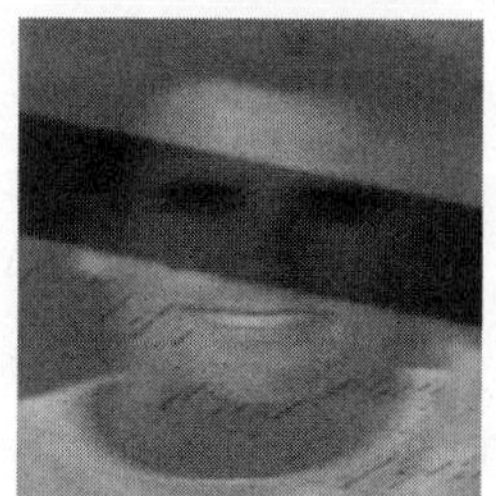

FROM SUSTAINING CULTURE TO CULTIVATING COMMITMENT THROUGH DIVERSITY

Culture is created first with a proclamation of values and vision. Then, as Dave described in Chapter Two, it is sustained with story, image, and ritual; that is, language, pictures, and action that overcome the barriers to culture. Whatever your sphere of influence, whether you are the designated leader or not, you can use the principles outlined here to continue to build the loyalty and commitment of those who work with you.

Collect the stories of events that support the application of the cultural values and norms. Publish them, or at least use them as you talk about your department's accomplishments and reputation.[1]

Find—or better yet, create—images that are meaningful and supportive of the culture and display them regularly. Posters will do, but the most effective images are personal: pictures of people in action or videos of actual customers or employees.

Consider the rituals in your group—particularly the rituals you take for granted like regular meetings, processes, offsites, and celebrations—and make a mental audit of them. Do they support the culture or are they run in a way that is inconsistent with the values you want to promulgate? If they do not reflect the atmosphere and rules that you believe in, change them.

Make sure that your hiring criteria include an inventory of the candidates' values in addition to their skills and experiences.

Sustaining culture takes constant attention and communication. You are, after all, deciding who belongs and who doesn't, what behavior is acceptable and what behavior isn't. These decisions are easy at the extremes (most companies won't hire people who openly incite violence, or those who are abusive), but they get progressively more difficult as mere matters of personal style and social custom might seemingly conflict with the corporate culture and dominant style of people in an organization. In the next chapter, we explore how that blurry line between congruence and conflict can become more distinct. Is there any advantage to diversity in a values-driven company? How does a company operate to assure that the culture remains intact and that, at the same time, it enjoys the breadth of experience and points of view that it needs to compete? How can a company ensure that the glue of corporate culture attaches to all variety of surfaces and forms a strong bond?

The word *diversity* is so often and so carelessly used that it is nearly bereft of meaning. Few subjects have generated more clichés, and few concepts have been used as much as diversity to support strong advocacy for radical change *or* for clinging doggedly to the status quo.

"Diversity" was first heard by many in the business world as a euphemism for affirmative action. But diversity arguments differ from affirmative action arguments. While the term *diversity* was and still is applied to the racial, ethnic, and gender mix of a given company, the rationale for its adoption is not only the moral ground of fairness, it is the practical ground of good business.

Consultants presented a case that strongly suggested that a workforce mirroring the client base was the best way to achieve competitive advantage within that client base. While that certainly makes sense, the arguments for the support of diversity that are the most useful to me are not the ones that focus on market share or individual decision models. They are rather the arguments that focus on the stimulating nature of working with people from significantly different backgrounds who bring significantly different perspectives to bear on a business.

Of course, *everyone* is different. Even a group of white male bankers is diverse in terms of background, parentage, and proclivity. But they are not *significantly* different and, as a result, they may not disagree on matters of substance. Their differences aren't very interesting and therefore they don't offer much to a company that wants to remain creative and passionate.

Bill Sonnenschein, a colleague of mine at Cal, suggests some advantages of diversity that actually have an impact on the fire, excitement, and quality of everyday interchange. He says that diversity

> Enables a wide range of views to be present in an organization, including views that might challenge the status quo from all sides.
>
> Focuses and strengthens an organization's core values.
>
> Is instrumental in organizational change.
>
> Stimulates social, economic, intellectual and emotional growth.
>
> Helps an organization understand its place in the global community.[2]

These advantages of diversity speak to those aspects of a company that keep it a vibrant, exciting community, a place where people can do their best work and are stimulated and excited about growing into new areas rather than clinging to old models. For example, one advantage Sonnenschein mentions is the strengthening of values. He isn't suggesting that diversity itself is a value. He is suggesting that showing interest and support for diversity affirms the company culture inside and outside the firm itself. A company cannot claim "empathy and teamwork" as values and not make the effort to engage everyone at work, regardless of their propensity to speak up. Likewise, a company cannot claim "fairness" as a value and ignore elements in our society that prevent fairness from being practiced. The value of "fairness" doesn't end just before the advertisements for recruiting are written. If it does, then employees who depend on those values for inspiration are quickly disillusioned and will soon leave.

Finally, globalization itself, and globalization's primary tools, technology and the Internet, create an environment that is strictly competence-based and therefore blind to differences that spawn prejudice, such as age, sex, ethnicity, and race. Technology, at this point, is an objective science. We know when something works. We don't need to know anything about the person who made it work . . . our judgment can be strictly impersonal. Ironically, these very technology tools that make impersonal communication prolific also provide a shield against the worst aspects of personal contact—judgments based on irrelevant differences.

One would suspect that all this information-sharing over the Internet will lead to an eventual dissolving of cultural boundaries, a flattening of the static wave that occurs when cultures combine. This may happen in a couple of hundred years, but right now there is research that points in just the opposite direction, data suggesting that the Internet is, ironically, creating a world of specialization of human beings even as it facilitates the globalization of information. "In order to maintain intimate communication, and in order to keep up with our own sophistication, we fragment into tiny clusters within our global skyscraper."[3] In other words, we specialize, finding and talking to more and more people who are interested in what we are interested in. This fits our experience, doesn't it? As we'll discuss in Part Three, this increased ability to sort information and contacts according to our own interest or expertise is one of the most powerful marketing aspects of the Internet. It makes it possible to market to each individual exactly what that individual has shown interest in before. Chat rooms and forums are organized around specific interests, not general conversation. So the Internet at once creates the possibility for globalization of cultures and the possibility of even more isolation, or of the clustering together of people with the same perspective.

This balkanization is precisely the opposite of what is needed to foster more informed general business decisions or greater innovation. Yet it creates an interesting and challenging backdrop against which we can try to create a diverse workforce.

To garner the cultural benefits of diversity, we have to want them badly enough to not just tolerate diversity but embrace it, to demand it as part of our culture, as part of our competitive advantage. And once we do, we have to adopt the policies, practices, and personal discipline that it takes to get the most from it. These are areas in which Dave has considerable experience, as we'll see in Chapter Three.

I teach a graduate elective course in leadership communication at the Haas School of Business at the University of California, Berkeley. The primary requirement of the course is that students must develop a message and speak about a change that they want to implement, one that is based on their values. The issue must also be something that they have had some personal experience with—they cannot merely wax lyrical about what they have read or about another's theory or experience. I add to their task by suggesting that they need to say something new about the topic. They have the luxury of eleven weeks to reflect, refine, and relate their thinking and feelings on the subject.

I give you this background because "diversity in the workplace" is the most popular student topic—and the most difficult to work with. Yet when students are able to tap into their own experience, new expressions about this topic come easily. The students eventually recognize that to intellectualize the issue is to miss the richness of possibility. It is an issue that calls not just for new ideas but also for our personal growth.

I'll add one more idea to the mix. As for diversity, we don't have a choice. Being in favor of diversity is like being in favor of cold weather in a Minnesota winter. The fact is that the white American male dominance of all organizations is coming to an end. The question is not whether we will have a diverse group of colleagues. The question is whether we will have the skill to capitalize on the changing and exciting demographics that will form the workforce of the next century. Rather than freezing to death in denial, by embracing diversity we'll find new connections and strengths, new areas to explore and to cultivate.

THREE

CULTIVATING COMMITMENT THROUGH DIVERSITY

Terry has traced the history of the issue of diversity and offered a worthy challenge: to say something new and useful about it—for today and as we move further into the Internet age. He knows that Schwab has indeed instituted several programs to recruit and retain the very best people from the whole range of race, ethnicity, gender, age, and sexual orientation. Our efforts have shown some results in terms of increasing the richness of the mix of people in the company. Yet this does not set us apart, for other companies are doing many of the same things. I want to rise to his challenge and offer more than statistics or program recommendations. These simply are not enough to weave through the maze of confusion around this subject.

WHERE ARE WE NOW?

Each year, *Fortune* magazine tabulates the fifty best companies for minorities to work for. Other publications publish similar ratings. The criteria are simple, objective, and apt; they include percentages of minorities in senior management, on boards of directors, and as new hires. These measurements clearly reflect the results of a company's policy and practices. *Fortune* asks companies to apply for consideration; we have not yet done so, but other larger investment firms have. Only one ranks in the top fifty: J. P. Morgan at number forty-eight. Of this ranking, the *Fortune* editor comments: "It speaks volumes about the industry that J. P. Morgan, Number 48, is the top Wall Street firm in our rankings. Managing director Ron Gault lives in South Africa, where, among other duties, he trains local blacks for careers in finance."[1]

This ranking does indeed say volumes about our industry, and it makes it imperative to ask just what it will take to make *sustainable, long-term* progress in gaining and keeping a diverse group of people. I imagine that many of you are looking for the distinctions that will make a major difference in this area just as I am. I consider this challenge a personal one—and also one that is critical to our being able to maintain a competitive advantage as we continue to grow.

The data underscore a major fact about our industry: Diverse groups of people have not traditionally used our products and services in the same proportion as Caucasian males. Financial services has been an elitist industry. Yet, in fact, our company is founded on the idea that the industry should *not* be elitist. Chuck started the company because he saw an industry that was not fair to customers in general, even to those with access to markets or with money to invest.

So financial services is not like groceries, pharmaceuticals, cosmetics, or clothes. There have been structural and cultural barriers to minorities and women in this industry, and that fact creates more obstacles as well as more opportunity. For Schwab, breaking this barrier is not just a matter of creating better programs, it is a matter of educating people to actually use our services and thereby to become engaged in what we do.

As Terry said, I have had some experience with this issue that has kept me active in seeking answers. Based on that experience, I believe that the roots of our success have to grow in our company culture, not just in the programs that we create and implement. Here is the syllogism: It is absolutely necessary, in the world of idea competition, to have contribution from as many people in the company as possible. Passion for the work makes people contribute. Passion comes from engagement. Diversity is a fact. Diverse people get engaged when they think they are able to personally contribute to something worthwhile.

If this line of reasoning holds true, then the key to attracting and really engaging a diverse group of people is making sure that they know they can contribute, and making sure that their contribution is worthwhile . . . that they are expressing their values in a demonstrable way.

We have had some success in this area of diversity development. In fact, we have had the greatest success in the industry in building a *gender*-diverse company. As of this writing, nearly 80 percent of the people in our company report to women executives. Our management committee is composed of fourteen people, six of them women. In 1999, we received the Women in Technology International CEO Recognition Award for our accomplishments. While this award does not speak to the overall diversity of our company, it is an important milestone. And by recognizing the benefits of our success with one important segment of this issue, we can analyze the possibilities for other segments.

We have learned a great deal from our success in integrating women into our company. A particular benefit of diversity is demonstrable: There is a fundamentally different atmosphere at Schwab than at other financial services companies, precisely because we have done well at recruiting and promoting women. I have experienced this difference at other companies (and I serve on the boards of several right now)—Schwab's style and decision processes feel fundamentally different from those at the other companies. I've also heard the unsolicited remarks of new executives at Schwab, both men and women, that indicate that we enjoy a much more collegial atmosphere, much more dialogue, and have an easier time focusing on customers rather than focusing on personal career advancement, precisely because our culture is not overly charged with aggressive personal competition. Outside observation is very important, because I suspect that we are enjoying some of the benefits of a diverse group of people, and that those benefits may be transparent to us. This is as it should be with all differences in gender, ethnicity, race, physical ability, age, or sexual orientation. I wish I could say that the company had achieved the same level of natural comfort with all categories of diversity, but we haven't. But because of our success in achieving gender diversity, we have some experience in how it will feel when we are successful in other areas.

HOW DID WE MOVE TOWARD GENDER PARITY?

This small success did not come easily, nor was I the prime mover in it. But in light of that success, Schwab has taken a very long-term and I believe successful path toward the workforce of the future. Programs are only what the public sees, and I think the story that underlies our approach will be instructive.

Like most people my age, I was introduced to the world of organizational diversity through education about affirmative action programs. In my first job (it was in public health), we were keeping track of numbers and worrying about diversity from the standpoint of compliance with certain goals. It was a real distraction, because I believed then, as I still do, that there is a moral imperative buried in the broad subject of diversity. I was inspired by my mother's activity in nursing to make a difference in any way that I could. She and Dad raised my brothers and me to recognize our responsibility to help others, and I thought that the public sector offered the most opportunity. In public health we talked a lot about equal opportunity—and public health was, in fact, an early bastion for talented and smart women. When I migrated to financial services, I noticed a marked difference. Most of the conversations were about hitting the right numbers rather than doing the right thing. I didn't think much more about it until I came to Schwab in the early 1980s.

In the interim, the thinking about affirmative action and diversity had begun to shift. It had become obvious that population demographics were changing in such a way that white males would not dominate the numerical measures of the workforce for much longer. The same demographics were creating potential segmented markets in financial services that were gender- or ethnic-based. Chuck had also made it clear that he wanted the employee base of Schwab to "look like America." This in an industry that had been identified with backroom dealing by Wall Street power players, all of them . . . you guessed it . . . white males. There was nothing about this industry that provided minorities or women with any prospect of succeeding.

The stage was set for my education. In the next few years, my attitude changed from tolerating diversity to valuing it; from looking at diversity as something that was morally good and difficult to implement to thinking about it as something that is absolutely necessary—and more difficult to implement than I ever imagined. This evolution started with a hard lesson.

In 1989, I was managing all of the retail operation for Schwab, which included a national branch network. At the time, about 40 percent of the branch managers were women. We had grown so big that I needed to hire six regional managers for the branch managers to report to. I thought I needed real professionals who had been in the financial business, and I didn't think any of our own branch managers were qualified, so I asked my colleagues to hire from outside the company. I told them to try to find qualified minorities and women as part of the mix. They came back to me with five white males and a single African American, also a male. I asked them why they had not found any women, and they replied that qualified women were hard to find. I agreed to hire the people that they recommended.

In short order, my boss came to me and said, "You're hiring too many men." I was really defensive about it. I told him that I had tried, but couldn't find any women . . . that qualified women were too hard to recruit. He said, "I don't care. You need to hire some women regional managers." I thought he was picking on me.

I didn't think that for long. There was a revolt among the women branch managers. They expressed a ton of anger about what I had done. Fortunately, there was enough good will that we could bring them all together and listen. I was defensive and angry at first, and then the more I listened to their perception, the more my own lights went on. "Look up on the stage," they said. "All you see are men." They were right. The more I listened, the worse I felt.

Shortly after that episode, I watched an ABC *20/20* program called "True Colors." The network had followed a Caucasian male and an African American male—both equally financially qualified—into a new city, and filmed them trying to establish credit, buy a car, and rent a house. The results were appalling. In every endeavor, the black was stifled, interrogated, or simply refused the same courtesy and respect given to his white counterpart. I began to realize what it must be like to be in a minority in the United States, and I began to shift my thinking about it.

As with most epiphanies, timing was important. Just then, listening to the women at Schwab and seeing that video moved me from tolerating the idea of diversity to promoting it. It was clearly a moral consideration at that point, and I can't say that my own standing as part of a religious minority hadn't given me some special sensitivity in this area. I decided that it was time to learn what we could about this issue. Few companies were having a great deal of success, particularly in our industry. I started by forming a special high-level study group within the company on diversity.

FINDING THE RIGHT GOAL: PASSION-DRIVEN DIVERSITY

We debated the purpose of the group at length. There were advocates for a "numbers" approach to the issue, who felt that the group should first focus on programs to increase the populations of minorities in our company. Because we believe so strongly in the role of passion and engagement in growing our company, we eventually defined our purpose as "exploring, articulating and creating the kind of environment necessary to support a diverse employee base." We wanted the company to be a place where *every qualified person who shared the fundamental values of the firm,* regardless of age, race, ethnicity, sexual orientation, or gender could be productive and feel safe and fully included. We wanted the purpose of the group to be visionary, an aspiration that would guide decisions about the internal environment.

It's important to note the limitations to our aspiration. We did not want to focus on numbers for numbers' sake. While we were eager to measure progress, I was convinced that the issue in the industry, and the issue at Schwab, was one of values and cultural integrity. We also limited our range to "qualified people who share the fundamental values of the firm." We had no intention of weakening the culture of our company to accommodate those who wanted to practice or advocate different values, and we made that clear from the outset. We knew then and know now that a vibrant culture balances freedom of expression with adherence to a core set of values. We did not want a "cult" at Schwab, but we did want to make sure that we kept both new thinking and perspective alive in the organization. *This* kind of diversity, different thinking combined with adherence to our values, is vital to our success.

The groundwork was laid for progress. We agreed that we would be aggressive in creating that atmosphere. I believed that by being passive about diversity, we would run the risk of creating an underground of misunderstanding and indifference. Conversely, I believed that by moving toward diversity aggressively while articulating the reasons why diversity makes good business sense, we would have the possibility of creating *the* place to work in the next couple of decades.

Linking diversity to our values and our strategy goes on to this day, and will continue. As we address new markets, both in the United States and abroad, the issue will become more obviously critical. While I still feel a moral mandate, my purpose in talking about diversity is to create better practical understanding of the business issues and urgency. As we include diversity in the front of our efforts, there are two clear points to make, and they are not mutually exclusive: the impact of diversity on business results, and the importance of diversity in keeping integrity with our values.

THE BUSINESS CASE FOR DIVERSITY

The demographics are very clear: minorities and women will be the majority of new entries into the workforce in a very short time. (They already are in California.) If we don't expand our capability to recruit from these growing pools of talent, we will find ourselves competing for a rapidly shrinking pool. When people look up in the organization, they want to see people like themselves in positions of substance and importance in the company. If they don't find anyone at all, or the people they find are all in stereotypical non-revenue-producing positions, they are discouraged and in fact might be driven away.

According to a survey conducted by Korn/Ferry International, more than half of minority executives are likely to leave their firms to find more challenging positions. The survey also revealed that nearly all of the respondents look for a racially diverse cadre of senior executives when evaluating their own chances for success.[2] This is not surprising, yet it poses a clear challenge to any firm—in order to attract minorities, a company has to *have* minorities.

New Employees, New Customers

We also know that women and people from ethnic minorities will be the fastest-growing groups of customers for our services. Two years ago, I was visiting a branch in Southern California when an older Asian woman walked in carrying a shopping bag. She stopped short of the counter and looked around the lobby and behind the desks that were in the front part of the branch. She spotted a young Asian broker, and immediately walked up to his desk and asked, "Can you help me?" She proceeded to show the broker her bag full of stock certificates, which she wanted to identify and leave in a new account. Had she not seen a face that gave her confidence, she would have gone elsewhere. The presence of an Asian broker made a statement to her, at least about this branch, if not about our company. We would expect her to want to be comfortable in our surroundings. Other companies have this experience. One of *Fortune*'s "best" companies, Union Bank of

California, has a workforce that is 54 percent minority, roughly the same percentage as their primary market in California. They know it makes a difference, particularly on the front line. "We do awareness studies. We ask customers. The answer is 'yes,' it makes a difference."[3]

Emerging Culture-Specific Markets

A physical presence is not the only factor that makes a difference. Decisions about specific offerings in the many diverse markets are far better when they are made with the participation of members of those markets. Perhaps there is no single ritual that displays differences in markets more acutely than the way people deal with money. Money is intensely personal, and our ethnic and social cultures teach us different rules about spending, saving, and investing. The Asian woman who walked into our branch in Southern California demonstrated a need to speak to someone who could not only speak her language but also understand her culture's nuances. We learned, years before that episode, the power of being able to serve cultures very specifically, and it became part of our effort to demonstrate that we are serious about a connection with diverse cultures, not only as a recruiter, but also as a financial partner.

After the severe market correction in 1987, we had to reduce expenses fairly sharply, and we chose to close the branch we had opened in Hong Kong. The operation had grown fairly rapidly to over $1 million in revenue, and we wanted to keep as much of this business as we could. We moved the manager, Larry Yu, to San Francisco, and he installed toll-free lines from Hong Kong to make it possible for clients to continue to do business with us. Naturally, he staffed the operation with people who could speak Mandarin and Cantonese. He saw an additional opportunity to build business among the Bay Area's substantial Asian community as well, using the same approach. We produced a number of Chinese-language television advertisements featuring Larry, and sure enough, people from the Asian communities began to call.

While we had intended to be opportunistic and to leverage our Chinese capability to serve our customers, the community also saw our efforts as a commitment to their culture. Asia/Pacific Center is now a major factor in our retail operation, with seven branches nationwide as of 1999 and several hundred native-speaking brokers, customer service representatives, and managers. We offer multilingual automatic telephone service. In 1997 we reopened in Hong Kong; early the next year, we introduced Web trading in Chinese. Having learned from our customers of their needs, we also make sure that there is a mix of people in our branches that reflect the customer base.

Clearly, our Asia/Pacific experience served us well in demonstrating our desire to connect with other cultures. We have since opened a Latin American center in Miami with Spanish-speaking capability, and we are learning the significant differences among Spanish-speaking cultures. We have also begun a specific development program based particularly on the needs of women. We believe that as we demonstrate our interest in helping customers with specific needs, we are signaling our interest in them and appealing to their desire to do business and work with our company.

The most difficult group for us to recruit has been African Americans, and I count it as a personal failure not to have made more dramatic changes there. At Schwab, we help people make their financial dreams come true, but the truth is that African Americans are disproportionately poor, and although that condition is changing for many, there is not a rich history of successful investing that serves as a cultural role model. To me, that makes it even more important that we find a model to serve this customer group, and that we recruit successfully from the culture. Accordingly, a few years ago, we began to execute a plan similar to our approach to the Asian community, building trust in the community of customers first.

In 1997, we sponsored the first-ever national study of African American investment preferences and habits. Our partner was Ariel, an African-American–owned mutual fund group. It showed that there was a heightened interest in investing in the African American community, and that African Americans were more likely than Caucasians to have participated in investment education activities. Accordingly, we followed the study with a series of seminars around the country expressly for African Americans, explaining the research findings and suggesting ways of expanding possibilities. The seminars were extremely well-attended, and we believe that the community recognized them as a real and culturally specific service. We completed another round of research with the same partner in 1999, and a similar series of seminars, this time on specific investment instruments and their relative importance in a model portfolio. The research shows that African Americans are more conservative as a group, and less likely to trust anyone in the financial services business, than their Caucasian counterparts. This is an appropriate challenge for a company based on values, and it reconfirms that our approach of trust building is the correct one.

Internet Egalitarian

The Internet is still another aspect of the business case for diversity. It is weaving its magic around the issue of diversity in a number of ways. First, as we will see in Chapter Eight, technology is blind to any characteristic except ability, so careers in technology are much less susceptible to racial and ethnic bias. Second, groups with similar values can form virtual investment communities on the Net. Support for specific interests and cultural cross-talk can easily be accommodated by the Net. Education about investment, research on companies, planning models, asset-allocation advice, even assimilating culture-specific portfolios—these are all available to anyone willing to operate a keyboard and mouse. That group is broadening daily.

The demographics of the Internet are rapidly moving to more than match the diversity of the population of the United States. Forester Research Inc., the most credible Internet research source, predicted that by the end of 1999, "32 percent of black households in the U.S., 43 percent of Hispanic, and 67 percent of Asian-American households will be online. These proportions compare with 39 percent of white households expected to be online by yearend."[4] Since much of our business is on-line, we believe our diversity efforts will benefit from this trend.

Does Diversity Mean Better Decisions?

It seems obvious that individual market decisions are better when members of the group being targeted are heavily included: women know best about women, African Americans know best about African Americans, Europeans know best about Europeans. It isn't as obvious that a diverse group will make better decisions about the business as a whole, and it is very difficult to prove. I think that is because of the way in which the proposition is put forth. The fact is that in the current business environment, groups don't make decisions very well; consensus is not a very good model for most decision making in this rapid-fire environment. It's just as obvious that more points of view will result in better decisions by the ultimate decision maker. Do we aspire to sit in a room with a diverse group of people and argue until we have consensus? No. But we *do* aspire to have input from as diverse a group as possible in order to make the best decision overall. Different people approach problems in different ways, and it is always valuable to see as many of those ways as possible before making any decision. It just makes sense.

So for us, the business case for diversity is strong: more diversity in the labor market; more diversity in the customer base, particularly for our products and services; better decisions in growing culture-specific markets; better input for general decisions as we grow into an international company. Diversity means more opportunity for growth—and for excellence in executing that growth.

INTEGRITY WITH VALUES

The business case is compelling to the mind, and for many, it is enough to induce a decision to work toward enhancing our diversity. But emotional commitment comes from equating a quest for diversity with the values of the company. Having established the company values as the basis for decisions, we make it clear that being "fair, empathetic, and responsive" and "worthy of our customers' trust" requires that we do everything we can to make customers, all customers, welcome. We could hardly earn the trust of customers who see no one, or only a very few people, in our company who look like themselves.

Equal access is fundamental to fairness. It is easy to see that our economic system, although the greatest in the world, has created conditions that are not inviting to certain minorities. People could certainly disagree on the nature of remedies for this condition, but the growing disparity between our richest and poorest is a matter of fact. It is as though our economy is like a boat race where one boat is manned by eight strong professionals with oars, and one is manned by eight neophytes with no oars. It is not hard to see who will win the race. These conditions are unfair, and we need to do what we can to correct them. Many people see and talk about the answer as "leveling the playing field," as though the answer is in providing more boats. But the answer is not only in putting more people in boats, it is in our society's providing oars and training and support to everyone. Accordingly, our own company programs are geared first of all to show broad evidence of commitment to all the communities we want to serve more fully, and then to help them get the tools to succeed.

BUILDING INTERNAL SUPPORT: LEARNING FROM THOSE WHO KNOW

It is vital to give the same level of support to employees as we do in recruiting customers. One of the first outcomes of our high-level study group was the formation of Employee Resource Groups, composed of members of particular minority groups of Schwab employees. Their purpose was threefold:

- Provide a familiar and safe group for other members of the minority group.
- Guide and, when appropriate, provide mentors for members of that group.

- Act, from time to time, as a focus group to provide insights into the company from their perspective.

We provide facilities for these groups to meet and encourage them to recruit new members from their particular constituency. The groups provide a forum for frank discussion in a safe environment. I meet with them frequently, and speak to them when I am invited. My personal support of these groups sent one of the first signals that, as a company, we wanted to learn, we wanted to make rapid progress, and we were willing to trust the good will of everyone in order to move forward.

Frankly, I got a lot of advice against forming these groups. The industrial relations consultants felt that the groups looked and felt like union bargaining units. That seemed shortsighted to me. First, my experience has been that people who want to complain will find others who want to complain whether there is an official group or not. Second, much as it was seemingly hard for some people to grasp, we actually wanted to hear negative feedback! How else could we improve?

One of the first things we heard was that minorities want to see evidence of a company's commitment in many ways. They want more than to be recruited, and they don't want tokenism: the same minority pictures on brochures, or a single minority executive featured in every annual report. They want signs that demonstrate a broad and long-term commitment. One way in which we demonstrate our commitment is through the Schwab Foundation, through which the company makes annual contributions to more than five hundred different community programs that encourage diversity and community. These investments are often initiated through our branches or call centers as a way of supporting local efforts and maintaining our presence in the local areas that we serve.

Our foundation's rules are designed to encourage the people of Schwab to contribute their own money and time in the same way. Unlike most foundations, ours double-matches employee contributions. To encourage individual volunteerism, we match volunteered time with money as well. Schwab employees care about these communities; their involvement is visible evidence of their individual interest—and, through the foundation, our company's interest in the communities becomes visible as well. Demonstrating this interest and building this commitment are, I believe, fundamental to building sustainable diversity in any company.

EXPANDING POSSIBILITIES

Competing with other companies for the same qualified minorities is close to a zero-sum game. Recruiting from a fixed pool results in higher and higher bidding. More to the point, a bidding war often results in only a temporary increase in numbers for it provides very little chance to build loyalty. Naturally, we will recruit opportunistically, but we have also taken a broader developmental approach that we think will bear more fruit over the long term. There are more and more data to support the usefulness of such an approach.

In 1997, California passed a ballot proposition that prohibited the state's university system from using race or ethnicity as criteria for admission. Many people who had championed affirmative action programs for years were angry; some groups sued to get the proposition overturned. The University of California took a very positive approach. The chancellor looked for creative ways, not to clandestinely work around the law but rather to make the law irrelevant. He reaffirmed that an overall goal of the university was to recruit a diverse population, not necessarily to create preference for minority groups. In 1998, the university spent nearly $40 million to expand the pool of eligible minority students through outreach programs in the high schools, secondary schools, and even some elementary programs, and will spend a similar amount for the next few years. In 1999, Berkeley's minority enrollment is up 30 percent, largely as a result of these programs, and faculties and students alike are applauding and participating in what they now see as the chance for diversity without the zero-sum calculus of affirmative action.[5]

In like manner, we at Schwab are developing relationships early and nurturing them over a longer period of time. Larry Stupski, the former president of Schwab, has become one of the leading authorities on "school to career" programs in the United States. He has helped us fashion a very aggressive summer intern program for both college undergraduates and high school seniors. In 1999, we hired more than three hundred such interns, more than 30 percent of them minorities, as a way of building their skills and beginning to develop what we hope will turn out to be a long-term relationship. We also have created focused hiring programs for college undergraduates and MBAs, both of which stress the value of job rotation and mentors as components of making sure that we are not just filling jobs but building careers of broad perspective.

We see these specific programs as part of our long-term effort to demonstrate our strong commitment to diversity and our respect for the differences among cultures. Community involvement and sponsorship, specific hiring and internship programs, and market-specific research, education, and product offerings form what we believe is a tapestry of effort to demonstrate something more than the desire to make numbers look good or make brochures and other advertisements look politically correct. These are Schwab's ways of demonstrating a desire to become a more diverse company, inside and out.

CHANGING FROM WITHIN

The business case for diversity and the fact that diversity is consistent with our values are easy to communicate. People embrace these two propositions and move from tolerance to acceptance, and then to action. But it is much more difficult to build *real appreciation* for differences—to inspire others to seek out differences, to welcome constructive conflict, to suggest that with different perspectives comes richer, more meaningful dialogue, more innovation, and ultimately better decisions. Finally, even after reaching such appreciation, it is still more difficult to build the skills to leverage diversity, to encourage the flexibility and empathy in communication that will bring out the best in everyone, regardless of their cultural norms or habits.

Because we are asking people from various social cultures to come together and contribute fully, we have to find a common ground worth the effort. In our case, we hope the glue is the vision and values of our firm.

Everyone, not just members of the majority, must change to make diversity actually pay off. It is not an assimilation process, it is an integration process. Some minority employees may have to be willing to take the risk of speaking out when they may feel that it is not safe. Others may have to learn how to communicate their views in a way that others can hear them without defensiveness.

Every one of us has to recognize that our own habitual styles—the result of our own cultural uniqueness, whether we are male or female, raised on the streets or in a mansion, the product of a loving home or a dysfunctional one—and our ethnic and racial biases will ultimately act to prevent us from recognizing someone else's value. We have to see the blind spots and limitations of our own backgrounds and counterbalance them every day.

By no stretch of the imagination do I consider myself disadvantaged. Nonetheless, my cultural uniqueness included some habit-forming experiences, including intense athletic competition and the daily physical competition of three brothers. I grew up in a Jewish family in a predominately white Catholic neighborhood in New York; mine was the first generation of our family to go to college. Eventually, because of that background of competition, I had to make changes in myself in order to get the best from my own group of executives, and ultimately the best from myself. I had to learn the effectiveness of a considered approach, of asking more questions, of listening more, of more collegial relationships. I had to learn that while there are still many times that I need to be direct, I can get the most from myself and others by being sensitive to what is appropriate, and encouraging others to be the same. It takes nonstop effort on the personal and on the corporate level to bring ourselves to an attitude of appreciation for others rather than competition with them. I realize that others have more intense experiences and much more difficult histories to overcome, but this work is still worth doing, and it is never done.

As with most things that matter, we start change by a declaration of values, then we take action to change the way things are, even if our old habitual feelings remain, and then we graduate, if we really want the benefits of change, to a deeper level of engagement and commitment in the process. Managers and executives have to fully understand the difficulties inherent in diversity, be willing to acknowledge those difficulties openly, and then encourage everyone, regardless of their cultural background, to contribute ideas. Leaders have to adapt their own communication style, perhaps question more, or perhaps be more—or less—directive. The objective, after all, is to gain as much perspective as possible, to leverage the richness of diversity that is going to be an integral part of the business of the future.

Diversity is a long-term strategic issue, and we don't have it figured out entirely. We do know that *diversity reveals itself in expressed points of view, not in any other way.* Terry's ten middle-aged white male bankers might well express more diversity than another group that was "perfectly" mixed. It really depends on the courage and skills of the leaders and the people in the mix. Partially because of the industry we are in and partially because of our own learning curve, we are not yet where we want to be in creating rich ethnic diversity in the company. Nonetheless, I think we *are* building the proper base, one that will sustain our long-term success.

A culture based on the values of fairness, empathy, responsiveness, striving, teamwork, and earning customers' trust has to make an extraordinary effort to act, both inside and outside its walls, to gain as diverse a population as possible and to exploit that diversity to sustain itself. Just as Schwab now operates with a certain blindness to differences in gender, the company has to institutionalize other groups not in the majority. To do less is to risk stagnation—and risk alienation from a growing and diverse pool of talent and customers. It requires programs that build long-term relationships, and above all, awareness, leadership, and changed behaviors.

As Terry and I write this, it is 1999. I see diversity as I see "Y2K," only with a longer horizon. We are headed toward a condition of the blending of points of view, the richness of many competent voices contributing to success. Like the year 2000, it will arrive with certainty. Our only choice is to see the inevitability and use the opportunity. I am not yet one who subscribes to a "world community," but I can imagine it happening in the lifetime of my children. More practically, I can envision greater understanding and a greater role for business in bringing the disparate people of the nation, and eventually the world, together. Moreover, and more important to most, I see that goal as one that is necessary to flourish in this enterprise called commerce.

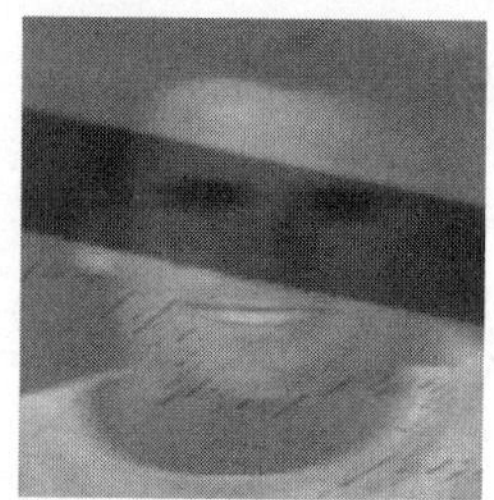

FROM CULTIVATING COMMITMENT THROUGH DIVERSITY TO LEADERSHIP PRACTICES

Dave started the preceding chapter by suggesting that although there are some programs and processes that a company can institutionalize to create more support for diversity, the critical element doesn't rest in the institution, it rests in the minds and hearts of the participants. Even with ideal processes, human beings can react to one another habitually, and depending on the source and nature of those habits, such reaction can destroy or enhance the positive effects of diversity. Leaders of organizations, whether departments or nations, have to demonstrate support for the kind of interaction that will bring diverse perspectives into play. It is too easy to merely get the numbers right, and then ignore the real prize.

Commitment. Diversity. Personal growth. These are goals that will pull us forward, goals that hold enormous potential. The path of building a diverse organization leads from tolerance to valuing. It leads a great distance, from recruiting with only the intent of making the numbers right to encouraging and supporting everyone in making a contribution that is as complete as possible. But for *most* of us, the steps on this path require real change, change from within that does not come easily.

How then do we put the passion into it? How do we wholeheartedly embrace ideas and practices that may disturb our comfort level for some time? We look at the horizon, decide what future we want, and begin. It helps to acknowledge some basics:

- Values and vision drive change.
- We all have to change, and it isn't comfortable.
- Constructive conflict is positive.

In the case of diversity, these are three significant issues that everyone has to confront:

Values and vision drive change. Why would people abandon cultural habits of communication? What would cause people to want to build trust with others enough to adapt habitual responses? After all, such work demands a great deal of awareness and understanding. But if people feel that what they want to do together is important and valuable, they will sacrifice their own preset ideas to contribute to it. Indeed, when there is enough on the line, we are willing to sacrifice what feels like a major part of our selves to contribute. Accordingly, companies with a compelling vision and a set of supportive and desirable values will support personal change much more effectively than others.

We all have to change, and it isn't comfortable. Everyone, regardless of their position on a team or in an organization, has to be willing to change, to be uncomfortable in order to garner the benefits of diversity. A leader cannot simply sit back and preach. Neither can a leader simply hire an accomplished practicing expert on diversity. There are none—and I don't expect to meet one anytime soon. Instead, each leader has to work at becoming one. It's appropriate that leaders, who are more aware of the potential benefits of change, have most of the responsibility for effecting that change. Accordingly, when an employee is communicating differently than we are used to, we have to quell our anxiety about style and listen carefully to what is being said. In doing so, we encourage others to do the same. More proactively, leaders have a responsibility to educate themselves about the different cultural norms among people in the organization, and to teach these differences to others, both as a way of creating knowledge and as a way of modeling the importance of diversity.

This does not apply only to those who have been in the majority. Those who do not consider themselves part of the majority also have to change. Sometimes it may be appropriate to speak directly, even if your habit is to be more obscure. In the name of contributing to the vision, you may have to overcome your cultural proclivity to accept authority or your personal tendency toward reticence. This last is an especially important point—and bears emphasis. Although leaders do have to listen more carefully and balance the loud voices with those that are more quiet, an unexpressed point of view is the same as no point of view. It is like a vote not cast. Those who remain silent have no right to complain later; they have simply opted out of their responsibility to contribute. Nothing is so frustrating as criticism from a person who was present during a decision point but chose not to speak. On the other end of the spectrum, you may have to be less aggressive to be more effective. You may have to find a way to constructively confront your boss. These steps take awareness, courage, and constant communication.

Constructive conflict is positive. It would follow, then, that no one will gain the benefits of diversity by being conflict averse. There is a legend about the late Alfred Sloan, chairman and CEO of General Motors for years. It seems that Sloan was in a board meeting, about to make an important decision. He said, "I take it that everyone is in basic agreement with this decision." Everyone nodded. Sloan looked at the group and said, "Then I suggest we postpone the decision. Until we have some disagreement, we don't understand the problem."

Now it could be that Sloan's board just wasn't diverse enough, but the story makes the point. In the physical world, we understand a subject best when we can see it from different angles—the sides, the back, the front. Ideas are the same . . . understanding comes from different points of view. A leader obsessed with peace and quiet, with consensus, with conviviality, will not gain understanding and will eventually make less than optimum decisions.

To begin to harvest the diversity dividend, leaders have to recognize their own biases, have the courage to change themselves, study and express appreciation for cultural differences, embrace conflict as positive, and be clear about the need for contribution. These are all unfamiliar, but when we do the unfamiliar and get predicted positive results, we have the potential to change our wiring, to actually shift the judgments that are based on forgotten programming. Undoubtedly, we all have a long way to go. Much to his credit, Dave is very clear in expecting nothing less of himself and those around him. The more leaders we have who feel and act in this way, the sooner we'll all get there.

Accordingly, in Part Two, we address the leadership practices that passion-driven growth requires. We see the importance of the leader as role model, the requirements and recommendations for leadership communication, and more specifics on how to stimulate ideas and generate innovation into the future.

PART TWO

LEADERSHIP PRACTICES

Inspiring Passion-Driven Growth

As an executive coach, I've devoted a considerable part of my adult life to the study of leadership. I'm fascinated and deeply moved by men and women who change history through their strength of will and courage of conviction. These extraordinary people find some internal calling to change the way things are, and they are able to inspire others to follow them, despite the odds. Whenever I go to Washington, D.C., I make a ritual pilgrimage to the Jefferson Memorial to stand in its rotunda and turn slowly to read the moving words of this most remarkable man: "We hold these truths to be self-evident, that all men are created equal . . . endowed by their creator with certain unalienable rights."

While we can marvel at the vision of a Walt Disney or a Henry Ford who created new modes of entertainment and transportation, only a handful of people have had the audacity to declare a new state of human rights. Before these words were written in our declaration, men did not have rights. Kings had rights. There was no special privilege to just being human. What an extraordinary act of courage it was to declare a new reality. And of course, it inspired men and women to action—ultimately to the action of war. People voluntarily gave their lives as they yearned for that freedom of expression, found it, and declined forever to forfeit it.

The feeling of passion evoked by this memorial has always been my standard for leadership, whatever the scale. I've felt that true leaders, through the integrity of their values, communication, and action, have been able to inspire others to act differently . . . not *forcing* them to act differently but creating a clear glass for them to see themselves, their deepest desires and finest motivations, and act accordingly.

Some mistakenly believe that leadership is only about creating change. The error of this idea is demonstrated, I think, by the fact that leadership is one of the most written-about subjects in the 1990s. Leaders do indeed drive change, yet in a world changing at warp speed, societies still feel they are missing leadership. The disconnect is that inspiration is also central to leadership. We are not missing change; we are missing inspiration, which provides the meaning of change.

In the world of business, inspiration has not always been necessary for success. Manual worker productivity isn't dependent on inspiration but rather on the efficiency of a system of doing work. But as technology has displaced manual tasks, businesses are correctly seeing that new ideas and the spirit to work on them are the primary capital of the enterprise. Accordingly, inspiration has become a requisite to progress. Even in companies that make material things rather than Web sites, ideas are more valuable than hands. Leaders of these companies have to be able to stimulate new ideas and new ways of applying those ideas in the workplace. Innovation is the output we are seeking. In such a world, it is more important *how* people respond to the leader than *if* they respond to the leader.

Metaphors for leadership are changing, from "general" to "coach," from "charismatic boss" to "orchestra conductor." Corporate leaders are trying not only to play the musical notes correctly, they are trying to create music that fills the room. In the fields of music and art and at the highest level of team sports, everyone can sense the difference between participation with energy and passion and just participation. To be effective, business leaders must now ask themselves, "How do I tap into that passion?" "How can I connect with the part of myself and of the other person that actually cares?" "How can I inspire . . . them . . . and me?"

Leaders are concerned more than ever with recruiting and motivating others to act as they would act if they were working for great personal stakes. In the new world of technology, *ideas, contribution,* and *innovation* are the key words. It takes a competent and trustworthy individual at the helm to develop the kind of atmosphere where the human spirit can speak with all of these results.

Today, leadership is personal, and it is public. A leader's actions and words—and the relationship between the two—are the primary tools of inspiration. This is new and uncomfortable ground for many leaders. In *Built to Last,* Collins and Porras examined this very point, reporting, "Some managers are uncomfortable with expressing emotion about their dreams, but it's the passion and emotion that will attract and motivate others."[1] This has been a rough go for many aspiring leaders, because it requires some personal involvement that was not required before. This kind of leadership does not start with a promotion, it starts with a personal decision about what is important and with the desire to be an agent, through inspiring and guiding others, to make that something real.

The information explosion and the use of the Internet have heightened the need for stimulating leaders. John Naisbitt coined one of the most predictive phrases of the century: "High Tech, High Touch,"[2] Naisbitt foresaw that to the extent that technology replaced humans in repetitive tasks, we would need new ways to effect human connection. Technology would not supplant connection, it would intensify the need for it. His prediction is borne out in listings of America's best-selling books of the last five years. As of February 1999, these best-sellers were led by *Men Are from Mars, Women Are from Venus; Don't Sweat the Small Stuff . . . and It's All Small Stuff;* and *Chicken Soup for the Soul.*[3] These books—and others like them—establish new ground rules for connecting with ourselves and others. They may seem sappy for business and to many business readers, but the people who buy and read them work in companies—many of them are us.

We want to connect; we care about human behavior far more than we care about the workings of our computer. While some CEOs decry the movement toward making their personalities as much a part of business coverage as the business itself, there is good reason for it. In *The De-Voicing of Society,* John Locke puts it this way: "The catch is that trust can only be restored through personal action. . . . and personal contact, the only means to deal effectively with declining trust, is also subsiding rapidly. On the other hand, the probability of people suddenly beginning consistently to exchange personal views and attitudes with others is unlikely under conditions of serious mistrust."[4]

I've worked with a number of executives over time who believed that trust was merely a matter of consistency. As they measured it, "trust" was the same as "predictability"—yet they found themselves with dissention among those who worked with them. It seems obvious that being predictably self-serving or thoughtless does not generate much trust. Robert Shaw's formula in *Trust in the Balance* is inclusive of my own experience. "Trust," says Shaw, "is a matter of getting results, acting with integrity, and demonstrating authentic concern."[5] Business schools teach us how to get results, but integrity and authentic concern are conveyed in our personal actions and words. Relentlessly, and wonderfully, economic reality is driving us toward deeper trust and connection. Leaders increasingly depend on others to provide ideas and actions to enrich and enhance the new reality they foresee.

The fundamental business need is for innovation. Innovation stems from expressed passion. Passion will be expressed for things we truly care about, and we will follow with our hearts only those we respect. Accordingly, this section on leadership practices is divided into three interrelated topics. Chapter Four looks at how a leader's life changes when she recognizes responsibility for acting in a way that others will want to follow. Chapter Five addresses the style, substance, and mode of leadership communication that inspires and encourages people to contribute. Finally, in Chapter Six, we look at the particulars of innovation and find out how a leader deploys herself, physically and through communication, to bring the best ideas out and get them implemented.

FOUR

LIVING LEADERSHIP AS A PERSON, AS A COMPANY

As Terry said, life changes as we grow as leaders. I will never stop marveling about the coincidence of my own maturing and my increasing responsibility. One clearly comes from the other. Until about 1992, each time I was offered more responsibility in business, I thought it was solely because I had learned more about that business and I could now make better decisions. Certainly, management competence is necessary to continue to grow in a company, but now I realize that three other characteristics, specific *leadership* characteristics, were just as important. One was the personal conviction that I was able to generate about the value of my work. A second was the ability to earn the trust of others through what I did and the content of what I said, and the third was the ability to communicate in a way that was inspiring.

I've talked about the importance of integrating personal conviction with work by using values as the basis of the culture. In Chapter Five, I will go into the details of leadership communication, dealing with inspiration in depth. Ultimately, whether we are discussing individuals or companies as a whole, what generates and destroys trust is what is actually said and what actually happens.

I have grown in my perspective of trust and its tenuous nature, and I have come to respect those who are capable of generating it consistently, day after day. I've also become a student of failure, and I notice, much more than I used to, when leaders make mistakes that affect their many publics. A recent series of incidents at another Bay Area company, widely reported in the *Wall Street Journal,* provides an example of the importance of recognizing that whatever a leader does and says is noticed by someone, and usually makes a big difference.[1]

PeopleSoft rose to great success as one of the pioneers of Enterprise Resource Planning software, and was known, as the article says, for its "aggressively informal and sensitive corporate culture." In telling the story of PeopleSoft's first layoffs, the article chronicled the company's rise and the role and some of the actions of its founder and CEO, Dave Duffield. This company had all the signs of success, with folks banded together in a mission of producing world-class product and seeing their stock price accelerate at a rate that created many millionaires quickly. Then hard times hit, perhaps because of their prospects' reluctance to add software before the turn of the century. The important parts of this story are the continued references to the "culture" of the company as the "antics and informality," and the CEO's referenced actions and words:

> Mr. Duffield leavened the merciless pace with beer blasts and parties at his house. . . .
>
> "Dave would start joking at the meetings about how people from Oracle might be double agents," says Rick Hess, a former head of PeopleSoft's international sales, who came . . . from Oracle in 1992. "A lot of us concluded that experienced businesspeople from outside PeopleSoft would have a hard time becoming part of the family." . . .
>
> He told a meeting of about 3000 employees that the company's new mission is to double the value of the stock in one year. He regrets saying that now.

Schwab is a good customer of this company. I consider its products first-rate, and I consider Dave Duffield a great human being. However, this story illustrates three very important points. First, it is vital for a culture to be defined in terms of values, not merely in terms of the style in which the company's people operate at and after work. Second, in this environment, the leader has tremendous influence.

And third, because of that influence, everything the leader does and says is noticed and reacted to. In this case, assuming the report is accurate, Dave Duffield created some impressions that he surely would not have chosen had he been aware of the impact of his words and actions both on the press and on his own people. It's also possible that he would have defined his company culture in terms of values rather than informality.

ACKNOWLEDGING A LEADERSHIP STANDARD

I have had similar experience. Perhaps because I have an excellent coach in Chuck Schwab, my own mistakes have so far not been as costly as Dave Duffield's appear to have been, or perhaps they just have not been as public. Nonetheless, I have learned the responsibilities for personal growth and demeanor that come with leadership, and the absolute requisite for the company itself to represent its values in the way it carries out its day-to-day operations. There is a standard for leadership, whether we like or abide by it or not.

I'm a sports fan, and I try to follow as many of the great basketball players as I can. On more than one occasion, I have heard Charles Barkley, basketball great with the Houston Rockets, speak about his reluctance to be a standard for behavior. He proclaims that he is not a role model for children, and encourages kids to look to their parents as their models. Well, Charles, you're out of luck. When you are in the spotlight, everyone can see you, and it places a special responsibility on you to act in a way that is admirable. When I became president of Schwab, and with every increasing level of responsibility, I have realized more deeply that I am on display, very visible, and under fairly constant scrutiny. I'll give some examples in the sections that follow.

Rank Has Privilege, Not Privacy

There is a perception among people in organizations that the folks atop the ladder have privileges those below don't enjoy. Of course that's true in certain respects: pay, perks, authority, power. But what's not commonly perceived is that the apparent double standard cuts both ways. With pay, perks, authority, and power comes a responsibility to manage perceptions—perceptions that may or may not have much in common with reality.

I can't possibly interact with every person who sees me or hears something I have said or that someone else has said about me. While employees at Schwab might be positively biased and interpret my actions and words in the best possible light, this is not necessarily true for the shareholders or for the public as a whole. People form their impressions from very little evidence—a newspaper report, a comment taken out of context, or an action without adequate explanation. Just about everything I say and do is amplified by the media, by the analysts, and of course by the rumor mill in the company cafeteria—and now on the Net. Accordingly, I have to manage my own personal and professional actions to make sure that the perception of everyone in the organization, and everyone in the entire viewing public, is as accurate and positive as possible. I have to serve as a model for the whole company and for our substantial public. I'm not excused from being a role model by whatever business talent I have or by my position. In fact, being a role model is part of the price of taking on the mantle of leadership. My standards have to be impeccable, because every gesture I make is open to interpretation. Like the forest in Huxley's *Brave New World*, the new world of leadership calls for constant attention.[2]

Earlier in 1999, I spoke at a conference of Wall Street analysts interested in the financial services industry. The speaker just before me in the program was an analyst with an expertise in electronic commerce. He commented during his remarks that the competition for electronic commerce in our industry was essentially over, that the discount brokerages had won, and that the banks were "losers." I was the next speaker, and as I promised my host, I spoke about Schwab's expansion on the Internet as well as some recent new business ventures that we had tried, including clearing mutual fund transactions for third parties and offering term life insurance. During the question and answer period that followed, one participant asked me if "Schwab would become a bank." I immediately quipped, "Why would we want to become a loser?"

Now, I made the remark as a joke, an obvious reference to the preceding speech, and it did get a laugh. But even as it was coming out of my mouth, I was picturing it as a headline, printed by a reporter who was in the room. I went on to answer the question more completely, and after the session, found the reporter. I told him that I realized how my "witty comment" would look quoted out of context, and that I clearly shouldn't have made the remark. He was gracious, said that he understood, and did not print the quip. But in the interchange and in my own reminder to myself, I learned again the care with which a leader has to comport himself.

In situations like this, it's easy to see why some leaders hire people to create and maintain their image. I don't do that, but I'm not as cynical about it as I used to be. Image-making and spin control may seem like a sham, but the need for some of it is clear. Many people will interpret such action as "it's all about appearances." There is a grain of truth to that. Does being careful about appearance mean that we are being disingenuous, inauthentic? It doesn't have to.

Appearances, Perceptions, Reality

As a business leader, I've all too often failed to appreciate the import of an act or comment, as I did at the conference just mentioned. But in my role as co-CEO at Schwab, I have become acutely aware that I have to consider appearances more carefully than ever before. This is not just to protect my own reputation. It isn't that shallow at all. Worrying about appearances gets straight to the essence of character. Worrying about appearances, and adjusting behavior to maintain the faith and trust of the people who listen to you and act on your suggestion . . . this is a profound act.

Appearance isn't the *first* thing to consider. Appearance alone can't maintain faith and trust. First I worry about the action itself and the motivation behind it. Then I try to err on the side of avoiding anything that might be considered OK for one of our typical employees but could be misinterpreted in a CEO. It's like a judge who dismisses herself from a case for even the *appearance* of a conflict of interest. Leaders have to set higher standards for their own behavior because appearances are indeed sometimes more important than fact. I used to ask myself, "Can I defend this?" Now I ask myself, "Could this be misinterpreted and held against me or the company?" "Could this be interpreted by an employee in a way that would shake her faith in the leadership?"

I had a conversation the other day with an executive from another company describing a decision he was in the process of making. He was going to spin off a division in a certain way, and I was uncomfortable with how that spin-off might be perceived. He was telling me why the approach made sense from a pure business perspective—why it was justifiable and defensible.

I said, "Let's think about how your worst enemy could use this story and put it on the front page of the *Wall Street Journal.* Could it be twisted, could it be used against you, could it be misinterpreted, and could it potentially embarrass you and the company?" He said, "I guess it could, but I could defend it." I said, "But you don't want to be on your heels defending it." That's how I feel. As a leader you raise your behavior to the point where it's above reproach, where even your enemies can't twist it or see it in a different way.[3]

Observers have to see a consistency of your behavior at the highest ethical standards. Behaving this way doesn't just mean you can't ever win an argument again, it means that you don't have to enter one. After all, people—our customers and our employees—are investing their future in this company. They have to see with absolute clarity that the values of the company start at the very top. Thousands of employees know me only by reputation, so in a real sense, my reputation is everything. Chuck has always been this way—he's modeled it for me. Now it's my turn to pass it on.

Shortly after I became one of the top executives at Schwab, I began dating an employee who was four levels of management removed from me. I knew that other couples had dated at Schwab, and some had married. I was single, so the notion that I might also date someone from Schwab seemed reasonable to me. We were discreet about our relationship and didn't flaunt it. But it got around.

Chuck soon told me I couldn't date any Schwab employee. His rationale was something like this: "I don't want people in the company spending their time speculating about your relationship with an employee when they should be doing their work. You're a very visible guy and it's just not right."

I had a very hard time with this notion because I felt singled out unfairly, and because this person was someone I deeply cared for. In fact, we ultimately got married . . . after she left the company. Later, when I thought over Chuck's message, I came to realize he was right. The rules for me as president of the company were different from the rules for other people. They were tougher. Even though the woman—Emily, my wife—was pretty far removed from my circle of daily contacts in the company, it was difficult for people who dealt with her daily not to think, in the back of their minds, about her pipeline to the boss. She and I have talked about it since, of course, and it was difficult for her as well. It created a real problem for her own managers, trying not to treat her special, but knowing that she was dating a top executive. All these issues made the situation turn on more complex ideas than just being single and available.

The perception of fairness extends to nearly every transaction between executives and their companies. It extends outside the company too. I had a very uncomfortable conversation with an executive whose spouse was a vendor to Schwab. I remember telling him it was awkward for us to deal with his wife. He said, "There's no reason it has to be that way. Treat her like any other vendor." And of course we always had treated her like any other vendor before they were married. But once they got married, it was impossible to manage the *appearance* of impropriety. At first, the employee could not understand. After all, nothing unreasonable was going on. I had a lot of empathy, but the fact is that it created a lot of difficulty within the company, and although this was a man of impeccable integrity, the situation caused employees to question his motives. Ultimately, everyone saw the logic of ending this vendor relationship.

So acting above reproach is important on every level: As employer. As boss. As vendor. On every level, modeling is important. Brain researchers tell us that given ambiguity, the human mind always seems to decipher what it perceives as negative. The brain's system has been programmed to protect us, to amplify negative presumptions and minimize the positive.[4] The higher you get in the organization, the more people notice you, and the greater the implications of your behavior are. You have to manage others' perceptions, not just your own reality. Jim Kouzes and Barry Posner call this "Modeling the Way."[5] Whatever you call it, it means setting a standard above reproach, inside, where it counts, and then acting on it.

VALUES: THE STANDARD FOR BEHAVIOR

At Schwab, we try to bind ourselves to our values. We try to make fairness, empathy, responsiveness, striving, teamwork, and trustworthiness the very foundation of our behavior. Leaders are responsible for making sure we have adopted the right rules—those policies that reflect our values—and that we carry them out ourselves. If responsiveness is a value, then we can't be behind our desks during times of customer crisis. We have to be on the phones, in the branches, or in some other way involved with the thousands of others who devote their lives to this value. Herb Kelleher, CEO of Southwest Airlines, believes in this idea so much that he often gets up on his flights and serves drinks to the customers; it is rumored that he works in the baggage claim area on Christmas and Thanksgiving to give some of his "teammates" a break. I've also heard legends about Sam Walton, founder of Wal-Mart. If Sam were flying from store to store, which he often did, and saw one of his trucks on the way, he would land the plane in a cornfield, flag down the truck, and ride with the driver to the next town. This may be hyperbole, but I don't think so. Kelleher and Walton are role models for the rest of us.

CHARACTER BREEDS PASSION–PERSONAL AND CORPORATE

We all want to believe in an ideal. . . . ("Where have you gone, Joe Dimaggio?") Although no leader that I know is flawless, the good ones take on the mantle of *trying* to live up to the ideal. In this age of speed and change, in this time when nothing seems stable, the leader's role is even more important. After more than two decades of writing about the qualities of leadership, Warren Bennis says it comes down to this, "in tomorrow's world, exemplary leaders will be distinguished by their mastery of the softer side: people skills, taste, judgment, and above all, character."[6]

Virtually everyone I've ever met wanted to work with people of impeccable character. Just as my own character determines my personal ability to generate trust, so it is for the company as a whole. I wonder how many people think of building an entire company that has strength of character as its foundation. Such a company will be a compelling place to work.

It requires focus on three aspects: responsibility, integrity, and what I call generosity of spirit. Each of these gets expressed by the corporate body.

Responsibility: Being Guided by Principle

Many companies, like many individuals, have public values. Being responsible for them means interpreting them as spirit rather than law. In that way, the values become a positive guide rather than a hindrance to be avoided. To see the values this way is to see them not as policy but as a body of ethics that created policy in the first place. We hear politicians say things like, "We play by the rules, and we all know that we need to change the rules." That is to admit that the body of ethics that guides behavior, the character of the individual, is subservient to the rules. That is to interpret the rules to avoid our own responsibility rather than to apply them as positive guides for our action. This garbage is unconscionable; it inevitably will ring hollow and not inspire any measure of loyalty or commitment from your people.

Responsibility does not mean never changing. But if change is proposed at Schwab, we are consistent with our fundamental beliefs. We are "able to respond" to what is needed without altering the basis of who we are as a company. As I write this, Schwab is going through a situation that highlights this responsibility. For years, we didn't offer investment advice. It was our feeling that offering advice and our values did not go together, and if we tried to offer advice we would automatically create a conflict of interest between the company and its customers.

At the same time, our customers told us in overwhelming numbers that they wanted us to offer helpful advice. We had to rethink our position, and in doing so, we realized it's precisely "no conflict of interest" that is core to our values—not "don't give advice." The way we constructed our advice offering—setting up a core of long-term investment principles, not paying commissions to employees providing the advice, a series of clear checks and balances to avoid self-serving behaviors, basing recommendations primarily on independent research . . . this formula would yield fair and responsive advice that would contribute to the creation of trust with our customers rather than detract from it. Bear in mind, we could have just blown the values off, or worse, not even considered them, and offered what traditional firms were offering. It was thinking it through and making the critical distinctions that made it a responsible extension of our offer.

Integrity Throughout

The second aspect of character is *integrity*—actually doing what we say we will do. It is the follow-through to being responsible. As one example, in the early 1990s, Schwab started the concept of the mutual fund supermarket with a program originally called the Mutual Fund Marketplace, and later branded as Mutual Fund OneSource. The idea was that Schwab would create a single source for investors to buy mutual funds from more than one fund company. The investor gets the benefit of a single statement rather than statements from each fund company, and (this was the proprietary feature) they get this service without a transaction fee.

Since our introduction of the concept, many of our competitors have created "me-too" marketplaces. So many that early in 1999 the *New York Times* printed an article about the number of mutual fund supermarkets that brokers and banks have created to serve investors. But there is a major difference. The funds available through our Mutual Fund OneSource service are all no-load funds. Through the years, we have added funds when our customers have asked for them and the fund companies will agree. The *Times* article reported that many of our competitors are adding load funds and splitting the substantial fees with the fund companies. In fact, many of these fund supermarkets are heavily weighted with load funds. Our competitors advertise that they have "more funds than Schwab," but what they really have are more load funds, which are more profitable for the broker but a more expensive choice for the customer. I was extremely proud of this article, because the head of our fund marketing group was quoted as saying, "We . . . simply offer funds that our clients want to buy. We don't willy-nilly add funds just to say that we have a lot of funds."[7]

Even further, when we created Mutual Fund OneSource, the real challenge for us was to be able to drive our costs down and volumes up in order to eliminate the transaction cost and still make a profit. When we first went to the funds, some said, "Oh, this will be easy. We'll just give you a different class of shares with higher expenses for customers. They'll barely notice and we'll pass it on to you." But we said emphatically, "No." Our intention was that our customers were getting exactly the same product they would get from the funds directly without any transaction fees. Selling them a different class of shares would have made our offer of "no transaction fee" a lie, and inconsistent with our values.

Has the way we chose made it harder to make money? Of course. What about our competitors? Have these programs that compete with Mutual Fund OneSource been true to the real promise of a mutual funds supermarket without transaction fees? No. Our competitors offer a different product although they set out to compete with ours. This is not an advertisable advantage for us, but our position was, to us, the right thing to do. Ultimately, I believe that customers are smart and they realize we are the real thing, and if we are responsible for the spiritual rather than literal interpretation of our values, if we are bound by the integrity of word and action, then this decision continues to make absolute sense and always will. The opposite decision might have generated more profit, but in the end, would slowly have begun to erode what makes our company strong . . . integrity between our values and our actions.

The integrity principle applies to what we do internally as well. For example, when we recently bought a facility in Phoenix from a blue-chip company, there was no covered parking. In Phoenix the summer sun is so hot it ruins paint on cars and bleaches out their interiors. The question was, Is it fair to ask our employees to paint their own cars every year when we could fix this problem with $2 million worth of covered parking? That's a lot of money, but it would have been inconsistent with our values to ask employees to dedicate their energy to Schwab while their cars were being ruined in our parking lot. This was an expensive decision, but one made easy by our insistence on being consistent with our value of fairness.

Generosity of Spirit

The final aspect of character is generosity of spirit, which has two distinct dimensions. The first is being able to maintain a perspective beyond what obviously serves me as an individual, or even beyond what obviously serves us as a company. The second aspect is a graciousness of attitude about one another.

Seeing Beyond the Boundaries. Developing a broad perspective results in our caring for all stakeholders, including the greater community. We believe that a healthy world, one that has strong possibilities for economic and cultural success for everyone, is within our scope of caring. That's why we structured the Schwab Foundation the way we did.

Despite getting lots of advice about structuring grants that would yield lots of public relations exposure for the company, Chuck wanted something different. As discussed in Chapter Three, he wanted the foundation to encourage all employees to find some cause they're passionate about and to contribute time or money to it. That purpose is what we emphasize; we downplay the corporate recognition that consultants tell us we should trumpet. After all, we didn't set these programs up as part of our marketing or advertising departments; we set them up to encourage the generosity of spirit of everyone who works with the company.

Assuming Good Will. The second dimension of generosity of spirit is more critical to us because it manifests itself day to day, minute by minute: graciousness of attitude. I spoke earlier about the tendency of the mind to assume the worst in situations that appear ambiguous. Doesn't just about every situation seem ambiguous in a world moving as fast as this one? Accordingly, we have to work at defeating the cynicism that will automatically creep into unexplained situations. In the next chapter, I will discuss the importance of providing the context of change as a way of mitigating the ambiguity, but providing context isn't always possible. Many times, we have to accept each other on faith.

Graciousness may sound soft, but it speaks to the heart of teamwork and support for one another, even as we discuss, disagree, and make tough decisions. We want to foster the ability to presume the best about fellow workers, customers, and other partners. Graciousness means that we willingly place trust in others, that we generate good will, belief, and faith in what's good, rather than focusing on failure or threats to our own existence.

The financial markets are a very good teacher of one reality: we can never calculate the future with certainty. With every decision we make, we risk an unknowable result. Regardless of how fine we make the calculations, the future will stubbornly remain unknown. "Of course," you say. But what is not obvious is that the chasm between what we know and what we can't know has to be bridged by an act of faith, and any act of faith will attract nay-sayers who demand more evidence. That kind of cynicism can erode relationships and freeze the action. When character is developed, decisions are based on the assumption that people will respond positively when they are trusted, supported, and cared for.

Here is how it works in reality. When we decided to award a year-end special stock bonus to all employees in 1997, we had no research to prove that this investment of $8 million would pay off. We didn't know what the result of providing covered parking in Phoenix would be either, and we really didn't know if fund companies would go with us if we insisted on one class of share for our customers. But we didn't hold our breath to see if these decisions would pay off. We had, and have, faith that these decisions were the right things to do.

Does this mean we don't need facts? Not at all. It means that as leaders, we cross the chasm of the unknown by adopting an attitude that assumes the best possible motivation on the part of others. We assume people will respond with higher motives, aspiration, and great accomplishment. It feels risky, it is tenuous, and it always works.

Do you remember the story in the beginning of this chapter about my own remark about banks? "Why would we want to be losers?" When I tell the story of that unfortunate lapse of judgment, most people hear a lesson, "watch what you say in front of reporters." But that is not the real lesson. The real lesson to me is one of generosity of spirit. It is "watch what you say that might in some way be hurtful to others." I shouldn't have made the remark, not just because a reporter was in the room, but because it was thoughtless, it was demeaning to any bankers in the room, and would reflect on me as a human being. Others who hear a remark like that could assume I am capable of making the same kind of remark about them.

Obviously, this notion goes right to the heart of the relationships that we have inside the company. In *Quantum Quality*,[8] William Miller tells a story about Frank Carrubba, head of the Hewlett-Packard Research Laboratory in the late 1980s and early 1990s. When Frank took over the lab, he was determined to create the best team possible. So he conducted original research on team effectiveness. He compared teams that failed to meet objectives with teams that attained good results, and then looked at "superior" teams that consistently exceeded expectations. He discovered that the factors that made the difference between mediocre teams and good teams were motivation and talent. Clearly, the good teams had better quality leadership and better qualified researchers.

But the difference between the good teams and the superior teams could not be accounted for by these two factors of talent and motivation. What is really impressive was that he judged the difference between good teams and superior teams to be in the range of 40 percent. What made the difference? Carrubba found that it was in the quality of the relationships between the team members. He found that this 40 percent increment in team performance was accounted for by the way they treated one another, by the degree to which they believed in one another and created an atmosphere of encouragement rather than competition. In other words, in this high-tech, competitive industry, vision, talent, and motivation could carry a team only so far. To fully optimize and expand performance, personal values such as caring for teammates and communicating with integrity and authenticity made the difference between plain success and extraordinary results.

Talent is insufficient to ensure the best results of a team. It takes generosity of spirit to bring out the spirit of the collective, and therefore the best results for the team. A leader's job is to make sure that atmosphere prevails by modeling it every day.

In this society of electronic everything, it would be easy to think that leadership is about information sharing or moving more quickly than some other person in your field. Terry and I will certainly discuss the positive influence of electronic communication. But precisely because the world is electronic, the leader's job has shifted to one of personal, values-based communication and action. I know how easy it is to get caught up in the tactical day-to-day of operating the company. I know how easy it is to move from graciousness to selfishness. But I realize that my responsibility demands that I spend a lot of time considering what Chuck and I stand for, acting in a way consistent with the answer, and then making sure that the principles of behavior are reflected in our company.

It is not our technology or our clever plan that have kept us growing. Our success is built on the same foundation as the Hewlett-Packard lab, or the winners of the great athletic competitions. It is our ability to act as a real team—the extent to which we believe in one another, creating an atmosphere of encouragement rather than competition. That takes strong leadership modeling by people of high character.

Yes, it is difficult for leaders to be so visible and be held to a higher standard than the rest of the workforce. But it is also a privilege and an incredible opportunity. I still do things I wish I hadn't, but I've learned to accept that as part of being human. I know what I need to do and I'm constantly looking for ways to improve, to further express my own belief in these principles rather than slipping back to pettiness, in my personal life as well as my life in the corner office. Doing so is challenging, certainly rewarding, and it provides an atmosphere where everyone wants to contribute, and usually does.

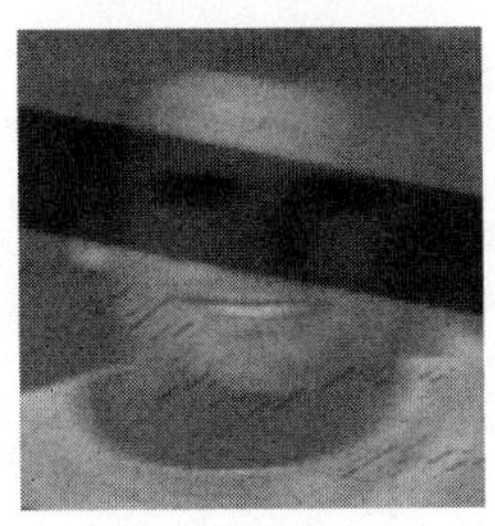

FROM LIVING LEADERSHIP TO LEADERSHIP COMMUNICATION

Dave's experience mirrors that of his peers. Modern communication media have made it nearly impossible for a leader of a public company, particularly a successful one, to have any modicum of privacy. What many of us don't consider is that we all have a public; we all have people who observe and judge us, whether we are actually leading a company or not. The office buzz is just as effective as the newspaper, and e-mail distribution lists have substantially enhanced the reach of office gossip. If you aspire to lead, or are in a position that calls for you to generate the trust of others on purpose, then the ideas in Chapter Four are important to you. The good news is that in this environment, and with this kind of scrutiny, a leader can influence more people than ever before, not only with her decisions, but with everything she does. Of course, that is also the bad news. More exposure, more at stake, more potential benefit and greater potential consequences—these conditions characterize the opportunity and challenge of the modern corporate leader.

We ask a great deal of our leaders, but I think in the wake of all of the political scandal we have failed to make the right distinctions about what we ask of them versus what we actually *expect* of them. What do we really need from a leader to give her our respect? What is really required to gain commitment in followers?

Jim Kouzes and Barry Posner have asked this question of more than twenty thousand respondents on four continents over twenty years. These respondents have consistently ranked four characteristics as more important than others on a list of twenty. We expect vision, competence, honesty, and inspiration.[1]

Vision is the ability to see what change is needed and how it will benefit people when that change is made.

Competence is the ability to manage the many variables that are necessary to effect that change.

Inspiration and *honesty* are related. To "inspire" is to "breathe life into" another, which means that life must first be in ourselves. So the task of inspiring others begins with self-discovery and self-development, in order to find out what matters to us, and to begin changing and refining the way we act in the world and the way we communicate with others. This self-discovery requires honesty, first with ourselves, and then in the projection of that self to others. That process of projection, or "deployment" of the authentic self is, in itself, inspiring.

Perhaps because we long for a model, perhaps because few really want to take personal responsibility for their own development and behavior . . . for whatever reason, we observe and reflect the behavior of people in leadership positions. Thus a position of leadership carries with it a responsibility to be aware of oneself, and to mold one's character to reflect that which will inspire others. The following activities can help in that process:

- *If you haven't already done so, spend time exploring your personal values.* After all, if you are to model in the culture, it is important that you are aligned with the company. If your company has no stated values, you have to determine the basis for the culture that you want to instill. This can be done with your mate, a coach, or on your own. You should be able to align these values with the company you are trying to lead or the changes you are trying to make in your sphere of influence.
- *Review your personal and business behavior and decisions over the past year and measure them against your values.* Were there inconsistencies? What was the underlying rationale for the behavior or decision?

- *Consider what characteristics are present in those you trust.* Continue to focus on developing these characteristics in yourself.
- *Ask your peers, your direct reports, and your boss to give you honest feedback on your own integrity, how consistently you act in alignment with your values.* (You can use one of a variety of "360-degree" instruments for this purpose.) Then ask those closest to you personally for the same kind of constructive feedback.
- *With every visible decision that you make, ask yourself, "How could people who would not like me to succeed twist this to make it look bad?"* Ask someone you trust to advise you, on a regular basis, how your actions could be seen negatively by others. Consider their feedback in both your professional and personal life.
- *With each decision that you make, notice if you are focusing on defending the action from the perception of others.* Consider how you could change the action so that it wouldn't need defending.
- *Take particular notice when someone interprets something you do as negative.* Fair or not, this is feedback. Rather than bemoaning the fact that you have been misinterpreted or misquoted, try to develop an appreciation for your position as a leader and your potential in that position to help others.
- *Take time to occasionally talk to those at different levels of the organization.* Ask their opinion, show them that you value their contribution. You know how good it feels when someone asks your opinion, and values it. Pass that feeling along to those who work for you.

These are practical steps; steps that you can practice overtly. Less definable, and therefore more difficult to change, is your manner, the way in which you undertake your leadership internally.

The most frequent observable act of a leader is communication. In fact, what the leader says and the way in which she says it is the leader's greatest opportunity and greatest challenge.

The former Chairman of Air Canada, Claude I. Taylor, commented about the link between communication to leadership. He said, "Certainly a leader needs a clear vision of the organization and where it is going, but a vision is of little value unless it is shared in a way so as to generate enthusiasm and commitment. Leadership and communication are inseparable."[2]

Leadership communication is my life's work, and it was our common interest in the subject that formed the basis for Dave and me to work together. Since he and I met in 1992, the ease and speed of the Internet and the other electronic media has raised major questions about how to optimize the balance of communication to enable people to do their best. Techno-communication is tempting . . . it is easy, and appears to be cost-effective. It can decrease travel expense, reduce the risk of more spontaneous communication, and is clearly easier to effect. But providing information, or even providing opinion, is not the same as inspiring. The central question for this next chapter is, "With all of the choices, how does a leader communicate, and through what channels, in order to generate the passion necessary for people to contribute with all they've got?"

In *Leading Out Loud,*[3] I focused on the public and more formal pronouncements of leaders. It is frequently in the formulation of speeches that a leader discovers what it is that she really wants to say. Preparing a speech requires conscious attention, so the speech is also an excellent vehicle to practice the principles of the kind of communication that is needed to inspire commitment. It is in the more common instances of communicating—real conversations in the halls, elevators, small meetings, lunches, one-on-one tactical encounters, and, yes, voice-mail and e-mail exchange—that the leader can make more frequent contact. It is also in these less formal environments that she is most vulnerable to unconsciously undoing all of the good that can be done with a thoughtful first statement of vision. Example after example could show that most of the leadership communication damage is done in less formal venues. (Remember the PeopleSoft case we spoke of in the last chapter?)

But the answer is not in close-mouthed caution. The answer lies in Dave's analysis of his "loser" mistake. The fundamental mistake was not that he "slipped up" in front of a reporter. The real mistake, as he quickly acknowledged, was that he was thoughtless, at that moment, about demeaning others. This analysis is a deeper one, an authentic one, and one that will, as he extends it into his life, separate him from other leaders who are more concerned with appearance than with authenticity.

Day to day, moment to moment, the leader's words influence those around her. In the next chapter, Dave will look at the few factors that make a difference in what that impact will be.

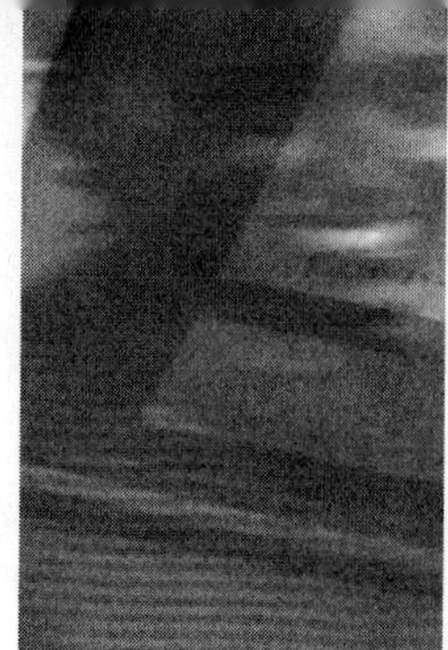

FIVE

LEADERSHIP COMMUNICATION

I look at our time not as the Information Age but as the Communication Age. The Information Age had its zenith the last two decades, when the world mastered the task of information accumulation and dissemination. Those companies that only collected and warehoused information are now gone, rendered practically useless by the Internet and the other technologies that we use to access the information available.

Clearly, our major task is not gathering information; technology will do that for us. Now our task is to make information useful and—most important for our purposes here—to make it meaningful. Many of us remember the skit on *Saturday Night Live* as the sports reporter begins, "And now for the baseball scores, 6 to 5, 4 to 1, 10 to 8, and a partial score from Minneapolis, 7!" This string of numbers is useless without the names of the teams, and it is meaningless unless the listener is a baseball fan. Usefulness is determined by context, and meaning is determined by caring.

Our job, as inspirer, as leader, is to make information useful and meaningful to others, as a way of moving them toward committed engagement in our company. Current business communication models don't help much. These models don't encourage dialogue, they rather try to facilitate an overload of volume and a corresponding overload of assumption about what people know and understand. The warp-speed sending and receiving of one-way messages, devoid of any intuitive or sensory feedback, is a condition that breeds ambiguity and the negative assumptions and frustrations that go with it.

The "commune" implicit in the defining word of our age doesn't really exist in our dominant ways of moving information. The practice normally referred to as the "communication profession" includes little two-way interchange; most of our society's so-called mass communication is still one-way. This irony extends to the corporate world. "Corporate Communications" is a discipline that has been historically fashioned to include public relations, press relations, and occasionally "internal communication." These groups are primarily vehicles to transmit declarations of position.

FREQUENCY IS UP, CLARITY IS DOWN

E-mail and voice-mail have, of course, exacerbated the problem in recent years. Unfortunately, for all their convenience, these innovations have made it much easier to believe we are communicating when we are merely informing. Like all technologies, they carry no intrinsic blame for the shortcoming in their use. Rather, they are misused by human beings who are at best unconscious and too busy, or at worst manipulative and self-serving. Bad enough that communication by voice-mail and e-mail is stunted, often ill-considered and knee-jerk. Worse, although they can do no more than move information between machines, these technologies suffer from a widespread presumption that they somehow transfer knowledge from one person to another. "If I have e-mailed you, you know it." This presumption frequently escalates from knowledge to understanding, then to consent, and finally to the delusion of wisdom.

One result is that people who stare at their computer screen inbox or listen to the prompting of voice-mail can feel overwhelmed and inadequate. The sheer volume is daunting. Of all of the comments about this frustration, I found this one of Seth Shostak, a scientist and manager at the SETI Institute, to be the most descriptive: "Masquerading as a better way to put everyone in touch, e-mail (and voice-mail) have become incessant distractions, a nonstop obligation and a sure source of stress and anxiety. I expect that a public statement by the surgeon general is in the offing."[1]

Many people at Schwab feel this way, even as these new technologies can and do serve us exquisitely. One reason for this feeling is the ambiguity of the one-way message.

Edward Hallowell, a psychiatrist at Harvard Medical School, took up this issue of techno-communication ambiguity in the *Harvard Business Review.* Hallowell draws from several of his own cases, men and women who developed deep misunderstandings from ambiguous electronic messages and then took action based on their own worst-case assumptions. One of the cases Hallowell cites has a CFO listening to voice-mail, and hearing that one of his best employees wants to transfer. He can't reach the person directly. His mind begins to fill in the blanks: "What if the employee complains that the CFO is a lousy boss? What if the employee plans to take his team with him in the move? What if, what if . . . ? The CFO becomes lost in a frightening tangle of improbable outcomes, a thicket that will ensnarl his mind."[2]

This may seem overly dramatic, but it is exactly what happens when high-tension messages are left without context, when there is no opportunity for dialogue. Unless personal trust has been well-established, the mind assumes the worst. Hallowell cites other examples of similar erroneous assumptions made in the absence of physical presence. He contends that for true trust-building communication to take place, we need moments with two prerequisites, "people's physical presence and their emotional and intellectual attention."[3]

As a leader, every day I try to remember that others will tolerate my point of view, but they will act only on their own. Accordingly, part of my job is to reconcile those points of view, to try to help everyone, including myself, gain a more insightful view of reality. In this work, listening is every bit as critical as speaking. Two-way communication is vital.

CONNECTING THROUGH PERSONAL COMMUNICATION

Direct, physically present communication encompasses the logical and emotional, it establishes links to corporate objectives and strategies and links to personal commitment and values. It conveys both clarity and depth. Making information useful and meaningful requires both.

I know, through Hallowell's research and through my own experience, that I could not use e-mail and voice-mail effectively or extensively until I had earned the right to do so. I had to first communicate enough with physical presence and attention that people could accurately assume the intent and meaning in these messages, despite my physical absence.

Effective leadership communication is made up of three separate elements: speaking, listening, and engagement. Speaking and listening are skills that can be learned. Engagement, however, only comes from an authentic interest and respect for other people and their points of view. Authentic interest in others makes communication a connecting art; when it is in place, the other elements, the skills of speaking and listening, can actually work to create a marvelous result. Unfortunately, authentic interest isn't something that can be taught. It has to be learned, and the learning sometimes requires a fair degree of failure.

SHOWING INTEREST IN OTHERS: THE FUEL FOR ENGAGEMENT

I was married and divorced twice before I dated my wife, Emily. My presumption coming out of two failed marriages was that I had a "wife selection" problem. Clearly, I should not get married again because I couldn't trust my selection skills.

I didn't like the scenario that had me single for the rest of my life, so I found a psychologist to help me sort through why I was having so much trouble picking the right mate. What I came to learn was that I didn't have a wife selection problem. I had a husband behavior problem. I had made a fundamental mistake about what a trusting and collaborative relationship would look like, and the extent to which my ability and willingness to really engage would affect the quality of any relationship, personal or professional. For example, I (emphasis on the "I") structured my first two marriages in a so-called shared-power situation, where there were certain things my wife was in charge of and other things that I was in charge of. We had respective areas of total authority. I thought my heart was in the right place . . . this was what I considered a good business model.

The psychologist challenged that notion, and said, "What kind of message are you sending? Did you ever consider really engaging with your wife—looking for a common solution together? You might come out with a better answer, and you would *definitely* come out with a better relationship."

Many of you are shaking your head at my naïveté. It dawned on me about that time that I had rarely engaged in such a process on purpose, I had never entertained the possibility of coming to a better solution through actually listening to someone else. I had treated my wife like a fellow employee of the same company—call it "Marriage, Inc."—and I had set up the distinct impression that we were two separate entities of that company . . . one subordinate and one authority, in all things. This model, of course, assures that you don't really have to engage at all. You don't really have to listen to the other person, all you have to do is determine whose turn it is, or whose area of expertise the particular issue falls into. There is precious little discussion, and no need for considering what the other person thinks or feels. In all cases, there is absolute submission to the authority of the agreement. You can imagine the level of interest that ensues in a marriage when this decision model is in place.

You can imagine the level of interest in a business that operates with the same model. The fact is that Emily and I really do come up with better solutions when we engage and decide together.

To really gain engagement and commitment in a business, we need a different standard of communication than one of "tell and instruct." Moving a new model into a business environment was a real challenge and took some modification. Ultimately, I want the engagement of everyone in the company, but unlike a marriage, the business requires that I also have the ability to move fast, to make decisions quickly when I need to. Business leadership is not only about facilitation or consensus, it is about ultimate responsibility. Even as I encourage dialogue and listen carefully to everyone who contributes, my responsibility is to make decisions that are the best for the whole of the business, and to continue to have the participation of those who disagree with me. It requires that I understand other people's points of view—and that I can acknowledge our differences.

Caring is also demonstrated by acknowledging points of view that are resistant to your own. I learned this when we were making the "Denver Decision" that I talked about in Chapter Two, and it has been present in my thinking ever since. Acknowledging resistance does not mean giving up your own point of view. It doesn't mean that other people have to have their way. It merely means that they know they have been genuinely heard and considered, even if the hearing and considering do not change your decision.

A few years ago, we decided to open our branches for a few hours on Saturday. Frankly, we did not have a very good decision process. First, we announced it without much input from our field managers. Second, the model did not differentiate between branches where potential customers would actually *appear* on Saturdays and those locations that would not get foot traffic on the weekend. To compound the communication problem, at the same time that we were looking at Saturday hours, we were "announcing" the opening of a call center in Denver, which would require many people to move to Colorado.

It didn't go down that well. Many people in the field operation were vehemently opposed to this idea; especially, and understandably, people who worked in branches that had no Saturday traffic. So we struggled with it, dictated it, listened to people threaten to quit, and finally got the idea. I had the opportunity to address the issue at a managers' meeting in Chicago. Here is what I said:

> When I decided to speak to all of you about these changes, I was quite excited. As you know, we have been considering both locating a call center in the Mountain states and opening the branches for a few hours on Saturday for some time. But as I reflected on the impact of these changes, it occurred to me that opening a new call center did not require me to move from my home, and in fact, I was not going to work any more hours on Saturday than I already do . . . [but] For many of you, an occasional Saturday away from the family will be something new, and certainly, these changes will cause some disruptions in the family patterns of your staffs.
>
> It also occurred to me that it was you, not me, who were going to tell your staff about moving or working Saturdays.
>
> Given these thoughts, I quickly realized that you might not be as excited about these moves as I am, even though these changes are for the good of the company and ultimately will create more opportunity for all of us.

I went on to outline the reasons for the change and the shifts we had made in the implementation before I took questions from the group.

The next day, I got a number of voice-mail messages from people at that meeting. Remarkably, their comments were much more about the "caring" part of the remarks than the "content" regarding the changes. It was a real lesson in leadership. People wanted to be heard and acknowledged. Eventually, we made changes to the plan that made it work much more efficiently. The move and the open-Saturday implementation went much better after that.

LISTENING TO HEAR RATHER THAN TO ANSWER

With engagement, listening itself takes on new meaning. Whereas many think of listening as a skill, I think of it as an attitude with a single focus: the more I *am known* by those I want to follow me, and the more I *can know* them, the greater will be our ability to do great things together. With this attitude, I put myself in a position to demonstrate to others that they are real partners in the enterprise. At the same time, I am letting them know that they are also accountable for the organization. They are not passive workers, they are responsible and engaged participants.

I was not always this way. I used to practice my public speaking a great deal, and part of that was a drill on "Q and A." My staff and I would rehearse the answers to questions that we thought were likely to come from an audience, and then during the "performance," our measure of success was whether we had correctly anticipated the questions. Of course, the intention of that drill was to look good and "fend off," not to really engage. Pretty dumb. Now I realize that every conversation, every interaction, is really a "Q and A," and I have tried to build listening skills that will help me engage the questioners, not fend them off. My objective can be stated simply. As a leader, I'm trying to respond to people rather than merely answer questions. People know when you are being authentic by a number of cues, including how actively you solicit comments (or whether you do) and how (or whether) you acknowledge what you hear.

Solicit Comments

Terry observed that people who work in big companies are not generally used to being able to offer ideas or ask tough questions. Many leaders really don't want to hear others' ideas; many others have just developed bad listening habits in the rough-and-tumble of clawing their way up some corporate ladder. Some, as I mentioned in Chapter Three, exhibit cultural barriers to speaking up. This means you have to go to them, rather than waiting by the phone or the computer and blaming them for not being forthcoming. Ironically, the people who are the closest to the customers have the best ideas, and they are often the people furthest away from the leader. Who knows more about what works and what doesn't work than those on the front line? I make it a point to go out often and ask what is going on.

Acknowledge What You Hear and What You Sense

Being authentic means being willing to respond to what is obvious, even though it isn't being said. In essence, this is like responding to the spirit rather than the word. The difference between the two is the same as the difference I spoke about on page 97—the difference between the law and the body of ethics that brings the law into being. Always being willing to hear the spirit of a message demonstrates true character.

Occasionally, silence itself creates noise. When I hear this kind of subverbal rumble in the company or in an organization, I don't ignore it. Getting to the bottom of it often results in correcting an error. It has for Schwab many times.

When we consolidated Web trading with the rest of the company in 1998, we were faced with some financial reality we didn't like. Analysis showed us that only a fraction of our customers were profitable for the firm; the majority of our accounts actually didn't generate enough revenue to cover the cost of servicing their accounts. The analysis team recommended a series of graduated account fees for our customers whose deposits fell below a certain minimum. We announced the changes to our customers and to our representatives, telling our internal audience that the fees were necessary to keep the business healthy, and then we implemented the plan.

Within the first couple of weeks, I started to hear rumbles about the implementation. It seemed that some of our reps did not think the fees were very "Schwab-like." After all, we were founded as a firm that helped those who had no access to markets. We had always encouraged people to begin to invest, even if they could only start with a small amount. Now it appeared we were going to charge them a fee just for doing business with us.

Bear in mind, the customers were not complaining. Neither had the press given us any criticism about the change. We knew that the stock analysts were supportive, as they assumed it would improve the earnings picture. But I felt like we had made a mistake. If people who actually deal with customers were uncomfortable, some cynicism was going to show up in their interactions with customers and fellow employees, and it would affect their belief in and commitment to our company. So at a meeting in San Francisco, I asked a large contingent of representatives and managers if there was truth to the rumor that many of them were uncomfortable with the changes. Even then, presented with the objective question, some were reticent about admitting their own opinions. It seemed they thought it was not the politic thing to do, that they would not be supporting the best interest of the company if they admitted to their discomfort.

Still, it was obvious to me in their hesitation. We went back to the analysis, came up with a plan that would give small investors an incentive to add to their small investment accounts rather than penalizing them for not doing so, and announced it. The result was a much better solution for everyone.

After the resolution, many of those who had been reticent about complaining were eager to confirm their support and to express their dissatisfaction with the original plan. Naturally, I would rather the objections had been brought up during the analysis phase of this change. And of course, I wished that the objection had been raised during the planning process by someone who was close to the customers. But in the end, I know that the final resolution was the best one for the company, and I know that the process set an example that will not soon be forgotten. The lesson here is not "don't raise fees." The lesson is to communicate about the discussions early, listen to points of view—and subsurface rumblings—and then reconcile those points of view with a common context. Within the company, we tell this story frequently to reinforce the necessity, and the reward, for people to speak up or to ask the tough question.

Sometimes this "sixth sense" listening happens in real time, and sometimes the message isn't subtle at all. Emphasis, tone, even a particular word can be a cue to the real question that someone wants to ask, but one that he is reluctant to verbalize directly. "*How* many people did you say were moving to Denver?" could mean "Why are so many people moving to Denver?" or "It doesn't seem like enough people are moving to Denver" or "Why am *I* moving to Denver?" or "Why am I *not* moving to Denver?" Finding the real meaning and responding to it makes it safe to ask the next question directly, and establishes your real interest in the concerns of the people you are engaged with.

A leader can usually draw out the real comments and concerns by listening carefully and stating what the other person just won't state directly. And much of this demands a physical presence. It would be all too easy to respond to the question of "*How* many people did you say were moving to Denver?" with a straight number, had the question come in over e-mail. In person, the unspoken question either jumps out or can be pulled out.

In more formal "Town Hall" situations, there is frequently an opportunity to engage in a discussion of hot topics—but to take advantage of it, the leader has to almost suggest the discussion. You will hear advisers say, "Don't state problems that the audience won't state themselves." That advice is only good if you want to avoid talking about what is really on people's minds. If you want to engage them, you occasionally have to prime the question pump. Opening comments like "I would imagine that some of you are feeling some apprehension about this change" or "If I were you I might be thinking—" will signal that there are no off-limits signs for the questions.

Listening and responding to what is really being asked are critical skills of leadership communication. Model this kind of listening, and before long, people will begin to respect your intention, and will come to you directly.

What you are willing to hear is a primary gateway to trust. What you are willing to say is another. We trust those we are closest to, those we know, rather than merely know *about*. As a leader, your willingness to address some fundamental questions will enhance others' perception of your trustworthiness.

SPEAKING TO ANSWER QUESTIONS AND CREATE MEANING

I commented earlier that the central challenge of leadership communication was to create use and meaning out of the sea of information available, and that usefulness came from context, while meaning came from caring. How can you create these two elements?

University of Michigan's Noel Tichy, leadership coach to some of America's top executives, claims that people who are deciding to make a commitment to a leader need some fundamental information, and they look for constant reinforcement of that information throughout the life of the enterprise. Among their questions are "Who are you?" and "Where are we going?"[4] I agree, but I would add a third that he does not include, a question that makes a significant difference in the potential for people's commitment. It is "Why are we going there?"

These are not the standard questions of business. In fact, most companies, most leaders that I know, focus on still a different question: "What are we doing?" Yet as important as this question is, the answer does not inspire passion and commitment, it only provides instructions. It is essentially a "how" question, and although it needs to be answered, the leader is not the best person to answer it. So whether you are a new manager in a small department or the long-time CEO of a major company, the "who, where, and why" questions need to be addressed constantly, in a way that those around you will take action on their own to develop the "what" and "how" and enhance the performance of the company or your organization.

Let's look at these fundamental questions one at a time.

Who Are You, Anyway?

"Who are you?" seems a fairly straightforward question for a leader, but the fact is that when you ask it, many people will give you their business card, literally or figuratively. You will get to know their company and their title. That's it. If they're a bit more forthcoming, you might get a résumé, a list of their accomplishments. But people will not passionately follow a résumé or a business card. (Imagine what Gandhi must have said in response to this question!) Rather, they are interested in whether you are trustworthy and competent in the context of what you are trying to do together.

In Chapter Four, we discussed the importance of consistency of action as a vehicle to generate trust. There are also signals in your communication that can greatly enhance others' perception of your trustworthiness. From my perspective, authentic caring is the most important aspect of being trustworthy. It is demonstrated day to day by your communication. Whether it is a positive or negative demonstration really depends on your willingness and ability to reflect your authentic self as you speak.

How would you assess your willingness and dedication in making your own values and the values of the company a constant centerpiece of what you say? How would others assess it? Are you willing to be vulnerable, to speak not only about your successes but also about the lessons you've learned and about the fundamental things that bind people together as human beings? Being open in this way does not signify weakness. On the contrary, it destroys any artificial barriers that have to do with hierarchy and signifies that you care about human beings as well as the bottom line. It opens the door for people to continue to come to you for help and coaching.

This connection is important, as retired Army General Colin Powell acknowledged in some recent convention comments:

> The day [people] stop bringing you their problems is the day you have stopped leading them. They have either lost confidence that you can help them or concluded that you do not care. Either case is a failure of leadership. If this were a litmus test, the majority of CEOs would fail. One, they build so many barriers to upward communication that the very idea of someone lower in the hierarchy looking up to the leader for help is ludicrous. Two, the corporate culture they foster often defines asking for help as weakness or failure, so people cover up their gaps, and the organization suffers accordingly. Real leaders make themselves accessible and available. They show concern for the efforts and challenges faced by underlings—even as they demand high standards. Accordingly, they are more likely to create an environment where problem analysis replaces blame.[5]

Who am I? I hope that through my actions and words, people decide that I am a human being who lives by the values of the company, who is vitally interested in their opinions and feelings about the business, who is motivated to do the right thing for our customers, who cares about them and their families' needs and who is capable of making the majority of decisions in a way that benefits all of us. These factors are a major focus of my communication.

Where Are We Going?

Unquestionably, the ability to see the future is a characteristic of great leaders. What we sometimes overlook is this: We only know the importance of vision because the really great leaders were able to communicate in a way that inspired others to make the vision a reality. It is not sufficient to be a visionary, but visionaries who can communicate possess two of the necessary talents of leadership—vision and the ability to inspire. Walt Disney, Henry Ford, Steve Jobs, John F. Kennedy, Martin Luther King . . . these are some of the great visionaries and inspirers of our time. They knew the importance of speaking in a way that people could see and feel the future, and see and feel themselves thriving in it.

So the answer to the question "Where are we going?" has to be clear and objective. Schwab's own vision is "to provide customers with the most useful and ethical financial services in the world." Although it is a noble vision, and it provides some guidelines for our business practices and products *(useful and ethical)* it doesn't answer the question "Where are we going?" in a way that people can see themselves creating it. We are constantly looking for compelling metaphors, phrases that we can use to describe our company in an active way. We are "the custodians of our customers' financial dreams," we are "entering the third era of Schwab," we are "reinventing full-service brokerage"—these are some of the phrases that we use to describe our vision in a compelling way.

In Chapter Two, I reviewed VisionQuest, the second ritual of the 1990s in which we reinforced the vision and values. This process was expensive, over $4 million, but it is vital in our communication scheme. Through it, we are creating a living metaphor for our future. The maps that we used during the process are full of images of Schwab employees "building bridges" to the future, customers crossing the "rivers of change" with help from our employees.

These maps help us make the differences in our company real for everyone in the company, from the chairman right on down. At the end of the process, everyone shares the "new language" of the vision, and for the next couple of years, these maps will form a common bond of vision. I will use the images in speeches, and we will all refer to the images in the maps in discussions of the company's direction. People will see and feel the answer to the question, "Where are we going?" This gets more and more difficult as a company grows, and it also gets more and more important.

Why Are We Going There?

If VisionQuest's only objective were to allow people to define their jobs, it would frankly just not be worth it. To be valuable, the process had to create meaning, a spirit that made people really care about making the vision a reality. The story of our progress, and the progress of the industry as a whole, provides a context of where we have been and where we are as a company, as a foundation for where we are going. This context then links values to action. Understanding context can compel people to respond to change. I'll give you an example.

In Chapter Four, I recounted the decision that we made to begin providing advice and help to our customers. Thinking through the distinctions and making sure that our action was consistent with our values was vitally important. It was a matter of reinforcing the character of the company. Naturally, the communication of that decision was of primary importance. We had to be sure that everyone not only understood the decision but could eagerly implement it in their own job. It had to have meaning. It had to be done as an expression of the values of the company, not just because we could make more money doing it. Remember that our company had been grounded on the idea that "conflict of interest" and "giving advice" were synonymous. In fact, many of the people who are now officers of the company were recruited on the basis of our firm's not giving advice.

Clearly it was possible to give advice that was sound, ethical, and based on a customer's own criteria, but because we had been imprecise in our earlier characterization, we needed to clarify the move carefully. Employees were asking for meaning in the change.

We had to first tell the story of Schwab customers' changing and accelerating needs. Next, we needed to describe the profile of future investors to demonstrate that what we currently offered would not provide effective answers for them. Finally, we needed to carefully differentiate "Schwab advice" from the advice of the full-commission brokerage. This task fell to all of us. The question was, "What are the differences between the advice that a traditional brokerage would offer and what we intend to offer at Schwab?" The fundamental answer was, of course, in the objectivity of our advice, in *the consistency of our approach*, and in the fact that it would be given in a way that supported the values of the company.

During VisionQuest, employees traced this history themselves, and confirmed these key distinctions. People now understand that by providing ethical advice we are actually supporting, not compromising, the values of the company. They are eager to engage and learn what is necessary to bring this new level of service and expertise to our customers. I feel that we have successfully communicated context. The change now has meaning to our employees, it is consistent with their values. The result is agreement and engagement rather than mere understanding.

Keeping that context of meaning in front of people is the express purview of the leader. It makes no difference what task a person is performing, the right answer to the question "Why are we doing this?" creates meaning in the job.

REINFORCING THE VISION—CONSTANTLY

Every time I go in front of a group of employees, I am trying to energize them, raising the vision from being flat to being textured, adding dimension so that people can connect with a piece of it, so they will want to contribute their own ideas. I recently had the opportunity of speaking in London to a group of managers from Schwab Europe. International operation is new to Schwab, and we are very careful not to confuse style with values. Our European operation was born from merging our own tiny London start-up with a six-hundred-person British firm, and we have gone to great lengths to honor the traditions of that workforce while we export the parts of Schwab that we think are most valuable and nonnegotiable.

I had always heard that the English were conservative compared to us brash Americans, and I didn't want to come off as overbearing. Still, on this particular trip, I couldn't help but be enthusiastic about the vision and values of the company, and about how we had grown to become somewhat of a haven for customers in the United States. I talked about a similar progression around the globe, that we had the opportunity to export this idea of fairness in investing throughout the world. Then I reviewed some of the recent changes we had made in their company and explained the "why" of those changes. I talked about the history of events that made those changes necessary, and related the work we had done to make sure that the changes were consistent with the values of the company. Everyone was interested and involved, and there were many questions.

Afterward, we had a discussion about their responsibility to pass this information along. I speculated that they might not tell their staffs everything I had shared. Sure enough, many of them felt that those who worked with them had no "need to know." In other words, they felt that the information that I had passed along was not important for employees to be able to do their jobs.

They were right, of course. Few people would actually use the information that I had given them to do their current day-to-day, minute-to-minute work. But these managers all agreed that they found what I had said to be interesting and provocative. They were happy that I had taken the time to come to London to spend the time with them, to share with them the thinking behind our plans. They agreed that it made them feel important, and it made them feel part of something that was much bigger than a 9-to-5 job. Still, few of them had considered their own power to affect their own employees in the same way.

How many of them actually went back and engaged their own groups with a larger context? I hope most of them did. People want to know more than they simply have to know. They want to know because they want a sense of ownership and perspective. The leader is the message. Someone who tells people more than they technically need to know to do their jobs is behaving in a way that reinforces the real message: "You are important, and I want your contribution to this enterprise."

At the end of the day, effective leadership communication is personal and attentive. It provides meaning, a sense of continuation of a quest based on the best in everyone, and confidence that each one of us, in conjunction with everyone else in the enterprise, can make a difference in the world.

I am only a passing student of Abraham Maslow and his hierarchy of needs,[6] but I suppose that most people who work in this environment are not worried about their next meal or having a roof over their heads. Ultimately, we won't find inspiration by talking about stock options or big bonuses, as important and even as motivating as they are. Of course, compensation does have to be consistent with the values of the firm, and it can actually provide incentive for people to do more work. But people are inspired to work by needs that are less basic. They want to belong, they want recognition for their achievements, and they want their own individual contribution to make a substantive difference to others.

With few exceptions, people working in big companies have not, up to now, expected to have those needs satisfied by their work. That is one reason why "work and life balance" has become such an important topic in business discussion. The theory, and still the dominant practice, is that people can't have meaningful work *at* work.

The workplace will never replace the love of a core family or the loyalty of dear friends, but it can and should provide something more than forty hours of distraction a week and a paycheck. Whether it does or not largely depends on the leader's ability to communicate enough of the "why."

I began this chapter by maintaining that corporate communication had to shift to an emphasis on two-way communication. What we need is "give-and-take" rather than just "give." All of the leadership communication that I've described—listening, demonstrating caring, describing the future, and providing context—is aimed at creating a dialogue. When people in the company feel like they are part of it rather than just an incidental "human resource," when they know the company is doing meaningful things in the world, and when they know that the leadership really cares about them and the customers they serve, then they will speak up. Then they will contribute their ideas and their criticisms . . . and that contribution is both the prize and the key to ongoing success of twenty-first-century business.

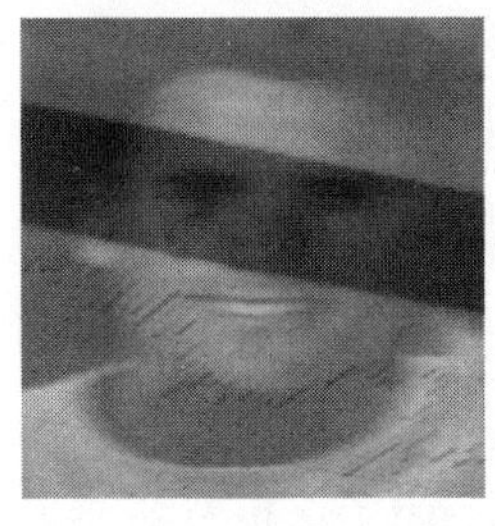

FROM LEADERSHIP COMMUNICATION TO GENERATING INNOVATION

As a consultant and teacher, I chose to specialize in leadership communication because I judged it to be the discipline that needed the most improvement, and because I judged that improvement in this field could make a great difference in the lives of people at work—in their productivity and, most important to me, in their sense of fulfillment and community on the job.

Leadership communication starts with the simple idea that employees need to know who "leadership" is and where "leadership" stands. They want to be engaged, to know what is in your heart, to know where you're taking them, and to know if they can trust you to take them there. After they know these things, then and only then can other media including the Internet be used effectively for inspiration.

The Internet and its attendant technologies provide ample opportunity to spread information around. But the greater the volume of information pushed by technology, the greater the need for integration, and the greater the need for relating the pieces to a meaningful whole. The task of leadership communication is to convert the volume of exchange from crazy-making to meaningful. To build passion and commitment to a business mission in a world dominated by information, and to build the atmosphere that compels participation and contribution, leaders have to deploy themselves even more frequently, even more personally, even more skillfully. Whether you lead a company or a small team, here are some principles:

- Make leadership communication your number one priority.
- Develop a sincere interest in and commitment to learning from others. Dale Carnegie said it in the 1940s and it is still the linchpin of building relationships at every level. If your first reaction to others' ideas is to justify your own, practice suspending not just your verbal reaction but your mental and emotional reaction as well.
- Consciously monitor how many times people ask questions when you speak about change. If you are not engaging others, ask them why.
- Solicit feedback actively from people who are closest to the business. Avoid waiting for their ideas—and avoid blaming them for not being willing to come forward.
- Develop a practice to hone your ability to hear what is below the surface of comments. Practice bringing the hidden meanings and feelings to the surface. Ask questions for clarity.
- When you are answering questions, use new measurements: Did the person feel heard? Did I respond to the person or merely answer the question?
- Reveal more of yourself than you think is necessary, not just your accomplishments, but your own personal hopes and fears as well. Even if you don't believe in being social with those who work for you, learn more about them as human beings.
- Practice stating the vision of your organization as a metaphor so that others can see and feel themselves involved in its accomplishment. Use images generously as you communicate about what you see for the future.
- Focus on values every time you speak about the future of your enterprise. Don't allow your business unit to be totally focused on the bottom line without some greater sense of accomplishment that comes with financial success.
- Write the history of your enterprise or industry that has led to any changes you want to make. Share this context liberally, noting the

key distinctions that make continued change necessary. Communicate the context every time you speak about the future.

- Deploy yourself generously. Strive at all times to be authentic, and use the new technologies to establish informal dialogue.
- Use e-mail and voice-mail to pass information but not for opinions or emotionally charged communication. Be complete in these media. Imagine yourself as reader or listener. What is missing? What questions would you be asking if you heard your message as the receiver? Would it be wiser to use these media to set up actual conversation or face-to-face time?

These behaviors will start you on the road to a new standard of communication for your organization, and over time, you will begin to notice a new level of interest and excitement about your leadership. The payoff, however, is not just in compliments for your communication style, it is in active participation by others—participation that signifies increased productivity for the whole organization.

How is that increased productivity measured? For the knowledge worker, the true measurement is innovation. Peter Drucker, the dean of management practice who has helped us anticipate and make changes for forty years, claims that "while the more than fifty-fold increase in productivity of the manual worker was the greatest achievement of the 20th century manager, the most important work of the 21st century is to increase the productivity of the knowledge worker."[1]

Drucker goes on to give us the major factors that will determine knowledge-worker productivity. To me, the most significant one is that the worker is seen as an asset rather than a cost . . . that she wants to work for the organization in preference to all other opportunities.

It is the requisite for willing participation that defies all purely structural solutions to the problem of knowledge-worker productivity. Organizational consultants have been hard at work on this problem of willing participation for more than a decade. The word *empowerment* has stuck like bubblegum to the sole—and soul—of the human resource professional. Many have spent half a career creating organizational and communication models that will facilitate people's taking responsibility for the business. Still, for all of our efforts at getting the organization and communication right, many people, if not most, simply won't express their ideas in the organization, won't offer new thoughts for innovation for the company. It is rare to see an employee opinion survey in any established company that reflects an eagerness on the part of employees to express opinions freely. Why?

Most people, it seems, come to a company with a built-in filter about expressing their opinion, and those who don't soon develop such filters or leave. People who are willing and able to express contrary opinions will start their own companies, work in smaller companies where they are clear that their voice is really making a difference, or will distinguish themselves by speaking up and eventually sit at the top of a large company. Such potential heroes and heroines are sprinkled throughout most large organizations, but to keep such brave and competent folks and to develop more in a large company, the leadership must be very skilled and aware. Depending on natural selection isn't enough.

Now here is the irony. The work of Karen Stephenson of UCLA[2] and many others suggests that even in the worst environments, where opinion surveys indicate that people don't feel safe enough to offer suggestions for the good of the company, they *still* express themselves. This research fits with my own experience. It takes tremendous tyranny and constant watching, listening, and punishment to prevent people from self-expression. Opinions always get expressed, but they rarely get expressed in ways or in places where the expression will be effective in actually changing things. Rather, new ideas are expressed as complaints in hallways or bathrooms, and are often voiced to people who can't help implement change.

According to Stephenson, these expressions occur in all natural networks, in every organization. The operation of these natural networks, however, is based on the perceived level of trust, not on organizational hierarchy. Whether opinions are expressed openly or clandestinely depends largely on the trustworthiness of the leadership. The natural network lines don't often correspond to the actual organizational structure of the company. In other words, innovation does not happen in organizations in which there is not a high level of trust in senior management, or if it does happen, it is the result of the good ideas of those senior managers themselves.

Ideas only get expressed to fulfill a compelling purpose. Generating new ideas is first a matter of aspiration, of common dreams for the future. Without a compelling vision and the inspiration to serve it, organizational changes themselves are meaningless, and to pretend otherwise is to pretend that a bad marriage can be fixed with a new house.

Just as the organizational structure can't compel participation, reward systems, suggestion programs—even formal and institutionalized forums for generating ideas—are impotent by themselves.

Many companies have decided that the physical plant itself can influence the sharing of new ideas. At Intel, for example, and at many other Silicon Valley firms, everyone works in a cubicle rather than a private office. These changes can all be useful, but again, are not sufficient.

The starting point for innovation is interest and commitment to the issues. People are creative when they care about something getting better. It is up to the leader to create an atmosphere that coaxes these creative impulses to the front. That's why the subject of innovation belongs with other leadership topics, because leaders must not only create an atmosphere in which people care, they must also "make it safe" to offer criticism of current procedures or to suggest entirely new ways of doing things, and then protect and nurture the implementation of ideas.

In 1997, Xerox Corporation endowed the first chair of knowledge, at the University of California at Berkeley's Haas School of Business. Its first appointee, Ikujiro Nonaka, was also the founding dean of the Graduate School of Knowledge Science at Japan Advanced Institute of Science and Technology. At the first Berkeley forum on the subject of knowledge management Dr. Nonaka introduced the philosophical concept of *"ba,"* roughly translated in English as "shared space for emerging relationships." "'Ba' provides a platform for advancing individual and or collective knowledge," says Nonaka. "'Ba' is the context which harbors meaning. Thus we consider 'ba' to be a *shared space* that serves as a foundation for knowledge creation."[3] (Emphasis mine.)

Now I admit that this concept might sound esoteric, and might also provide the basis for some loud guffaws in the rough-and-tumble world of financial services. But Nonaka's philosophically grounded concept is not substantially different from the ideas of Gary Hamel, one of the most popular and flamboyant purveyors of business wisdom. Hamel, from the London School of Economics, a specialist on corporate strategy, has been suggesting for some time that strategy is no longer just about doing a plan. "Strategy is revolution," says Hamel, "everything else is tactical."[4] He goes on to suggest that revolution can only come from innovative ideas, ones that change the rules of the game, and that therefore the task of leadership is "to create the field where new voices can have new conversations, to create new passion and conviction, and spawn a raft of new ideas." Hamel's "field" and Nonaka's "ba" are the same.

While there might be more perceived risk in suggesting the breakthrough to the boss than to speak up about a small change in process, it appears that both types of innovation are dependent on the right field being created—not merely the right organizational structure or physical plant.

Authentic leadership communication and the leader's observably living the values of the company are the cultivators of this field. These two, when coupled with the leader's demonstration of competence, create the atmosphere of competence and trustworthiness that brings others to a decision to follow and a commitment to participate fully. That participation certainly comes in the form of hard work, sometimes *long* work, but more importantly, it comes in the form of a contribution of ideas . . . innovation.

In the next chapter, Dave tells us how a leader can nurture this field to sprout new ideas, both incremental and breakthrough, and what we can do to recognize and implement the most important ideas when they do come to light.

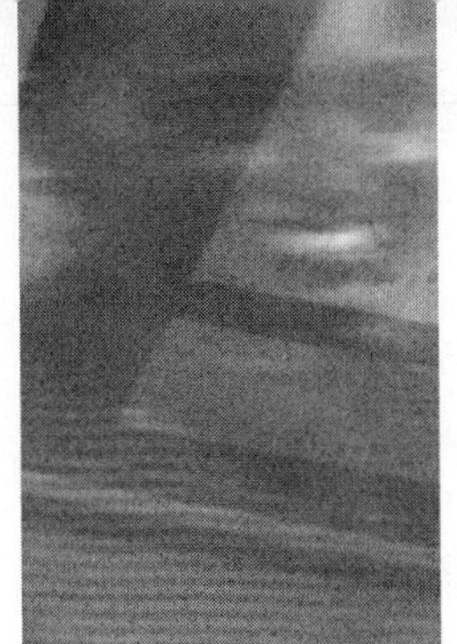

SIX

GENERATING IDEAS AND INNOVATION THROUGH LEADERSHIP

I wish that being a role model and creating great communications were enough to guarantee that everyone in the company would become passionate, contribute new ideas, and that the best of these ideas would be effectively screened and implemented. These leadership practices will start an organization on the path to accomplish the dual objectives of getting ideas and implementing the good ones—and it still takes much more.

As Terry pointed out, while I can inspire people in a broad sense and I can certainly set a tone for the company as a whole, most people are personally removed from the CEO. My own activities and communication might be appreciated, but when it comes down to day-to-day activities, people appropriately look to their direct managers for guidance and signals about what is OK and what is not OK. Frankly, even if their own manager is fully aligned and fully skilled, many people still harbor a fear of speaking up, much less offering an idea about the future of the company or a suggestion for departmental change. In a growth company like ours, many newcomers have a history in a totally different kind of enterprise within the industry. We are different from start-ups and second-stage technology companies in that regard, because we often hire financial services people who are used to playing by different, less dynamic rules. Technologists, as a group, are used to rapid innovation as a demand of their job; most bankers and brokers are not.

Financial services is an old-line business, and there was relatively little breakthrough innovation in the first few decades of the century. In the mid-1970s, Merrill Lynch introduced a Cash Management Account that turned the brokerage industry, and indeed many banks, on their ears. About the same time, Schwab was actually born as an innovation, a discount broker that only did transactions. Because Schwab is seen as revolutionary, we have depended on breakthrough innovation to drive our growth. Many sectors of our industry have felt that stability is most important, but innovation is vital to Schwab's success. We are, as Clayton Christensen has described in *The Innovator's Dilemma,* on the leading edge in adapting "disruptive technology"[1]—that is, initiating practices that change the very basis of an industry. We have tried to bring new rules to financial services, and it has resulted in products and services that many customers don't even know that they want.

Terry alluded to Gary Hamel's "field of innovation." I've become friends with Gary and consider him an outstanding thinker and consultant in both strategy and innovation. While he is a proponent of revolution, he also recognizes that ideas that incrementally improve tactics are invaluable, and often lead to breakthroughs. So the first order of business is to create the field where new ideas of any kind can emerge at a rapid rate.

TRANSFORMING THE CULTURE FOR THE FUTURE

Like most other firms that are in established businesses, we have had to transform our culture to encourage contribution. Schwab started as a transactions-only company; we just did trades, we gave no advice and didn't try to develop relationships. Excellence was defined as "doing it the same way every time." So we had a long way to go to get to a culture where innovation and knowledge sharing were the dominant themes. I think we are like many other firms in that regard.

Additionally, because we started out with this "same-way" culture, the source of our wonderful innovation has created some concerns that I think are also typical for any company in our stage of growth and transformation. Specifically, until recently, the big innovation has largely come from the top of the organization. When I look at the dozen breakthrough ideas that have moved the firm a great distance in a short period of time, most have come from the executive offices, from the top ten or twenty people in the firm, many of them from Chuck himself. In a traditional model of business, this is quite natural. After all, executives have two requisites for creating and implementing breakthrough ideas—the right perspective, and control of the purse strings.

Perspective: Customers Drive Innovation

At Schwab, perspective has been particularly important, because we were the first firm, and perhaps still one of the few in our industry, to focus on what is good for the customer as the basis for innovation. The customer and the investor always drive investment; but some companies don't learn this fact until they try to drive investment some other way. When the customers don't want what you offer, it affects performance rapidly and investors get grumpy. It's that simple. Chuck has trained all of us to make the customer our first and last focus. Even in changes that we make to improve productivity, we want to be sure that we don't detract from the benefit of our customers. The larger our company becomes, and the more layers we add to the organization, the more difficult it is to maintain that perspective throughout the enterprise, but doing so is absolutely necessary. Dick Notebaert, CEO of Ameritech, puts it succinctly: "When innovation is ingrained into your culture, you're living your brand. It's just a way of life. You do things with your customers because you're trying to look at it from their perspective, not yours."[2]

It is the leader's task to drive this perspective throughout the firm.

Controlling the Purse Strings

We are still small enough to be able to make most of our major investment decisions at the top, and of course, that practice has tended to heavily bias breakthrough innovation toward projects spawned by executives. Each decision to invest in a more dramatic innovation is weighed against decisions to invest in projects that primarily improve upon what we know makes the customers happy. This is the "innovator's dilemma" articulated by Christensen. "How can executives simultaneously do what is right for the near-term health of their established businesses, while focusing adequate resources on the disruptive technologies that ultimately could lead to their downfall?[3]" Most ideas that are really breakthrough don't present themselves in a neat spreadsheet. If the data were available to assure success, then someone would have done it a while ago. So to make great ideas pay off, we also have to make sure that the mechanism of the organization allows resources to flow to the right ideas, wherever they come from, and sometimes despite the business case . . . yes, *despite* the business case.

The Internet Multiplier

Amid all these demands of speed comes the Internet, which has raised the innovation bar to a world-record height. Companies that started out as "Internet companies" already think in terms of "Internet possibilities," but we started out as a brokerage, albeit one that was innovative. When we adopted the Internet as a channel of distribution for our customers, it was invasive to our old paradigm of telephones and branches. We are just now in the process of understanding its transformative power. To our customers, we wanted to make the Web a channel of information and distribution of our products. Internally, we want it to fundamentally change the way we relate to one another. We want to be more like Cisco and 3-Com, companies that were forged in the Internet crucible, than like Neiman Marcus and Target, companies that use the Web primarily as a source of customer information and advertising, something additive to their enterprise, rather than encompassing it. We want to use the full force of the Internet to help us encourage, gather, sort, and implement ideas that will continue to move the company forward as the industry change-agent—yet we don't want to mistakenly use it as a substitute for the direct interaction between people.

TACKLING THE CHALLENGES OF LEADERSHIP

So far, I've described in general terms some barriers to innovation in a traditional but growing firm: bias toward the ideas of the people at the top, shortage of resources to develop ideas deep in the organization, and keeping a balance between investing in what is already working and investing in new but unproven ideas. These barriers are daunting enough, the danger is that with the Internet multiplier on top, they can seem overwhelming.

And before leaders can tackle those issues, before leaders can begin discussing innovation, we need to be sure that everyone shares our aspiration as a company. That vision provides the pull that is necessary for people to care, to build the passion around their work.

Our process in 1995 and the more recent VisionQuest that I described in Chapter Two were designed to clarify the vision, reinforce the values, and help people understand their individual role in accomplishing our shared goals. The next step in innovation is to communicate about the vital role of constant renewal.

Success Through Renewal: Using the S Curve

A few years ago, I read the book *Jumping the Curve*, and it made an immediate impression—not because I thought Nick Imparato and Oren Harari had discovered something new, but rather because, like most good business writers, they had described a phenomenon in a way that could be shared with people who were not business students. The S curve they describe has many variations. The compilation I use is shown here as Figure 6.1 to demonstrate the importance of the idea and to demonstrate what I consider to be effective communication about the central reason that innovation is so important.[4] I'll review it briefly.

FIGURE 6.1 The S-Shaped Curve.

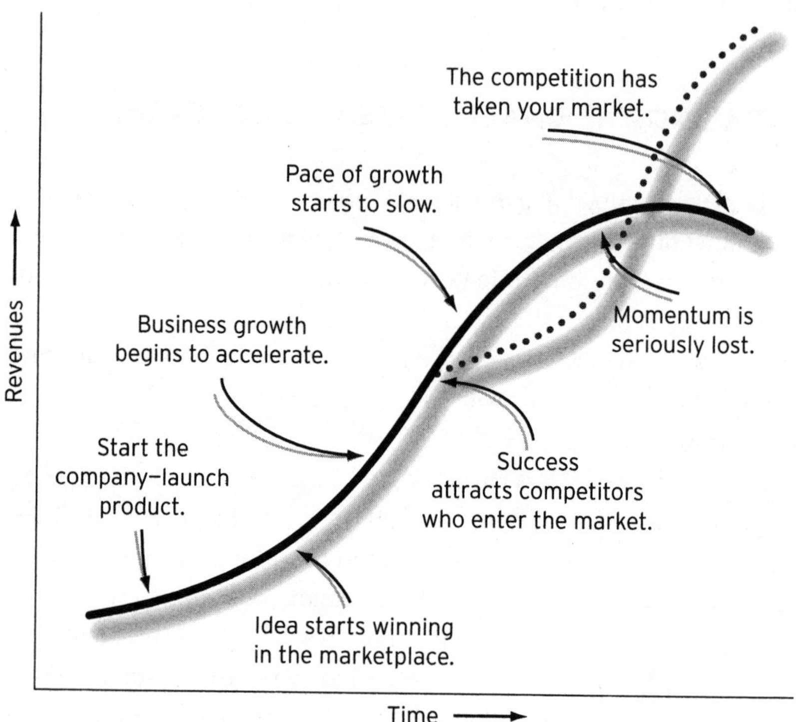

The S-shaped curve depicts a foundation of ongoing success in the marketplace. All businesses operate on a life cycle, and unless they take steps to renew that cycle, they will inevitably rise and fall according to the curve. As you start your new company your idea begins to gain favor in the marketplace. As demand increases, scale begins to help with costs. Business is good. As the product's dynamic approaches the middle part of that curve, growing revenue and profit attract imitators—either existing competitors or brand-new companies—who want to cash in on your model. They go for the fat—the product, the markets, the segments—where you're most vulnerable. They find ways to do what you have done, only they do it better, faster, and cheaper. If you respond incrementally, by only cutting costs or cutting price, you may indeed extend the length of the line before it flattens and then starts to go downhill. Unfortunately, incrementalism also gives your new competitors more time to improve on their new approach. When your own curve flattens out, it appropriately resembles your deathbed. At the same time, their curve accelerates and grows steeper. You lose volume, your unit costs go up. There is no need to follow the model to the demise of your enterprise . . . you get the idea.

There are lots of examples of companies "sleeping on the curve." Apple certainly snoozed as Microsoft, IBM, Compaq, and others moved in, not to build a better interface but rather to open up the PC architecture. In turn, IBM and Compaq were sleeping as Dell purified the manufacturing of the PC and accelerated past them. In retailing, Wal-Mart capitalized on the Sears idea, except they built in the places where Sears wasn't building, gave better service and charged less. They passed Sears and never looked back. At the same time, catalog companies like L.L. Bean and Eddie Bauer were claiming the most profitable niches in the mail-order business that Sears and Montgomery Ward used to own.

What were Barnes & Noble executives thinking as Amazon.com used the ordering power of the Internet to shoot past them? And of course, in brokerage services, Schwab did it to a whole industry, first with discount brokerage, and then with other products and services that we will use shortly as examples.

Virtual Cycle Times and Innovation

When I was in business school, the idea of business life cycle was considered a given, but one as dull as the saying, "The future lies ahead." It is a substantially more important idea now. Why? The cycle time once measured in decades can now be measured in months, even weeks in some industries. It isn't just companies that rise and fall with this cycle, careers and jobs do as well. A company will now go through many of these cycles in the life of one executive. The model used to describe an interesting long-term strategy problem—now it describes a dynamic management problem. Most employees don't know that or appreciate it, so it is up to the leader to communicate it, and I do, and will continue to do so.

I use variations on this idea to teach Schwab employees exactly why it's important to create breakthrough thinking as a matter of course. We've used these graphic concepts to share with employees throughout our organization so they'll understand how dangerous it is to get too comfortable—and how powerful it is to keep jumping to new growth curves at precisely that moment when it seems most unnecessary to change anything at all. But the most important lesson that I've tried to teach is that innovation is not an option, it is part of everyone's job. Ideas are the currency of today's worker, just as time or hands used to be. We still pay people for their time, but we really expect their ideas as well. In fact, the health of the organization depends on them.

When I communicate this message, I use examples that people are familiar with; for example, Schwab's introduction of Mutual Fund OneSource that we discussed in Chapter Four. This idea, the convenience of a single marketplace for customers without incremental cost to them, revolutionized the mutual funds market. Now nearly every brokerage firm, bank, and investment company has a similar marketplace, but our lead in announcing it—and our long-standing relationships with the funds themselves—gave us the position of having "jumped the curve" of the mutual funds market. Those who came after us are now trying to increment their way to success by adding funds to claim a bigger "supermarket." It's a story of our history that reaches into our future. The very act of communicating this concept and example has given life to our employees' appreciation for innovation. This awareness is the first requisite to stimulating ideas. With this awareness as a base, we then need to take on other challenges. Getting the ideas, sorting them out through the right questions and the right attitude, implementing and nurturing them, and learning all the while—these are leadership challenges of the first order. We'll take them one at a time.

ASKING THE RIGHT QUESTIONS

An innovation consultant came to our company in 1996 and tried to show that people were not really resistant to change. The consultant posed a question to Schwab employees (about 150 of them) in our auditorium: "How many of you went to the same place on vacation more than once?" Only a few hands went up. He went on, "and how many of you went on vacation to the same place four times or more?" No hands were raised.

"You see," said the consultant, "it's not true that people don't like change. When we are left to do the choosing, we all like a certain amount of variety and change in our lives."

Then, from the back of the room came a raspy woman's voice: "You misunderstand, sir. We do not take vacations!"

Hopefully, she was kidding . . . but it illustrates the point. What the consultant said had sounded good, but the interchange demonstrated that it didn't work in this instance; he hadn't asked the right question. Let's look at some characteristics of questions that stimulate good ideas.

From Boldness to Breakthrough

Timidity results in incremental change; boldness creates breakthrough. To create our Mutual Fund Marketplace, we asked the question, "How can we make it more convenient for customers to own funds from more than one family?" That question resulted in a modest success, but customers still had to pay transaction fees to Schwab for the convenience of consolidating funds from various families under one statement. We created Mutual Fund OneSource—the industry-changing product—by asking ourselves, "What could we offer our customers that would put us in the top three companies in offerings of mutual funds?" This question forced us to accept nothing as given, making it possible for us to conceive of a marketplace in which funds companies themselves paid the fees, and the customer got the benefit of a consolidated statement. Now, with the benefit of a consolidated statement and no transaction fee, customers couldn't wait to subscribe. These were fundamentally different questions that yielded substantially different answers.

Asking the right question often leads from an incremental change to a breakthrough. A few years ago, our "Chairman's Division" (Chuck's office, the area where customers complain as a last resort) had quite a backlog. Complaints were a mere fraction of our customer interactions, but with millions of interactions per month, the fractions added up. These customers were, by natural selection, those who were most upset—yet it was taking us more than two weeks, on average, to respond to them. The process was one of writing back to the customer acknowledging the complaint, contacting the branch or call center where the transaction was processed, investigating the customer's allegation (this sometimes meant auditing tapes of conversations), reaching a decision about who was right and who was wrong, and then writing the customer back with the resolution. As we approached the problem of a more timely response, we asked, "How can we shorten our response time by a couple of days, getting back to the customer in ten days rather than two full weeks?" That question yielded a streamlining of the process . . . getting the branch or call center to treat these complaints as a priority.

It was not until we asked ourselves, "How can we shorten our response time to a week?" that we really analyzed the process. One team member suggested that we call the customer rather than writing. An old hand at the Chairman's Division believed that it was a regulatory requirement to write the letter. We investigated, and found that there was no longer such a requirement. Suddenly, we were down to five days.

Finally, we asked, "How could we respond to these particular complaints in forty-eight hours?" This question called for breakthrough. When a question like this is asked, people start to question all the givens, all their preconceived notions and the fundamental "rules of the game." This is no longer about incrementally solving a problem, it is about redefining the problem entirely, and people begin to challenge even their own assumptions. In this case, we redefined the problem as "customer-retention" rather than "complaint response." What did the customers want? They wanted to have the complaint resolved in their favor, as quickly as possible. This conclusion then goaded us to analyze the cost of our responses. We concluded that we could concede any dispute that we could resolve in the customer's favor for less than that cost and make our target. Eighty percent of the complaints could be handled in this way, well within the forty-eight hours.

To complete the process change, we began measuring the department on "customer retention" rather than "complaint-response" time. Now, thanks to the right questions and breakthrough changes, the employees in the department are more spirited and they continue to improve the process. Our customers, as a group, are delighted with the result. It's a positive breakthrough for everyone.

Choose "And"—Not "Or"

One of the most useful and challenging questions has to do with the resolution of apparently conflicting ideas. Deion Sanders is one of only a handful of athletes with the talent and stamina to play more than one sport professionally. In 1995, when Deion was rumored to be signing with the Dallas Cowboys football team, one of the companies that Deion represented ran a commercial featuring the owner of the Cowboys, Jerry Jones, and Deion having a conversation. Jerry said, "So, Deion, are you going to play baseball or football?" Deion said, "Both!" Jones went on, "And when you play for the Cowboys, do you want to play offense or defense?" "Both," said Deion. "OK," said a chagrined Jones, "Is it going to cost me fifteen or twenty million dollars?" Deion looked at him, smiled, and said, "Both!" The interchange drew a laugh—and it dramatically demonstrates the attitude of many customers today. They expect to receive seemingly conflicting benefits—and they are often getting them.

Ironically, about the same time Deion was moving to Dallas, business best-seller *The Discipline of Market Leaders* suggested that focus was the key to market dominance. According to the authors, firms that tried to be many things failed, while those companies that used only one major strategy in a market could control their niche forever.[5] That book generated a lot of controversy around Schwab. At the time, we were actually debating our strategy and moving from a strictly discount company to a value-added company. We found ourselves saying things like: "We can either be low-priced or provide spectacular service," or "We can have branches and be 'high-touch' with our customers, or we can push them toward our automated channels and become primarily a 'high-tech' provider."

We learned a lot about innovation during this period. As we began to ponder our choices in strategy, our research was telling us that customers wanted *both*—and so did we. We wanted the strong deep middle of our market, and the middle demands it all: great service, great products, and fair prices. We didn't want to become a niche player because we felt that niche players in financial services were eventually marginalized and swallowed up. It was not going to be enough, in our business, to settle for *or.* We wanted *and.*

Since then, we have used a phrase coined by Jim Collins and Jerry Porras in their best-seller, *Built to Last,* to describe this ability to deliver seemingly contradictory benefits: "the brilliance of the and, rather than the tyranny of the or."[6] We believe that we can give great service *and* have great prices. We can be both high-tech *and* high-touch. We can be the premier provider of investment advice *and* have no conflict of interest with our customers. These are the hard things to do in tandem. These are the tasks of really great companies. So we frequently ask ourselves, "How do we do both?" to gain deeper insights.

Asking the right question can make a difference in the way people see a problem, in the way they analyze it, and of course, in the way they see themselves in the solution. Being bold and resolving apparent paradox can lead to great answers to very tough questions. Formulating the questions is the easy part, staying out of the way as people answer the questions is a bit more difficult and every bit as essential.

STAYING ALERT TO THE PERILS OF INCUMBENCY, INCLUDING YOUR OWN

There is always someone invested in the status quo. In the case of the "Chairman's Division," there were many people involved in handling our complaints who had set ideas, and certainly the system was conceived and had operated in the same way for years. Incumbency has its advantages, including stability and consistency. Indeed, turn the clock back as little as fifteen years and you find that incumbent companies ruled the roost of business. The top firms simply continued to be the top firms. Brand recognition, distribution systems, computer systems, manufacturing systems, sourcing systems, know-how, customers, relationships, scale advantage, vendor relationships, presence in the marketplace, deep pockets, sophisticated management systems . . . these all gave, and still give, incumbents some advantages.

But globalization and technology have changed the nature of incumbency from a decisive advantage to a selective liability. Increasingly incumbents are finding themselves trapped by their strengths—by the old ways of doing things, and sometimes by the sheer size of the systems dedicated to doing them. Their distribution systems might be old, expensive, sluggish—a liability. Their brand identities might be old, wrong for the times—can't change fast enough. Their technologies might represent millions, maybe billions, of dollars built into legacy mainframe technologies. These investments, both financial and psychic, are hard to ignore.

Breakthrough technology such as the Internet spurs the imagination. There were those who imagined the ability to cook an entire Thanksgiving dinner in the microwave oven. While others were claiming that the telephone had use only as a novelty, Alexander Graham Bell was seeing at least a neighborhood network of people chatting with one another in their kitchens. As with Bell, the mentality for the devotees of technology is one of infinite possibility: "It is possible to do anything better than it has ever been done before." Is it? There are literally millions of young entrepreneurs up to the challenge of finding out. The barriers to entry that used to be established by incumbency are now merely a challenge to a person with some imagination, a garage, and some technology talent. In fact, technology entrepreneurs specifically target the most sacred of cows, knowing that their pasture offers the tallest and greenest grass.

Just as incumbency hampers and helps companies, so it does with individuals. Generally, the older we get and the more success we have, the more invested we become in the status quo. Human nature works against change, because most people grow to like predictability and stability in their lives. We also become entrenched in our own ideas of reality, and might hear ourselves muttering, "That won't work, we tried it," or "That's not the way we do things." In fact, the status quo can become representative of our own personal legacy and therefore even more difficult to let go of. This kind of investment in incumbency, both with our companies and with our own ideas, can become a real burden to innovation.

For example, as you probably know, the financial services business was built on interest, commissions, and fees. There is what is known as a "banker's mentality" regarding the willingness to charge a small fee for nearly everything, including a fee for opening an account.

Accordingly, from the time Individual Retirement Accounts (IRAs) were created by the legislature, every financial institution charged a small fee ($25 to $50) to open such an account in their establishment. We were no exception. Then one day, a young vice president named Jeff Lyons proposed that we eliminate the fee altogether. He came up with that idea because we were looking for ways to accumulate assets from customers. His rationale was that if we wanted to stand for value, and if the assets were really important to us, we should offer to set the annual fee at "zero." Certainly, he reasoned, assets would come in.

You can imagine the debate. Everyone who had ever worked in a bank (this included nearly everyone except Jeff) considered his idea heresy. Give up a fee? We looked at the effect on the bottom line:

$9 million in reduced profits. His analysis showed that it would take $2 billion in new assets to offset the $9 million. He also pointed out that if our biggest competitor tried to match our offer, it would cost that competitor more than twice what it would cost us. We suspected that they would be hesitant to make that decision . . . like the monkey with his fist clenched so tightly around the bait that he can't escape.

Jeff was coming from the right perspective—the good of the customer—and he suspected that even if our competitors followed suit, they would appear to be late and greedy. Of course, he was right. We advertised "No-Annual-Fee IRA" heavily and quickly blew by our projections. Our competitors waited, not wanting to give up the bottom line dollars, and lost credibility as well as assets.

This is a case where incumbency could have kept us from doing the right thing. There were executives in the firm, including me, who were not as enthusiastic because of their own preconceptions, and we were dead wrong. The trap of incumbency can stifle the changing of systems, processes, or even shifting the fundamentals of an organization, when to do so would be the best course of action.

Many people don't know that Schwab was the first company in the electronic bill-payment business. In the early eighties, we launched a software product called "Financial Independence." It was a stand-alone banking product that allowed customers to manage their personal finances on the computer. Problem? It wasn't built around an easy-to-use check register. That was the equivalent of forgetting your hiking boots as you left for five days of backpacking. The product was a little ahead of its time, sold very few copies, and was never resurrected. Why? Because I convinced Chuck and Larry that we were in the brokerage business rather than the financial services business. But for those who recognized the financial services aspect, the market was ultimately there: look at Quicken now. (Maybe this wasn't my best recommendation!)

I'm not suggesting that every product is worth pursuing forever. It isn't. But it is absolutely necessary to give up attachment to old ideas to be able to see the new ones that will hold the success of your future.

We use our diversity of ethnicity, age, experience, and function to help us remember that everything we have—systems, organization, and especially our current products and services—can be potential barriers to innovation, and also as mulch for the new ideas that we will need to continue to grow.

Leadership establishes the field for innovation by holding an aspiration that everyone wants to accomplish and then communicating the urgent need for everyone to play. Innovation can then be stimulated by asking questions that are expansive enough and inclusive enough to bring out unique perspectives. It is necessary to ignore incumbency, including your own set ideas, and to find and encourage the widest and most diverse set of eyes to look at each and every issue. These practices can help get ideas out. Getting them implemented involves other practices, some of which are not part of the traditional business bag of tricks.

ENCOURAGING NOBLE FAILURE

One never goes to a motivational seminar or speech without hearing at least once that failure is the primary ingredient in learning. It has certainly been true in my own life, yet I cannot say that any of my bosses have been particularly gracious about my failures. I'm not criticizing them, it's just that the prevailing response to failure is punishment. Success by failure is the hardest plank to install in a culture, because it is so counter to our instincts of "survival of the fittest." There are few companies where failure in the lab results in enormous success (as it did for 3M's Post-it notes). Innovation, however, will only be prolific to the extent we are able to create some kind of assurance that risk of failure is not only acceptable, but expected, in fact, encouraged.

Realistically, I can't walk up to an employee who has just botched a project and say, "Thank you. Here's your promotion and bonus." But I can make finer distinctions than just "success" and "failure." It seems to me that the largest impediment to a healthy attitude toward failure is our inability to distinguish between just plain being stupid and failing on the way to great success. We need a good model to be able to communicate the difference so that we can encourage the kind of "noble failure" that can spur innovation forward. The distinction involves doing the homework, establishing "learning" as a primary goal, starting small, and stacking the deck in your favor.

Do the Homework

Larry often told me, "Don't let the power of intuition be an excuse for laziness in doing the analysis." He was right. The first hallmark of noble failure is that the analysis of the pros and cons is actually done: we don't take risk as a matter of whim or seat-of-the-pants navigation. New ideas, particularly ideas that are disruptive in their potential, can only be marginally analyzed for their impact before we have to go to actual test, but they *can* be analyzed. The fact that the generator of the idea has done the analysis shows that she is taking innovation seriously, not merely brainstorming, implementing, and hoping for the best.

Frequently analysis does involve some intuition. For example, when we did the analysis of "No-Fee IRA," we knew we could not predict with any accuracy the increase in assets that would come in from customers. What we could do, however, was calculate the worth of assets we would need to have the plan work financially. Then we could look each other in the eye and ask, "Do we think we can hit or exceed this number?" This type of analysis is not as scientific as we would like, but our reaction gives us some sense of the possibility. If one or more persons says, "No way!" it's probably time to reconsider.

Play to Learn, Not Just to Win

A few very special ideas defy analysis altogether. These ideas are for products and services that simply don't exist. As Christensen said, "Markets that don't exist can't be analyzed."[7] (I wish I had read his book before I met Larry. I would have had a great comeback to his incantation to "do the analysis.") Actually, of course, the newer the idea and the more disruptive it is to the status quo of the customer or product set, the less it will yield to any analysis at all. There simply isn't any data, and there are no situations on which to base questions about possibility. This is usually true for products that are the first in their class, or services that customers don't know they want: the first telephone, the first television, the first personal computer. But the lack of data doesn't mean that a product or service should not be moved ahead. As Christensen points out, "markets for disruptive technologies often emerge from unanticipated successes . . . such discoveries often come by watching how people use products, rather than by listening to what they say."[8]

TeleBroker is our touch-tone brokerage system, a fully automated system that provides quotes, does trades, and now even responds to voice commands. But it didn't start out as a trading system. We introduced it as "Schwab Quotes," a way of giving people stock quotes without involving a human being. By watching the way people used it, we have expanded its use many times throughout the years. Hardly anyone called for just one quote, so we added stock lists to the individual quotes so that folks could get all the quotes they wanted with a single keystroke. We found that many people whose first language was not English used TeleBroker because the touch-tone quote request didn't require strong English skills. This observation was a precursor to our efforts to provide segmented language-specific services to Chinese- and Spanish-speaking customers, both of which have evolved into very successful programs. A simple idea of providing quotes by phone has turned into a highly productive system that gives great service and lowers costs dramatically.

New, dramatic breakthroughs are doomed to failure if they rest only on the details of the original idea. In fact, they are frequently abandoned as failures because they didn't live up to the expectations of the implementer. IBM's first entry tailored for the home computer market was the "PCjr" (vintage 1983). It was criticized as a toy and ended its short-lived career as a flop. IBM didn't launch another model specifically for the home market until the PS1 models in the early 1990s. I suspect that had the company merely learned from the first entry, rather than expecting huge IBM-scale success, it would have moved forward more rapidly. Apple made a similar mistake with the Newton, expecting instant market rather than instant learning.

With an attitude of learning rather than one that demands instant success, the chances for a favorable implementation increase. Both IBM's and Apple's chances would have been greatly enhanced had they wanted to learn rather than merely sell. They would not have flooded the market with heavily advertised products in markets that were ill-defined.

Start Quickly, Start Small

The principle of starting quickly and small is a corollary of "playing to learn." Thanks to technology, the cost of prototyping and testing products in the real marketplace is coming down. Not long ago, depending on the complexity of the product, we had to actually build a reasonable likeness of the product or service before we could test it live. Accordingly, we didn't test much until we were quite a ways down the road toward a major investment. Now, technology gives us the ability to simulate, and the Internet gives us the opportunity to build a site with computer code rather than with expensive steel and concrete. We can run tests almost immediately, and we can run a variety of trials, testing something in market "A" and something different in market "B." We can actually get customers' reaction in the real world of decision making before we have made a major commitment to investment. When we launched the first models of our electronic brokerage division in Florida, we actually had multiple offers, testing each one in the virtual environment of the computer in order to fine-tune the offering.

This flexibility makes it much less expensive to fail, and consequently it encourages people to try. This "starting small" approach proves particularly valuable when the whole thing actually blows up, when the customers don't like it. The lost investment in a trial is not nearly as serious as the money you could lose in a full-scale rollout.

The same principle applies when the product is not high-tech. Let me give you a case in point. In the late 1970s, Chuck made a decision to add a branch office to our little discount firm because, even though we specialized in transactions-only, he suspected people would find it valuable to have a place and a face to meet where their money was concerned. He opened the first branch in Sacramento and in a few months recognized that it was growing at double the rate of the other markets without branches. We've been opening branches ever since. As we examined our success with opening new branches we began to recognize that our model only worked in large markets where a substantial investment (in some cases, as much as $400,000) could be paid back by large market returns. We needed a more streamlined model to expand into small markets.

We asked ourselves, "What's really important about a branch office?" And we suspected the answer for our smaller markets wasn't fancy furniture or lots of faces. It was one face. A human being you could talk to. So in the early 1990s we invented the one-person branch office as a test. We opened four of them: in Provo, Utah; Medford, Oregon; Fargo, North Dakota; and Boise, Idaho. They cost $10,000 each. We learned that even the smallest office needs two people for support, backup, and dealing with peak times. We learned we could do well in executive office spaces with a month-to-month lease. We learned we could make the technology work.

We also learned that offices that don't spend all their time on customer service grew much faster than those we clogged by transferring existing customers to them. Adding the existing customer base to these offices would have quadrupled the cost to $40,000.

Three of our first four small offices were successful—Provo, Medford, and Boise. Fargo wasn't successful—but it was a $10,000 mistake, not a $40,000 mistake, or the $400,000 debacle it might have been had we started large. And in that sense it wasn't a mistake at all. We have already opened more than a hundred of these smaller offices and plan to open more than a hundred more in the next few years—and we'll do it successfully because we started small and learned what worked.

Skew the Test Toward Success

I admit that the idea of skewing a test toward success flies in the face of the conventional wisdom. Most simulators want to try a worst-case scenario, or at least an average scenario, thinking that if you can be successful in the worst case or the average case, then the best case is easy or more profitable and you can go ahead and fully invest. But what if you fail in the worst or average case? What have you learned?

Real breakthrough ideas fail much more often than they succeed, so when we fail, we'd really like to recognize it as a failure. We would want to know that it is a bad idea in its current form, and we can only be sure of that if it is tested under ideal circumstances. If it fails, we don't have to say, "Let's try it again with better managers." If we have left some variables doubtful, we will continually be tweaking the circumstances to make it work. It is far better to either ditch the idea or challenge and rethink some of the basic assumptions before we try again. If under the best circumstances it succeeds, then we can analyze how to stack the deck in our favor as we go ahead. We really stacked the deck in favor of success for those one-person branches. We tried to find locations where chances of success were great. We found great people to run the offices. When Fargo failed, we knew it was because the location was not right, not because the idea itself was faulty.

"Noble failure" includes doing the analysis, playing to learn, starting small, and skewing the test toward success. There is only one requisite result of an effort that includes these elements: *new knowledge.* If the project fails, we still know more than we did before, and we probably know more than our competitors who didn't try. This is the essence of innovation management, and it is an important idea to communicate and live by. It gives people the guidance they need to know the difference between a wild idea that results in an undisciplined failure and a solid proposal that deserves the risk of implementation. By articulating these distinctions, a leader is making it clear that responsible innovation is not only welcome, it is part of the expectation for employment, and, as long as the elements are present, ideas can be implemented—not just talked about.

GROWING A CANNIBAL

Innovations that fit into the extraordinary and necessary category of "cannibals" deserve special treatment. These are ideas that have the potential to literally transform the existing practice of the company or organization, even the industry. In an established business, they will be in direct competition to other businesses you are in, businesses that are successful and could even be the lifeblood of your income statement. They are, by their nature, threatening. Such ideas are the foundation ideas for start-up companies that will become your most effective competitors, and we can all learn from their way of operating.

Start-up businesses are like incubators. They are safe, warm places for new ideas—ideas that might die in other environments—to hatch. The entire enterprise of a start-up depends on the successful nurturing and growth of those ideas. All eyes, ears, and brains are focused on the newborns.

Most established businesses are not like that at all. They can be inhospitable to new ideas for any of the many reasons I've outlined here; but the primary causes of casualty for the very best ideas, for the ideas that could revolutionize the business if not the industry, are rigidity, familiarity with the established ways of doing things, the arrogance of an establishment, the complacency of market prominence—many of the pitfalls of incumbency, and the really big barrier, posing a perceived threat to the bottom line.

Because these cannibal ideas are generally in markets that don't yet exist, there is little data to let us know what to expect. We do the best we can with the data available, start with a small test, set the process up to learn, skew the pilot for success, watch how the customers use what we offer, and adjust. If we are right about the idea catching on, then we will find out relatively quickly.

Such ideas simply can't easily make it in the mainstream of a company. It takes a focused effort by a group of individuals who are not invested in the old ways to give these ideas a chance for greatness. At Schwab, we have learned and relearned this in the last few years—most dramatically, when we decided to move full-scale into Internet trading. It was successful in large part because we employed the same principles.

e.Schwab in the Incubator

By the winter of 1995, we knew that there were more computers being sold in the United States than television sets. This was an important turning point for us. We had been offering on-line trading for years, but over special network connections to Schwab with some specialized software, first named Equalizer and then StreetSmart. The Internet was still being used primarily by academics and a few other technology whizzes who could actually understand and code in UNIX. But the slight breezes were there that portended the storm to come. We could not see the total impact, but it seemed that the Internet would be a perfect delivery system for the financial services industry. It could deliver information and it could do transactions. It was like being presented with a brand-new broad-band worldwide telephone system intact, without having to invest a penny or wait a day. If it was ever to be secure, it could represent one of the greatest breakthroughs in our business since the inception of the first stock market.

As we considered our decision to fund a project that would get us into the on-line brokerage business, we knew also that it would be threatening to our main business. The decision was painful, but it wasn't hard. We knew that someone would do it, and that our business would either go to them or stay with us because we had done it better. The primary questions revolved around how to organize this new effort to give it the best chance for success.

We knew that this project would take a great deal of passionate involvement, so we put Beth Sawi, one of our best executives, in charge of the project and located it away from the main body of Schwab as a way of giving her free rein to develop the market as it presented itself. This group had a clear aspiration, an inspiring mission that felt and looked like pioneering work. They knew that other start-ups as well as established, highly focused companies were already working on this same opportunity. Our group had to be just as focused and develop the same passion as a start-up.

There were three additional reasons for isolating the work. First, the main body of Schwab's customers were not demanding this service, so investment could not be justified in the traditional way. Second, the new enterprise was going to use a different model for making money than our traditional business, and we didn't want the comparisons to form the basis for measurement of success or failure. For example, e.Schwab's per-trade revenue would be less than half that of the mainstream of the company, and that could be seen as a drain on resources rather than a response to what customers would be using in the future. In order to minimize dissonance, we felt it was wise to keep the group isolated on their new and special mission.

Finally, we could size the operation to fit the market that we initially expected, and focus everyone in the organization on the goal. An alternative organization would have had people competing for resources in the company as a whole, and the small potential that was evident in the new operation would not compete well in the larger Schwab constituency.

Over the next two years, we tested, we learned, and we grew to become the largest on-line broker by a factor of almost three. As I look back critically, I see improvements we might have made to the plan and to the incubator. I think that we could have tested more effectively earlier, but we were still constrained by the expectations of our own business plan, a remnant of our own incumbency. Had we been a start-up, we would have had no concern whatsoever about the profits of the "other" business, and while we tried to operate like a start-up, the old habits were tough to fight.

Even so, within a few years, we found that on-line investing was in the mainstream of our customer base. So we fully integrated electronic brokerage back into our company, and organized our pricing and availability so that every Schwab customer has the ability to deal with us through any channel.

Integrating the Cannibal

In 1998, when we integrated electronic brokerage into the main body of the company, we learned yet another lesson in innovation. Like the "no-annual-fee IRA," this integration was going to cost us at the bottom line, except it was $125 million rather than the $9 million cost of the IRA program. But we recognized that the principles of innovation were still intact. Customers still drive innovation. By offering two separate services, we were confusing our customers. They did not want electronic trading or branch trading, they wanted both.

We were able to ask the right questions about this change. "Can we create an entirely new model of full-service brokerage, one that provides value pricing, conflict-free advice and help, great service via the Web or by people, and remain consistent with our corporate values?"

Part of the answer was to offer every customer access to this powerful tool called the Internet, and to share with every customer the substantial savings that it can offer over a more traditional model. The integration, once again, was a financially painful decision, but not a difficult one.

Passion-driven growth requires almost a frenzy of contribution from people in helping customers realize the dreams that they bring to our company. If we are able to create a field of caring, and grow in it a confidence that every idea counts . . . if we can demonstrate that there is a predictable process for implementation and that it requires and rewards responsible analysis, then we will truly be overwhelmed with innovation. We are still working on it at Schwab, and we are confident that we have at least some of the right ingredients.

This chapter suggests that with a strong shared aspiration, customer-first perspective, a sense of urgency, and effective communication people will come forward rather than keeping their ideas to themselves. Then implementation can follow a prescribed noble course that will ultimately lead to success, either from the market itself, from the knowledge you gain along the way, or hopefully from both.

Innovation is, after all, the signal of a human spirit that it wants to contribute to making the world a better place—to make it clear that we were here and made a difference. Whether we are in business or not, whether motivated strictly by profit or not, it is worthy of our efforts to bring it forth.

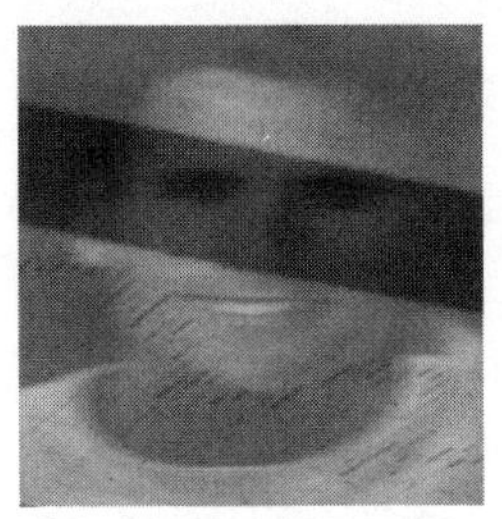

FROM INNOVATION TO MANAGEMENT PRACTICES FOR THE INTERNET WORLD

Wouldn't it be nice if customers automatically wanted what we had handy? Unless you are a barber or hairdresser, it probably isn't so. Even if you are, if you don't at least keep up with the latest styles, you will be obsolete in a very short time.

Customer-driven innovation is fundamentally a leadership issue. If the leaders of larger companies are not creating the atmosphere that can spawn new ideas into the production stream of the company, then their companies will lose to other, smaller, more nimble companies. Such small companies are often one- or two-person enterprises that don't have to worry about being far removed from customers. They *know* that their future depends on new ideas. They have no old ideas that have been their lifeblood. They have no rules or hierarchy that is different from the natural networks that spawn new ideas. Older established companies include many people who are not among the founders, and who perform tasks that might seem disjointed from actually satisfying customers. The older and bigger these firms get, the more difficult it is to renew innovation. The founders of such companies had a couple of good ideas at one point, and have ridden the S curve to the top. It is beginning to make its downward move, but they can't see it and don't want it pointed out to them. They still believe in their old ideas and old technology, and will do nothing to change the revenue and profit numbers that have resulted from these ideas. "After all, these are *my* ideas." It's an old story.

The best example of the century might be the Swiss loss of the low- and medium-end watch markets. The digital watch was actually invented by a Swiss engineer, who put it on display at an international show in Geneva as a curiosity. He had not bothered to patent it. After all, this was not a watch, it was an electronic display, a toy. His training, his bias, his entire career was based on an analog, precision, good-looking expensive device to tell time. The engineers from Texas Instruments and Seiko walked by, looked at the display, and saw the future.

The story had a happy ending, again as a result of leadership.

It took more than two decades for the Swiss to recover any part of the lower-end watch business, and they could do it then only through the vision of Nicolas Hyack, a watch engineer who saw the opportunity to compete with fashion rather than function, and put together the consortium that became SWATCH.[1]

Many of Schwab's changes weren't just incremental, they were breakthroughs that made it possible for people to do things they couldn't do before, dream dreams they couldn't dream. From the perspective of the 1970s tradition-bound financial banking industry, Schwab's innovations became nightmares that would force companies to change to compete. This is the stuff of true leadership.

If you are part of a larger company, you can do a great deal to stimulate innovation:

- Remind everyone in your group of the market's requirement for innovation.
- Remind them who the customer is, and ask them to establish at least one regular contact among that group. Do the same yourself.
- Go through an explanation similar to the one in this chapter about the growth curve of a business. Ask people where they think your group is on the curve with regard to your primary functions. Discuss new possibilities.
- Instigate a dialogue that includes these questions: Where would you attack us if you were our competitor? What ideas do you think

are being implemented by others that will make what we do less expensive or better?

- Ask a series of "and, not or" questions. If your strategy is "low price," ask how you could also add "highest quality." If it is "best service," ask how it could also be "least expensive."
- Explore all apparent paradoxes in your particular field. Analyze niche players' strengths. Try to use the resulting insights to provide customers, internal or external, with a whole new level of product or service.
- Explain the elements of "noble failure" to your group. Set up the necessary process to encourage small-scale, test implementation of new ideas. Set an objective for such implementation—per employee and per year.
- Make a list, with your group, of the ideas that you and they consider to be assumptions about what you do. Challenge these assumptions, investigate their etymologies, find out where they came from, and see if they are still valid.

As you can see, innovation is an individual's game best played within a team. It is the leader's responsibility to both promote individual courage and stimulate collaboration. In the innovative organization, people believe in the purpose of the group, and they are alert to possibilities for improvement. They share their own ideas and contribute to others' ideas. Does this sound ideal? It is.

My favorite recent book about innovation is *Orbiting the Giant Hairball,* written by a creative genius, Gordon MacKenzie. In the opening chapter, he describes the decreasing courage of children as they are criticized for their work. When first graders are asked, "How many artists in the room?" every child leaps up, hands waving. In the second grade, when asked the same question, about half respond—and they are more subdued. By the third grade, about ten of thirty would raise a hand . . . tentatively. By the sixth grade, only one or two artists remain. MacKenzie describes the cause: "We tame the little Yahoos. We teach them the meaning of the word 'no.' We teach them the benefits of boundaries. We teach them the value of our learned lessons . . . but we have been slow to learn how to tame the Fool without also interring the Fool's innate creativity and inborn genius."[2]

Some of those "little Yahoos" are corporate employees—in fact, some of them are us. But in the night, or in the closet, or in the bathrooms and hallways of our workplace, the creativity and genius comes out. It is a leadership task to coax it into the open. When you can create a field where people can contribute openly, you may be amazed at the number of them that want to play. I hope the principles of the chapter help you do it.

PART THREE

MANAGEMENT PRACTICES

Bringing Passion to the Internet World

In the first two parts of this book, we've focused on building and leading the most effective and inviting environment for the knowledge worker. A solid culture, grounded in values, focused on a compelling vision, and sustained with inspiring leadership practices will generate the passion that will bring the best ideas to the surface and get them implemented. Until the last few years, building culture and other leadership practices were considered "soft" and perhaps unneeded skills. In fact, before the 1990s, you would not find courses on these subjects in many professional business schools. Even today, business writers and critics are quick to point to "culture" as a distraction rather than as a contributor. The PeopleSoft case is but one example. In 1999, *Fortune* fundamentally blamed a disproportionate focus on culture as the principal cause of Levi's tough times.[1] Business has been fundamentally about numbers, and the professional manager's role was to achieve a good bottom line with the traditional usable resources of equipment, capital, and people.

The predominance of knowledge workers has shifted the balance of these three resources. While it was possible to replace many production workers with technology, and while we accomplished tremendous gains in productivity by doing exactly that, the same scale of substitution is not possible in the knowledge-based company. Certainly, as technology becomes more sophisticated, we will automate even more tasks that require judgment and selection. Even as we amaze ourselves with the level of intuitive selection and judgment that can be made by computer, the most critical parts of the "human resource" cannot be synthesized. These parts—the creative brain, imagination, and spirit—are what fuel this economy. The best companies are paying close attention to developing these elements.

Ten years ago, the idea of business process redesign, or reengineering, enticed us to take a totally fresh look at entrenched thinking about the traditional categories of business process. We were appropriately asked to look at the new capability of technology and redesign the very fabric of our profession. This was tremendously helpful, because it forced us to invent a new language of business, to change our habitual question from "How can I do this better?" to "Given the needs of today's business and the capability of technology, what do I really need to do?" The answers often required such upheaval that implementation was impossible without seriously hurting the morale of those who actually did the work, but the thinking process was extremely valuable.

This movement also strongly contributed to more fluid thinking by today's professionals. It is no longer possible to work in Accounts Receivable or Marketing and pretend that your work does not affect every other function in the company. To be effective, each person has to conceive of her task as part of a larger process that includes every aspect of delivering value to customers. This kind of holistic thinking ultimately allows each person to see the real impact of her work, for better or for worse, and to be engaged in it. If a company makes bombs, each employee will see her responsibility in the end result of the process of making bombs. There is a much greater possibility of generating engagement with the work; in this example, either to take pride in protecting freedom and democracy or to lament her part in injuring others.

Mastering traditional business practices is still critical for success of the enterprise, but while it's good for the economy to treat corporations as legal entities, it may be bad for the people who work in them. When we treat a business entity as a thoughtless, nonfeeling, sterile "person," it allows depersonalization of the numbers, and it allows us to refer to "the bottom line" as something that has nothing to do with us.

Years ago, Paul Hawken put this in perspective: "The bottom line is down where it belongs—at the bottom. Far above it in importance are the infinite number of events that produce the profit or loss, especially those that determine how a company approaches all of its constituents and what the company is able to give to them."[2] We can look at business practices differently, and we can design our use of them to remind everyone of their personal stake in the game. This transformation is especially important now, as we try more than ever to inspire contribution.

Three aspects of business practice have changed the most in this rapid-fire environment. First, until recently, performance measurement and compensation have been linked to produce results. Now, as cycle times for products shorten, and as the need for innovation grows, both measurement and compensation need to be reformulated to inspire commitment. Second, the management of technology (and technologists) has grown in importance much faster than our abilities to recognize or implement needed adjustments. And finally, the world of marketing has been stood on its head by the new ability to reach targeted audiences, by the integration of employee and customer messages, and by our ability and frequent need to change a message or emphasize a new message in a matter of minutes.

Just as new thinking about business process itself can contribute to the generation of passion, so too can a different perspective about business practices themselves. We merely need to ask new questions. For example:

- How can we rethink the traditional functions of budgeting, individual performance management, and other quantitative measurement practices that we use to set our goals and parse our progress toward those goals?

- What are the characteristics of compensation and incentive systems that actually build commitment, rather than merely fabricate "golden handcuffs"?
- What do we need to know and do differently when we manage technology and technologists?
- How can a shift in our thinking and execution of marketing and advertising programs help to create the kind of employee engagement that we are trying to build, while at the same time building extraordinary customer loyalty?

Dave and I are going to explore these questions of business management in this next part, and see what impact a few changes can have on the experience of our employees and customers. If passion is the key to growth in these times, and if inspiration is the forebear of passion, then it would seem reasonable that these questions are up for review.

They certainly have been in Dave's world.

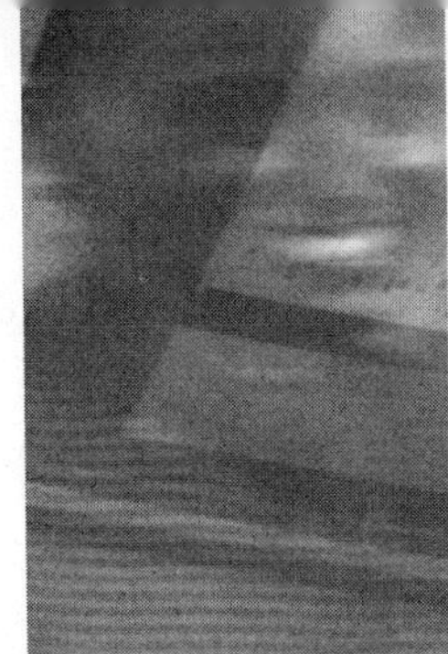

SEVEN

CREATING THE FUTURE WITH MEASUREMENT

Technology has had a remarkable effect on our ability to measure results in a business. It wasn't that long ago that we were merely assigning budgets and measuring results against those assignments monthly. But as we have been reconceptualizing business around globalization and the information economy, technology has done more than provide faster adding machines, it has become a tool for transformation. It has changed our use of measurements in two ways. First, we can categorize much more finely and therefore understand relationships between different datasets, and second, we can have the data in real time rather than waiting for month-end or year-end.

New software has allowed us to do intricate analysis of ratios and trends that we had not done before, and that can be extremely helpful in day-to-day management. In addition to measuring categories and traditional ratios, we can measure the relationship of every category to every other category, and we can do it over time. More holistic thinking has helped us see the direct relationship of front-end process to a seemingly remote variable at the back end; to measure, for example, the effect of product design on accounts receivable. New capability also makes it possible for us to establish targets in multiple categories and relationships—to measure the business down to a minuscule level.

Because the data can be continuously updated, we also have the ability to measure ourselves in real time and to make adjustments based on much less experience than was previously necessary. Daily, or in some cases minute-by-minute, sales reports help manufacturing companies time purchases to coincide precisely with what they will need. Companies can plan labor expenditure, balance workload, and respond to trends much more effectively than ever before. Every business unit, from the cafeteria to the warehouse to the showroom, can plan for goods and labor to arrive "just in time."

However, the new measurement technology by itself does nothing to spur the business on, any more than a speedometer makes a car go faster. Additionally, there is a big difference between measuring the business and measuring the effectiveness of the people who run the business. What I'd like to do in this chapter is to make that distinction clear, and to suggest some new ways to look at business measurement and individual performance measurement—ways that will create and sustain the ideal general manager, the rare combination called the organizational entrepreneur. I'll start by sketching my own learning about the fundamental business tool, the budget itself.

FROM BUDGET TO DYNAMIC MANAGEMENT TOOL

I first became a general manager when I became president of the brokerage company at Schwab. I "negotiated" for my targets with Larry Stupski, my boss and the chief operating officer, but essentially, I was given an expense budget based on projected growth in costs from the previous year. Naturally, I used the same process with my own subordinates: I assigned each of them what I considered to be "stretch" expense targets.

One year in particular, I was faced with growing costs from projects that I had started the preceding year, including more than two dozen new branches, and the revenue plan for the new year was not particularly aggressive due to a lackluster stock market environment. I calculated the expense budget the way I always had: last year's expenses, plus inflation, plus new things, minus an increase in productivity. I proposed this to Larry, and he simply said, "No."

"What do you mean, 'No'?"

He said, "The ratios don't work."

"Too bad," I retorted, "This is the cost. I opened the branches last year, the revenue from these new offices takes awhile to kick into gear—so I have to spend the money up front."

"You should have been looking ahead, knowing the impact. You planned badly, and you can't spend the money."

To say that I was upset would be like saying that the *Hindenburg* had a rough landing. My experience with budgets had been at Citi, where we negotiated only the expense side every year. At Schwab, the chief operating officer was the lowest level of person in the hierarchy to be measured on both expense and revenue and the relationship between the two. But what I was to learn was that in a growing company, the absolute costs don't mean much. It is the ratios that count. The expenses can only grow with the revenue, and with that, they can't grow as much or margins decline. I was about to learn about the key relationships: revenue per employee, revenue per customer, profit margin, and finally, the ratio of revenue to operating expense versus investment in the future. Understanding these ratios allows general managers to set targets that drive growth. It also builds responsibility and commitment for that growth in the entire management cadre.

As we continued to grow, and as I became the chief operating officer myself, we realized a couple of things. First, the only person who was getting trained in how to run a company was me. No one else was responsible for producing a bottom line, having to weigh revenues and expenses to get to a profit contribution. With the new ability to measure contribution by business unit, we wanted to push the whole responsibility down and have it owned by all the business unit heads.

Second, we realized that some of the businesses were going to grow at a faster pace than others. Some of the businesses were mature and big, and their relative percentage of growth was going to be smaller than some of the young starting businesses. So as we started to think through how to allocate budgets, we realized that everyone couldn't get the same budget increases or decreases. For example, we could not expect productivity to grow as fast in our labor-intensive businesses as we could in purely transactional, technology-heavy businesses. If the company was going to grow at 20 per cent, every business head could not expect to get a 20 percent increase in their revenue and expense lines. Getting the entire team committed to the entire business would allow us to adjust budgets to account for different potentials in different businesses.

Any of you who have had careers in growing businesses have probably learned these two lessons from your own experience. They come into play because it is important, at some stage of growth, to decentralize a business so as to build more talent and to maintain focus on the various aspects of the operation. At Schwab, we did this in 1995, dividing the operation into nine enterprises, with nine separate executives in charge. Some of these were support enterprises such as Corporate Services or Finance, and some were operating enterprises such as our retail operation or our operation that provides services to independent investment managers. At the time of the reorganization, I was trying to apply those two lessons, giving bottom line responsibility and applying variable expectations to different units. But I also wanted to focus on a third objective, one that was most important to me as I looked ahead to more growth in the future. It had to do with the development of people. It is necessary, in this environment, that the business heads are both entrepreneurial *and* team players. Not one or the other, but both. I wanted them to display individual initiative. I wanted them to know that their decisions made a great difference in their individual rewards. I also needed them to cooperate with others toward achieving our corporate goals and driving toward our vision. It was going to require a rare combination, one similar to Frank Carrubba's team at Hewlett-Packard labs (see Chapter Four). Since we were all working together, we could only maximize our combined effort through building the kind of relationships that would contribute to joint achievement *and* enhanced individual accomplishment.

THE PARADOX OF THE ORGANIZATIONAL ENTREPRENEUR

The term *organizational entrepreneur* seems antithetical to the image of the entrepreneur as a swashbuckling, solely responsible gunslinger, the starter of businesses, the taker of risk, the lone-wolf captain of industry. Within an established growth company, entrepreneurs are responsible; they are also full of spirit about what they are doing, they want to excel at it, and they are willing and able to take risks to accomplish their goals. These risks can be financial, but more often they are also risks with their corporate reputations and their personal view of themselves. Paradoxically, in the ideal corporate culture, they also work well on teams; in fact, their ability to do so is critical to their individual success.

Thomas Petzinger covered a rich variety of business stories for the *Wall Street Journal* for four years, and published the column under the heading "The Front Lines." He has since moved on to other assignments, and in his final column did an admirable job of characterizing his experience and commenting specifically on this paradox of entrepreneur and team player. In thanking those who gave him material, he said in part:

> You've shown me that in the new economy, everyone is an entrepreneur, I think of people like Bill Fulkerson, a staff analyst at Deere and Company, whose personal initiative and network of contacts in the science community helped Deere solve some of its most complex shop-floor scheduling problems. Or Tom Kozak of Panduit Corp., who used a junior-management post to unite the fractured electrical-products industry around a single set of e-commerce standards.

> And if every organization is full of entrepreneurs, every entrepreneur must join many organizations. Joe Marabito of Paragon Decision Resources relies on a vast confederation of other entrepreneurs who help him handle every aspect of corporate relocation. This year he and his collaborators will relocate about 10,000 families for many of the world's largest companies.

Petzinger finished his remarkable column with this experience.

> Time and again, you've shown me that business is a passion, a canvas for the artist in all of us. At a conference this week I ran into a high-school classmate I hadn't seen in 26 years. I remember her winning all the art awards. Now she's in satellite communications. "Still painting?" I asked. "No," she said, "but managing a complex project uses the same creativity."[1]

Petzinger has captured the essence of what the proper use of business performance measurement can yield: people who are individually passionate about what they do and skilled at it, who use all of their resources, inside and outside the company, to work in a team to solve a problem worth solving. These are the team-playing entrepreneurs we are trying to create. How can we encourage them and measure them? Measurements that encourage these dual attributes have two characteristics: they avoid zero-sum calculations and they encourage collaboration.

First, relational measurements, those based on the ratios I described and others, are not zero-sum. An individual manager can add to expense or capital budgets by bringing in more revenue. In addition to providing accountability, such a system gives individuals and the group itself inspiration and latitude to explore beyond normal constraints, and then rewards them accordingly. Second, goal setting and budget allocation are both top-down and bottom-up processes. There is collaboration, discussion, and agreement, and there is also authority bestowed by the team and exercised by the leader. This aspect of budget setting is more difficult to build, because it requires great trust in the process and in the other members of the team.

When we decentralized the company, we established the measurement procedure around some principles that encourage and feed that kind of trust.

PRINCIPLES FOR DYNAMIC MEASUREMENT

As we set up our first set of relational measurements in the new organization, we applied four principles, each of which I'll discuss in turn:

- Establish trust by agreeing on the basics.
- Put the vision first.
- Plan as a team, with full disclosure.
- Contribute to the whole.

Establish Trust by Agreeing on the Basics

The first and most fundamental agreement among the heads of all of the enterprises was that we could allocate exactly one hundred cents for every dollar that we took in, including allocations for profit and taxes. That may seem like a given, yet, in a more typical budget process, this agreement doesn't exist. Operators are pitted against a mythical "headquarters" as though it were a monster with an unlimited supply of funds trying to keep as much as possible for itself. By starting with the fundamental agreement, knowing that we can allocate every dollar of revenue, with all parties to the process knowing where each penny is going, we created a process of sharing and allocation, not manipulating and hoarding. To further discourage the typical "us and them" thinking, we decided not to *allocate* overhead expenses to the enterprises, as such percentages can appear arbitrary and cause friction. We use a concept of "transfer pricing" instead, so the general managers can focus on the real business of managing the growth of their enterprise.

Put Vision First

Every manager must buy into the corporate goals and have incentive to meet them, before she can effectively help in allocation of the budget or become committed to her individual goals. If everyone on the team is not committed to a common objective, then the budget allocation can sink into a discussion of "fairness" that pits one enterprise or department against the others, rather than a discussion of their relative contributions to the strategic growth of the enterprise. As long as individuals feel as though they are competing with one another, the budget process will be undermined by gamesmanship and numerical engineering. This produces bad budgetary choices, reduced teamwork, and distraction about who the real competition is. When there is a real sense of buy-in to the vision, the budget allocation is much more likely to be based on the most efficient way to move toward its accomplishment.

Compensation structure must reinforce this fundamental idea. We award stock options and bonuses—more than half of an individual executive's bonus—tied to the company's overall performance. This method of bonus application is modeled throughout the company, and it stimulates true teamwork. Each person is really interested in how the others perform, because much of their compensation depends on everyone doing well.

When we have built a solid foundation based upon a common vision of where we want to take the company, a teamwork style of operating, and a compensation structure that rewards us for operating in this fashion, we are ready to create a meaningful plan and budget. We start with a revenue dollar and set aside the return we want to give our shareholders, the target percentages for profit and taxes. Then we set aside a percentage for bonuses, driven by that performance. The next step is to agree on the allocation of the resources necessary to deliver that performance.

Plan as a Team, with Full Disclosure

We agree on the balance of the ratios as a team. Every company will be different in its calculations of these ratios, depending on the industry or nature of the operation. If companies hope to outgrow their competitors and gain market share, they must typically spend a greater percentage of every revenue dollar on development projects, technology, and marketing than their industry average, and hopefully more than their best competitors. Certainly, technology garners a relatively high—and in our case, growing—percentage of the revenue, and as a team, we understand the importance of leveraging that investment. What is left to allocate is the cost of human delivery and operations.

We make these allocation decisions together. Naturally, conditions occur that make it necessary in a given year to allocate a greater percentage of the dollar to one group or another. But overall, we are committed to hold the line on these ratios, and challenge one another to increase growth and productivity to make up the need for extra service. We look at these ratios of cost to revenue as a way to see if we are making progress.

This is a fundamental concept of measurement in a growth company. To make it work, we simply have to grow, because the absolute cost of things that don't contribute directly to bringing in customers continues to get bigger. In our company, every single function, support or "revenue-producing," looks at the ratio of employees to revenue and performs against its relative targets—its contribution to the whole. We want to be putting our money toward building the customer experience, toward bringing in more customers. So all of the fundamental operating expense is measured tightly. It isn't easy, and I often find myself in the position of my former boss, who said no at the right time.

A few years ago, I met with our general counsel, who explained why she needed a greater percentage of the revenue to grow her own enterprise. The world of litigation was growing more complex, there were more regulations. And I agreed with her. I could not argue at all with her facts. But in the end, I had to ask her the same questions that Larry asked me. "Where does it come from? If you get a greater percentage, then who do we cut in order to make it happen?" Every single department can make the same argument . . . and it is growth that gives people the money they need. This kind of relational measurement makes it possible.

Contribute to the Whole

These allocation decisions are all made as a team. The budget-setting process now becomes one of balancing the revenue expectations from new and established businesses, large and small businesses, businesses that contributed smaller margins and ones that have some room. Every year, the revenue-producing managers forecast their businesses, with smaller, faster-growing ones helping to pull the overall percentage growth average up, and larger ones trying to maintain and increase their growth rates as well. This is not zero-sum thinking, since expenses and some development budget items are based on a percentage of revenue rather than absolute amounts. As executives increase their revenue, they can also increase their expense allocation, consistent with the goals of the company.

After five years of administering the budget this way, we were not really doing much battle over the targets. This is not to suggest that the process isn't hard—it is. But by planning together, we rely on our mutual ambitions for our corporate and our individual enterprises, rather than the ability to haggle. All the top executives see each other's budgets. No one wants to appear greedy, and no revenue leaders want to appear to lack ambition or creative ideas to grow their revenues.

This openness stimulates team play, not only during the budget process but during the year as new challenges come up. For example, from time to time, sharp volume spikes in the market make it impossible for the retail operation to maintain a high level of service for our clients. But the other enterprises know that the retail business is the backbone of the company. Accordingly, they are ready to contribute people to help answer phones and take trades during such times. The spirit is high, and the feeling of cooperation is felt universally. We know, too, as a group, that developing our Web capability and moving into more global opportunities are critical strategic areas, so we adjust accordingly, and we do so willingly.

This process of budget allocation stimulates teamwork. What about the "spirit" side of the entrepreneur?

PROVIDING INDIVIDUAL INCENTIVE FOR RISK AND GROWTH

Two final elements of the budgeting process are left after the growth targets are assigned. One is the allocation of the budget for developmental projects and the other is the establishment of individual bonus targets. While these elements are set in conversation with others, I administer them using my somewhat broader perspective and the decision authority that the team has given me. I use both of these measurements to differentiate between members of the team and to inspire them to do their entrepreneurial best. If used well, these elements can help generate cooperation during the process of setting targets.

Developmental Projects: The Stretch Capital

We always have a long list of project proposals, all with very specific estimates for net present value (NPV), or payback. In theory we should simply fund the projects in decreasing order of their NPVs. The best paybacks would be funded first; it would be easy, and we would be done early. But such an approach fails to recognize a number of crucial realities, and again, falls short of our commitment to make the allocation process contribute to inspiring our executives.

First, different projects have different levels of risk. How sure are we, even when the NPV is forecast, that the project can be done within the financial and time constraints of the proposal? What's our confidence factor, taking into account the additive risks of time frame, scope and definition clarity, technology newness and familiarity, scale, and our ability to manage the project? What businesses seem to have the best prospects for growth? Finally, and critically, which executives have the most difficult targets? Which individuals obviously need the investment to meet their targets and maintain the momentum?

To some extent, I use the discretionary project money as a way to reward managers who consistently set ambitious goals. I factor in the passion-building recognition that the corporation is betting scarce resources on these managers. They know it, and it builds their own engagement and commitment to the project and to the business.

Individual Incentives: Plans Versus Goals

I also establish different targets for the executives' personal bonuses than the targets that are in the plan for the business. In a contentious process, this vital element would be impossible to implement, and the result would be unrealistic planning in one arena and ineffective goal setting in the other. There is a conservative bias in business planning, as no one wants to be constantly running behind plan and explaining shortfalls to analysts. Conversely, there should be an aggressive bias toward individual goal setting. I want to set the targets for individual performance, because I want each person who works for me to set and communicate "stretch" goals, goals that are inspirational, attainable only with breakthrough thinking and performance. Goals *can* be set too high, so high that they are demoralizing. When goals are overaggressive, people leave. Proper goals are set to inspire something more than just "last year's performance plus some" effort. Such goals have an impact on the individual, not just the business. If I don't take this approach as a leader, then the intelligent thing for my colleagues to do would be to set the goals low and blow through them. I don't want that. I want them to inspire their staffs to shoot very high, to really stretch themselves. After all, which is going to be more inspiring and gain more engagement: setting a low target and knowing that it is easily achievable, or setting a stretch goal and having to inspire others to hit it? I think the latter. So I try to use the budgeting and measurement process to stimulate inspiration, on my part, and on theirs. This is not always comfortable, and it requires a high level of trust.

In the late 1980s, we started a business of providing services to independent investment advisers. In the early stages of this business, it was difficult to forecast growth. We were always underestimating it. Every year, John Coghlan, the leader of the enterprise, and I would do a dance: I would push for high goals, he would suggest something lower, we would compromise. Then he and his team would blow through the goals, he would maximize his bonus, and I would pound my fist into my desk, muttering, "He got me again!" There was nothing clandestine or hidden about this process. It was a new business; we really could not predict the growth rate, and John was a very good negotiator.

Finally, one year, I got serious with him, and told him that I wanted him to commit to a bigger goal. I gave him two reasons. First, low-balling the plan was not the best thing for the company because it gave me less leeway with his colleagues who ran the other enterprises. If one person on the team seems to excel every year, others begin to question his candor, and cooperation begins to wane. Second, I believed that a more aggressive goal would inspire him and his team to really stretch themselves. As noted in Chapter Five, innovation sometimes springs forth from a breakthrough question—not "How can I grow by 20 percent?" but "How can I double the business?" I knew that this new business was not as predictable as others, but I wanted him to generate that kind of inspiration.

To make it really fair, I agreed that his compensation should be tuned to the greater degree of difficulty in the goal. In other words, if his group really attained the big goal, the reward should be immense. If they missed it slightly, then John and his group should be rewarded just as though the goal had been set slightly lower. In other words, there would be an "inspiration dividend." He agreed with the logic, and based on the trust built up through the years, set a very high goal for his group.

They missed it.

I hate to admit it, but when it came time for me to award John's bonus and review his performance, it was very difficult for me to remember that earlier conversation about inspiration. I had to recall that I wanted to reinforce the message, "Set high goals to inspire yourself and your team." I had to look at the year-on-year numbers to remind myself that John had done a remarkable job and deserved to be richly rewarded for it.

Bonuses must provide incentives, not just rewards, as this example shows.

We schedule "special award and recognition" events for people who excel during the year. One of the highest-prestige Schwab events of the year, the "Chairman's Club," is for select employees and their significant others. The qualification rules are clear at the beginning of the year, and the eligible managers and their staffs are keen to qualify. And every year we have the same discussion . . . shall qualification be limited to the "top 20 percent" of the performers, or should qualification be rewarded for performance against set criteria (for example: "all who achieve 125 percent of their goal") regardless of how many people qualify? In case you haven't guessed, I am very much in favor of the latter. The former would pit one participant against another. Like any zero-sum program, it would not provide incentive at all, but only a reward garnered after the fact. And that would be a reward for outperforming peers rather than stretching oneself beyond perceived personal limits.

I can remember setting big goals in 1995, thinking that if we were to exceed those goals, we would have done incredibly well. I remember saying, as we set those goals, that we wanted as many winners as we could get. Then when the goals were reached a year later, when we should have all been celebrating, some people were wringing their hands because we had "too many winners" and therefore by definition, we must have set the goals too low. The only thing more deflating to the spirit than issuing zero-sum bonuses is to ignore the rule of relational measurements for recognition events . . . the trips and other premium incentives that often mean more than money.

As a company grows, there is pressure to make special recognition incentives into fixed rewards (for example, "only 20 percent can win"). Programs like this are easier to plan, more predictable, and much more economical. Unfortunately, they do *not* accomplish the purpose of inspiring teamwork and the excitement of sharing best practices and winning ideas during the year. Financial compensation is important—in fact vital—as a symbol of accomplishment. Likewise, the financial measurements of a business are invaluable as tools of diagnosis and prognosis. But beyond their role in helping us to form judgments, these financial systems can act as incentives and tools to inspire the passion, teamwork, and excitement that energize people to excel in a fast-paced and competitive environment.

THE LIMITS OF TECHNOLOGY: MEASURING PEOPLE

In mid-1999, interviewer Charlie Rose hosted a televised panel of experts on the future of technology and its probable impact on our society. Among the panelists was Ester Dyson, certainly one of the foremost thinkers on the implications of the Internet for business and for society as a whole. She said, "The limitation on the application of technology will never be ideas or capital. It will be people . . . enough of them trained and excited about taking the ideas of the technologist and making them real in the world."[2]

Without a doubt, Dyson is right: great people are in short supply. For precisely this reason, the most important measurement device of the new economy is the individual performance appraisal. As an instrument, it strongly signals the traits, skills, and behaviors that are required to reinforce the culture. As a process, it reinforces trust and support in the relationship between a subordinate and her boss.

As a technique, it is significantly more difficult than its corollary, measuring the business. At the beginning of the chapter, I made a distinction between measuring the business and measuring the people who run the business. The business itself is relatively easy to measure, and much of the time, sophisticated measurements, when read correctly, can get a good manager 90 percent of the way toward the best decision for correction or optimization of a business. Implementing it, through people, is the critical part. Measuring their effectiveness requires attention to form and ritual.

Performance Appraisal: Form or Relationship?

The appraisal process can be easily misused, or even become irrelevant if it is allowed to devolve into merely a form or process, rather than the documentation of the relationship between two people. The early iteration of the appraisal was designed in the 1960s for the system of Management by Objectives and consisted primarily of a left-brain instrument that documented first the objective goals and second, a numerical representation of the degree to which the subject had accomplished those objectives. In its early form, MBO made no mention of *the way in which* the objectives were accomplished. That objectivity was its elegance. Ideally, the "appraisal" could be done by computer, as the form itself merely called for check marks in boxes . . . reminiscent of the primary-school report card. While performance appraisal has changed substantially in most companies, many people (and I have done this myself) define at least part of their jobs as "boss" to find the weaknesses in people and bring them to attention, not just as a method of development, but also as a way of reminding others, "you still have a lot of areas that need improvement if you are going to reach my standards of excellence."

Change the Ritual, Change the Result

Of course, if we are trying to stimulate commitment rather than only the performance of tasks, then, as suggested in Chapter Two, this appraisal ritual has to change. Especially in this time when effective managers and dedicated people are at a premium, the ultimate objective has to be to develop rather than merely to criticize. We simply must make personal performance review a positive, constructive, trust-building process.

PRINCIPLES FOR APPRAISAL

I think you can tell from my own story that I grew the most when I received objective feedback for improvement. To improve my own performance, I welcomed the introduction of 360-degree feedback, and looked very carefully at the way my peers, direct reports, boss, and subordinates viewed my effectiveness. Many times I didn't like it. It just felt bad to be criticized, especially if the criticism was not offered in the best spirit. But no matter how I felt or how it was given, much of it worked.

In the last few years, as I've seen my role change toward having more responsibility for the development of people who work for me, I've gotten better at helping them grow. That means first that I've learned that positive reinforcement is just as valuable as putting the spotlight on "developmental opportunities." Second, I've gotten better at giving people real, constructive feedback. Occasionally that feedback has resulted in their leaving the organization, but rarely has it ended our relationship. Along the way, I've learned some principles for appraisal that have served me in maintaining the trust of the people who look to me for leadership. Primary among them is the fact that this is a human process, not a purely objective one. The performance appraisal can be used to develop and extend the bond of trust between two people. Accordingly, the leader needs to apply all of the principles of leadership communication that were discussed in Chapter Five—and others that relate directly to appraisals.

Separate Numbers from Development

Numbers digitize reality for convenience. They provide an excellent representation of what has happened, but they are not, in themselves, anything more than a convenience, a shorthand way to report. They contribute to, but can't replace, the discussion of the traits, behaviors, and skills that are more reflective of the person's personal growth needs. The numbers are the measure of the business, and of the person's past accomplishments, and they are indicative of where to put more leadership attention. But numbers only point the way, they do not prescribe a remedy.

If you and your colleague agree on the numerical accomplishments of her business unit first, then you both can enter much more easily into the discussion of the "how." It's this part of the discussion that will give you the chance to reinforce what's working and offer constructive observations and suggestions regarding development needs.

Avoid the "Doom Loop"

It was hard for me to understand that even if I agreed with my colleague on the constructive nature of the interview and even if there were smiles and nods, chances were very good that a constructive interview will be perceived as negative. As Harvard professor Chris Argyris puts it: "Because it represents the one moment when a professional must measure his or her own behavior against some formal standard, a [negative] performance evaluation is almost tailor-made to push a professional into the 'doom loop.'"[3] Argyris is commenting here on the tendency of human beings to let criticism or suggestions for improvement amplify their own fear of failure. We all know the trap of defensiveness, but Argyris contends that, despite this knowledge, defensive reasoning is more pervasive among highly competitive leaders than other groups, and that when they hear criticism, they default to defensive behavior to remain in control. Often, this includes their own desire to stick to the numbers and be rational.[4]

Your purpose is to give real, objective constructive feedback, both positive and negative, that will help the other person improve rather than demoralize her. Because of this built-in default of defensiveness, even the best of reviews from the most keenly insightful of bosses can be a blur to the recipient. How can a leader mitigate this tendency to tune out? This will sound familiar: through caring, contact, thoughtful review, and through focusing on the future.

Use the Antidote of Caring. The best mitigation for defensiveness is genuine caring. In Chapter Five, I suggested that the most important aspect of leadership communication was "authentic interest in others," that such interest was what made communication a "connecting art," rather than merely an ability to pass information along.

Ability to work together depends on the strength of the relationship. Nowhere is this more important than during the process of appraising performance.

Create a Broad Foundation of Regular Contact. Like the business measurement process, the individual measurement process is becoming more dynamic. In a growth company in the Internet world, everyone is always learning and developing. Even seasoned executives who may know the business functions cold are learning new things in this environment; if they are not, they are falling behind. Given that dynamic, I want the evaluation process to include my judgment about how much executives are developing themselves. Of course, as a CEO I have regularly scheduled discussions with each of the enterprise presidents. Some are more formal business reviews, but some are less formal, consisting wholly of conversations about their personal goals or their personal needs for development. This part of the process is vital, as it gives me a chance to ask more indirect questions and to answer their questions that might not pertain directly to the operation of the business.

These regular meetings are not the only informal conversation that we have. We have ongoing e-mail and voice-mail dialogue as well. But there is no substitute for the face-to-face meeting, so that we can read each other better, sense the urgency behind comments, and act on the multiple cues that only present themselves face-to-face.

Make Even the Formal Review a Thoughtful Conversation. If this foundation has been built, then the annual review can become a deeper, more effective tool for development. Given the pace of business, I have adopted a procedure of writing, reviewing, and revising that includes both parties in a dialogue. It gives us an excellent opportunity to review, with as much authenticity as we can muster, the executive's strengths and the areas where growth will be required. I write my reviews, and then give them to my direct report to look over, making sure that the words "preliminary draft" are clearly written across the top. I want comments and suggestions, but most important, I want to give my subordinate the opportunity to absorb and consider, for a few days, what I've said. Especially when I have something particularly critical to say, I have found that this "absorption period" helps get past the initial defensiveness and move toward understanding.

Focus on the Future. The competencies that make up an appraisal have to focus on future development, using the past only as the launch-pad for prioritizing. Too often, just as the appraisal process is formalized, the appraisal form is developed as boilerplate, and emphasizes what your company or other companies have found important in the past. These measurements may or may not have relevance for your company in the present, and for sure, they are incomplete as characteristics that will be needed in the future.

I have to admit that I absolutely hate doing performance appraisals. It's uncomfortable for me to sit in judgment of my colleagues, whom I've worked with as a partner all year. It's easy to brush off appraisals as no longer necessary in the fast-paced Internet world, an anachronism of 1970s management techniques. But it is just not true. No one becomes a champion without a coach who tells him honestly what is good and what is not good. Yes, a continuous stream of feedback consisting of pats on the back and constructive suggestions is vital to individual growth. But a once-a-year, bottom-line documented appraisal is a healthy and important part of management measurement.

Certainly, there are many specific measurements of the business available, and there will be new ones in the future as we learn to gather even more data. But in general, the measurements of leadership, of individual executive effectiveness, remain constant. They boil down to what you would expect: competence, honesty, vision, and the ability to inspire. The first, competence, is a moving target as business gets more complex. But the other characteristics are timeless. Emphasizing them in a forthright conversation reminds everyone in the enterprise of their importance.

We are moving toward a dynamic real-time measurement system for the business. Our capability at developing and sustaining relationships with our key partners has to match the honesty and currency of the business metrics, so that the measurement and growth of human effectiveness can keep pace.

In a world that depends on both passion and skill, both conviction and intelligence, measurements cannot be passive yardsticks of what has happened. They must be forged and administered actively to bring out the very best in everyone.

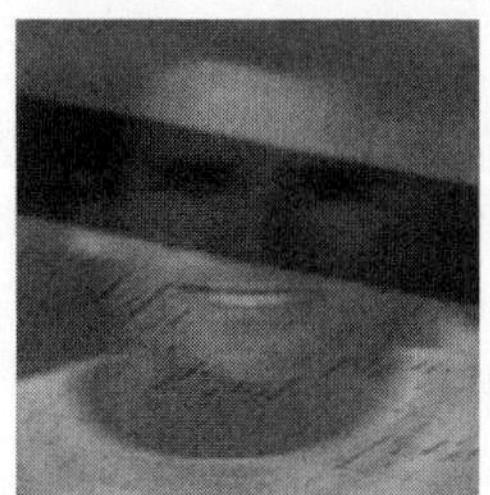

FROM MEASUREMENT TO UNDERSTANDING TECHNOLOGY

Budget. Measurement. Compensation. Of course, we need to use each of these tools on our way to the future, to ensure that we can meet the goals we set for our companies. But they seem far removed from risks, results, and relationship—the lifeblood of those fastest approaching that future. For that reason, any company that still measures its business or its people the way companies measured in the early 1990s will be working with measurements that make little difference in its success.

In the introduction to Part One, I defined values as the "nonnegotiable tenets against which we measure the worthiness of our choices." (For emphasis, note "against which we *measure*.") If we are to build an inspirational measurement system that works for the business *and* for the people who run it, we need to base it on the values of the business and the people. Very few of us, in our own statement of values, would include "to increase the market share of my product by 2 percent." And if asked what values we would like to pass on to our children, few of us would include "become senior vice president."

In a world that demands passion and commitment, we need to adapt. We need to inspire. And we need to rethink what traits, skills, and behaviors it will take to bring disparate people together and hold them together in the world of tomorrow. In 1999, Schwab reformulated future leadership needs into a list of "core competencies." The purpose of the process was to more closely align individual performance measurements with Schwab's future needs. While Dave uses these competencies to frame discussions with his own colleagues, they are also the basis for recruiting new people and for assessing current employees for increased responsibility. They include

- *Has Passion for Service:* Focuses on customer as the first priority. Strives to exceed the expectation of all stakeholders, including employees and shareholders.
- *Inspires Trust:* Maintains a high standard of personal integrity, follows through on commitments, is widely respected as a direct and truthful individual, respects and advocates Schwab's core values.
- *Communicates Effectively:* Promotes a free flow of information and communication throughout the organization, and encourages open expression of ideas and opinion. Communicates frequently and deeply in person, and inspires others to contribute on their own. Delivers clear, well-organized presentations, actively listens, writes effectively, and communicates well one-on-one, in small and large groups. Effectively represents company to outside constituents.
- *Seeks Self-Development:* Is personally committed to self-improvement, looks for new challenges and learning opportunities, actively seeks feedback, gains insight from experiences, demonstrates awareness of own strengths and weaknesses.
- *Drives Execution, Demonstrates Results Orientation:* Sets and pursues aggressive goals, demonstrates a strong commitment to success, is able to marshal resources to accomplish projects, and handles multiple projects simultaneously. Demonstrates a consistent bias toward action.
- *Builds Organizational Relationships:* Understands the primacy of interrelationships and cultivates community across all enterprises. Networks outside the organization and stays in touch with employees at all levels. Willingly shares credit for wins and successes.
- *Leads Change and Innovation:* Champions new ideas and initiatives, challenges existing processes, and removes barriers. Helps others respond positively to change and ambiguity. Initiates, directs, and sustains efforts to ensure continuous learning and improvement.

- *Inspires and Develops Others:* Attracts and selects high-caliber people of diverse backgrounds and perspectives. Provides constructive feedback and develops world-class successors. Nurtures commitment to a common vision and shared values, provides opportunities for others to grow and achieve, creates and maintains an environment that is rewarding and full of learning opportunities.
- *Creates Vision, Thinks Through Strategy, Correctly Judges Tactics:* Develops and articulates a clear and consistent vision for the organization. Defines strategy clearly, and maintains a long-term, global view. Demonstrates superior judgment regarding large tactical choices.
- *Encourages and Manages Differences in Hiring, Dialogue, and Development:* Understands the implications of a diverse global population on Schwab's business. Seeks out different points of view, encourages direct and tough debate, works through conflict constructively, and creates clarity from ambiguity. Projects credibility and poise, even in highly visible, adversarial situations.
- *Manages Resources Effectively:* Acquires and allocates resources to maximize profitability and productivity. Understands meaning and implications of key business performance measurements. Allocates resources consistent with values to optimize the interests of all stakeholders.
- *Manages Technology:* Understands the basis of technology development, and is conversant in the language of technology. Has an appreciation for the possibilities and limitations of technology in raising productivity, serving customers, and complementing the effect of human interaction. Is skilled in these distinctions and communicates these distinctions to others.

Separating the measurement of these core competencies from the more objective reporting of the business results allows room for a real dialogue. None of these competencies can be mastered in a vacuum, none can be perfected as one would perfect the process of putting wheels on a car or balancing a cash drawer. Some have to do with character traits, some have to do with relationship skill, and some have to do with behavior. All have to do with the development of a person rather than the fine-tuning of a worker, and all are relevant to the world in which change is the constant management challenge. Far from being set in stone, some of these measurements, particularly the ones dealing with skill, will evolve, changing over time along with the company and its technology.

Not coincidentally, skill in technology management is an important part of these measurements, just as it an increasingly important part of the future of all growth businesses.

The last time I heard Tom Peters speak in public was in the summer of 1996. It was a multi-speaker event, beamed to several hundred locations at once. He was one of three business gurus holding forth on a number of topics for an international audience of several thousand. Peters has a way of giving the audience pithy statements that bounce around in the brain for a few days, even occasionally generating an operable insight. This particular day, the comment that stuck was something like, "Every CEO should look for a Chief Information Officer who is under the age of fifteen." The comment got a laugh, but since I am the father of three, two of whom grew up with their primary sources of inspiration being a golden retriever and a Pac-Man video game, I knew immediately what he meant. All of my children are much more comfortable with technology than I am.

Because of my background at IBM, I am relatively free of the fear of technology, unlike some of my peers. I had my first XT in 1985, and was one of the first few thousand people to have a CompuServe account. Later, in 1989 when I started teaching at Cal, I was introduced to the Internet through the university system. This was a few years before any kind of graphic interface with the Net. So I dutifully learned enough UNIX commands to get around, if sparingly.

But my kids' generation takes this technology for granted, and therefore they are not in awe about its operation. My youngest son was one of the few people I knew who got to the fifteenth Pac-Man screen. (It's blue and the music is terrific!) Additionally, they are knowledgeable enough about the fundamentals of programming and computer operation and have grown up with such rapid change and progress that they don't marvel much at the potential of new technology. They aren't easily impressed, two of them can design Web sites, and I'm sure that if a live cat walked out of a video display into the living room, they would say something like "Cool!" while I was heading for the bomb shelter.

Why is this relevant? Because the leaders of most companies that we would call "traditional" are closer to my age (mid-fifties) than my kids' age (late twenties). And the leaders of most companies that we would call "emerging technology" companies are closer to my kids' age than mine. It's hard to ignore that the market capitalization of "their" companies is greater than that of "our" companies.

So Peters's comment had three instructions to me. First, I had better find in myself the courage and capacity to learn technology like a fifteen-year-old. Second, I had better redevelop the inquiring and "anything is possible" attitude of a teenager, and finally, I had better have an understanding of what this young person feels like, acts like, and cares about if I am going to successfully manage an organization of technologists.

Now, to keep myself out of trouble, I must clarify that I am not saying that technologists act like kids. I think their ranks are probably typical of the population as a whole in that regard. I'm suggesting that they operate in a slightly different world, one that puts a premium on technology itself, and that parallels the world of *technology application,* in this case, the world of business. The real leader is able to build a bridge from the business part of the organization to the technology part of the organization, walk across it, and teach others, both technologists and business-types, to walk across it too.

There was a story going around in 1999 that had a hot-air balloonist lost, floating about thirty feet above an open field, when he spotted another person on the ground. He shouted down, "Excuse me. Can you tell me where I am?"

The person on the ground looked up, looked around and considered the question . . . then replied, "Yes, you are hovering about thirty feet above this open field."

The balloonist yelled, "You must be a technologist."

"Why yes, I am," came the reply. "How did you know?"

"Well, everything you just told me is technically correct, and it does me no good at all!"

With this, the technologist shouted back. "Oh, I see. You must be a business manager."

"As a matter of fact, I am," shouted the bewildered captain. "And how did you know?"

"Well, you don't know where you are. You don't know where you are heading. You asked me for help. You are no worse off than you were before, but now it is my fault!"

Whichever side you identify with, if you have ever been in a project planning meeting, then the laugh at that situation probably got a little stuck in your throat. The communication difficulties between technologists and business managers have existed since the advent of the computer. But they have been magnified, beyond my ability to express it, by the Internet, by the World Wide Web, and finally and forever by the advent of e-commerce. These have created two central differences in the world of data processing and the world of network technology. One, the need for passion and commitment to generate innovation, we've been talking about. The other central difference is this: The customer now has direct access to everyone's systems.

When I was selling equipment and applications for IBM in the 1970s, mistakes were kept inside the business; the systems' frailties were only known internally. When a system went down, there were frequently long nights and heated arguments, but the *customer* was never a party to those discussions. With on-line, real-time access and transaction processing, the customers know every single glitch in a business system, and they are able to judge and choose who they do business with on the basis of the reliability of the system over time.

Because of this central change, there is now a premium on good communication between those who are responsible for business results and those who design and build technology. We are now building systems as tools to be used directly by customers who will not expect to read a users' manual. Accordingly, both technologist and general manager now have to be concerned, not only with efficiency, but with the nature of the customer experience.

The roles of technology and business have traditionally been split within a company. The CEO of a traditional product or service business (as opposed to a provider of high-tech equipment, components, or direct service) rarely came from the ranks of technologists. Rather, they were promoted from the ranks of general business operations, sales and marketing, or some aspect of finance and were installed in the "ivory tower" of the business. This newly critical need to be conversant and appreciative of technology's capability and project management puts added responsibility on these generalists—first to envision the full potential of what is possible, and then to understand, to question, and to contribute to the definition and execution of technology projects.

Likewise, the technologist traditionally had been in the basement of the business, creating the infrastructure that executed and measured operations. They were like specialists in lab coats, hunched over their workstations, working out the possible by applying their keen understanding of the inner workings of the computer. They could then place those limitations on the dreams of the businessperson. But now, to be truly successful, they have to understand more about customer behavior and preference, more about the tradeoffs between speed of development and market timing, more about customers who are not at all conversant with the technical jargon of the electrical engineer. In addition to understanding programming language, they have to renew their use of the everyday language of conversation and apply what they know to make it easy to bridge between the two.

In Chapter Two, we commented about the challenge of bringing together different natural abilities and cultural biases in one company, about focusing people of different skills and communities around a central core vision and set of values and maintaining their excitement about them. The most difficult pair to bring together is that of the technologist and the generalist. This need is a late-twentieth-century phenomenon, and Dave's career pretty well matched its growth in importance. Let's see how he did.

EIGHT

UNDERSTANDING TECHNOLOGY AND THE PEOPLE WHO BUILD IT

Terry stated the dilemma well. Blending technology and the more traditional business disciplines has always been a challenge, one that I recognized in my early days of business at Citibank. I volunteered to do a job in what was then "data processing," generating projects and managing them, primarily to run the internal systems of the business. I was not invited to attend meetings with the heads of the operating units. I was not embraced as part of the business, but rather operated in my own little domain. I almost had to invade their business sanctum to get them to give me the help I needed to work on the projects I was asked to work on. I had a hard time getting their attention, and this experience began to teach me some important lessons.

I learned quickly that those who included me in their meetings, who helped me clarify what outcomes were actually needed from the systems . . . these people got the best results. The ones who refused to help, who treated me like a necessary but unwelcome appendage, got the worst outcomes. Their projects were delayed, inadequate, and more expensive than we had planned. More than anything, we always underdelivered on what might have been possible had the cooperation and understanding been better.

It seems so simple, but it apparently wasn't. I kept thinking, "Why are we being treated this way?" I concluded, at that time, that it wasn't intentional, and it wasn't passive-aggressive behavior at work. It was lack of context. They couldn't appreciate the potential of their involvement.

Many of the business operators didn't see technology as integral to their business; instead, they saw it merely as a tool. They thought, "Well, I don't know technology." "How much value can I really add spending time with you?" and my personal favorite, "Why can't you just do your job?" I discovered later that these thoughts were all code for, "You work with this stuff that I don't know about, and you ask me questions that require me to think harder than I want to."

I think this was typical of the thinking in the 1970s and early 1980s. Having learned this dynamic from the technical side, I was determined to make it different when I went back to business operations at Citibank, then at Shearson, and finally at Schwab. In fact, many technology people recognized and appreciated the difference in working with my group at these companies. I believe it's because I embraced them, invited them in, got them involved, and made their jobs easier and more rewarding. It was a partnership. Consequently, when technology moved to the forefront of the company, when it became primary to the way we interfaced with our customers, it was easier for me to operate than for some others. My experience also came in handy when we began to see the Internet as the next major integral delivery system in our business.

THE ROAD TO PARTNERSHIP

The first principles of generating engagement, partnership, and passion are the same for technologists as for everyone else: Get them behind the vision of serving customers, and make sure that everyone is conversant with and aligned with the values of the company. When that alignment and understanding is in place, then both businessperson and technologist will be open to using their respective skills toward the same end. But inside that commitment, there are fundamentally different points of view determined largely by the different nature of the technologists' work. These differences simply have to be understood in order to smooth the process and make the partnership secure. In the last few years, I've worked with Dawn Lepore, a chief information officer at Schwab, who appreciates this need for partnership. She has helped me learn some characteristics of technology projects and good technologists, and I've applied what I've learned to maintain that partnership and apply it in the best interest of the company. In this chapter, I'd like to spell out the differences between the world of technology and the world of the business operator and offer some help in dealing with those differences, actually using them to build commitment.

The stereotypes of business generalists and technologists that are characterized in the story of the hot air balloonist come from the different nature of the work and the people who choose to do it. Like all stereotypes, they can be handy for general understanding. They can also be damaging when applied to anyone specifically. That said, I'd like to look at some of the differing characteristics brought out by the nature of the work and the relative ages of the professions.

Literal and Granular Versus Metaphorical and General

It's stated as fact: *Technologists are literal.* The balloonist comments, "Everything you have told me is accurate, but it does me no good whatsoever." And of course, the "accurate" part is true. To be good at defining instructions for a computer, a person has to think in literal and granular terms. *Every* case in a business function has to be fully described. The computer does not deal well with approximations, nor does it do well with variables that are not defined in the programming. As we will see later, being literal is only a skill, a way of thinking that has much to offer to business. But to those of us who are not so literal, it can also yield some pretty funny stories.

Dawn (the CIO) is married to a technologist, and she was remarking to him over dinner that being literal can really cause some misunderstandings, and can even result in a lack of grace in personal relationships. She was recounting her day, and told him the story of arriving at a meeting at a local hotel. She had remarked casually to the meeting organizer that she had been traveling and had come to the hotel directly from the office after dropping off her bags.

Later, during a break, she was engaged with the same meeting organizer in a side conversation about Automatic Teller Machines, and mentioned the difficulty she had experienced with a transaction that she had attempted at the local ATM on her way to the hotel. The organizer, a technologist, said, "I thought you told me that you came here directly from the office." Dawn was somewhat taken back, but explained that she had made a brief stop at the sidewalk ATM on the way. The technologist then implied that the statement about coming direct was inaccurate at best, a prevarication at worst.

Dawn was telling her husband the story with a touch of disbelief, as an example of "being literal" run amok. She remarked incredulously, "Can you believe that she considered this a lie?" Her husband (a technologist) thought for a moment and said, "Well, you know, Dawn, she was technically correct!" One can only ponder, like the balloonist, whether that information was useful or not!

There are two points to be made here. First, to have the skill of critical and literal thinking is a plus, but we cannot apply that skill too liberally to our personal relationships without running the risk of discounting the human tendency to approximate, to automatically screen out the trivial. In fact, "thinking in a literal way" is a more appropriate description of the skill than "being literal." To pretend that "literal" is a characteristic of a human being might lead us to pretend that technologists can't be inspired but can only be motivated by digitally measured incentives. Companies make this mistake, and as a result, they offer only greater monetary rewards. They can get trapped in a cycle of turnover that could be mitigated by remembering that technologists also want to make a difference. They too want to contribute to something greater than themselves. They want to use their specialized knowledge just as the rest of us want to use our own gifts: to make sure that the world is different because we have been here.

Second, in identifying technology project requirements, business leaders have to adapt their thinking to match that of the technologists. Generalists typically operate with a much bigger picture, while technologists have to operate at a very granular level, a level that is uncomfortable for most businesspeople. When we talk to a technologist about the business rules in a functional set, we can't talk about 98 percent of the cases. We have to talk about 100 percent of the cases. The stereotypical project definition meeting goes something like this:

Technologist: Could anything else happen?

Operator: No.

Technologist: Are you sure?

Operator: What do you mean?

Technologist: Is there even a 1 percent chance of something else happening?

Operator: I don't know, we'll figure it out later.

Technologist: No, we can't. We have to figure out all of the cases before the design can proceed.

This is not what business generalists do best, but it is a discipline of thinking that is the technologists' lifeblood. Business operators are asked to think harder, and to spend the time to identify as many variables as possible. When a system doesn't quite work, it is because the business sponsor didn't think quite specifically enough, and the technology designer didn't ask quite enough questions. Both bear the responsibility of inadequate functional design specifications, which lead to less-than-optimal operation.

Complete and Complex Versus Sufficient and Simple

Just as the technologist will consider the granular, it is up to the businessperson to provide adequate context in the world of the customer, to allow the engineers to apply the rules to the best advantage of the company rather than literally and "without exception." In the 1980s, at an *Inc. Magazine* conference in Reno, Nevada, I heard an executive from the Porsche Motor Company say, "A Porsche is built by the best engineers in the world. It will never be built by a focus group in

Los Angeles." Well, this executive engineer would not say that today. Customers ultimately dictate what is built. While I'm sure he is still justifiably proud of Porsche engineering, the car is now available in many models and many colors—all of them dictated by the market, not the engineers.

Engineers given a blank check and no market limitations will (and should) build the most complete systems possible, often the most complex. Such a system will take care of every single contingency. But the market might only need something functional and simple. In truth, there is no way for the engineers to know how much is too much if the business operator doesn't tell them. Let me give you a live example.

In early 1998, I called one of our National Investor Centers just to test the phone system, to hear what our customers were hearing. I was put on hold for about sixty seconds. This was not an unacceptable time, but I noticed that the "music on hold" was a recorded repetitive message of market news. I thought that it would be much more effective if we offered something more current, something that we could interrupt with live updates on our call waiting times or more timely business news. I thought that a repetitive message didn't seem so bad in normal times when waits are short, but in the busy market times we sometimes experienced, the effect of our recorded system would be brutal. A customer who was on hold for three or four minutes was reminded of how long it was by the repetitive message. And of course, in those hectic market times, everyone was too busy to record an updated message, so it became as much as an hour old, was absolutely out of date, and frequently wrong.

Changing to live radio seemed like a relatively easy project to me, with a good payoff. I called the responsible general manager and described what I wanted in typical general manager terms—something like, "We need to improve our customers' experience while they are waiting. We should be able to have a live broadcast that we can interrupt with frequent updates on our call-waiting times." She got technologists involved, told them that I wanted a better customer experience with our "hold" recording, and then repeated what I had said to her. The technologists set about the design and implementation of a system.

Six months later, the market was going crazy, and I got a letter from a customer telling me about how he listened to the same tape eleven times while he was waiting for a representative. I was frustrated and more than a little piqued. I called the general manager and asked about the status of the project. She told me that it was complicated, and that the group had been working on it with some urgency. Since she understood the technology fairly well, she called the project manager, and the three of us discussed it.

I learned a lot of reasons why it was very complicated technically to make it possible for us to have a live broadcast, and to be able to cut in at will, including the difference between voice and data bandwidth, and why live radio was difficult to cut in and out over phone lines that doubled as data lines, that we would have to move to satellite communication and wireless, and how much the network would get tied up . . . and on and on and on. Of course, the technologist was absolutely accurate. They were designing and building exactly what I had called for. So I said, "Wait a minute. Let's pick apart what you've told me here. We don't need a lot of bells and whistles, we just need a more current message to play over the phone and we need to update our customers frequently about the status of the wait. Lots of companies do that right now. We don't need all that complexity, we simply need to let the customers hear something besides a recorded old message while the market is going crazy, and we need to let them know how long the wait will be . . . that's all. Can't we just do that much?"

And sure enough, when the team went back to the designers and let them know the broad parameters of what we needed, they found a simpler approach that delivered about 80 percent of what we needed for an investment of 50 percent of the time and cost.

Now, I'm not blaming the technologists or the general manager at all. I was just as much at fault, describing a specific solution rather than giving broad guidelines. Also, I didn't communicate the urgency that I felt the project warranted. If I had, the general manager might have disagreed with me, and we could have discussed it. As it was, when she communicated the request to the system designer, it was more specific and less urgent than I had intended. All of our communication could have been improved. Given a request for a specific solution to a given problem, the engineer tried to provide the most complete one possible, just as anyone would expect.

Unfortunately, many business managers will take the technology answer as gospel, and not probe for a deeper understanding. When a technologist speaks in information technology jargon, some business folks get intimidated, or they feel, as in the old days, that they can't take the time to understand. They could say, "It's hard for me to understand what you are saying because I don't have your technology knowledge." "Can you put that in more layman's terms so we can talk about it?" "Maybe there are some compromises between the absolutely complete solution and the one that we can get implemented in a shorter time frame." But rather than saying any of that, many business operators will just nod to the technologists' comments. It causes overspending and underperformance. In most projects, as this one, there is a breaking point where we can build 80 percent of the value for 50 percent of the money. The rest of the money will get the other 20 percent of functionality. It is vital that the businessperson define the sufficient and simple requirements. Then and only then can the complete and complex solution of the technologist be fairly evaluated. Of course, in the case of the "live radio," we have all learned a great deal.

So in general, technologists see the ultimate capability of a system. They see the complete and complex answer, and they ask the questions that make it possible for the technology to deliver a flawless solution. They traditionally have not known enough about the context of the application to offer alternative solutions that might be more efficient. Conversely, businesspeople know the broader context of what is actually needed, know that compromises can be made to satisfy most of the need, but have not had the knowledge, understanding, or confidence to ask questions that would lead toward simpler, more appropriate solutions. These are different points of view with huge possibilities for coming together.

AIMING FOR SYNERGY

There are two main facets to a good leader's understanding of technology: understanding the people who build and adapt technology and knowing something about the technology itself. These are fundamental to bringing technologists into the heart of the company's purpose.

Acknowledge Age and Attitude

Naturally, with the explosion in demand for professional technologists in the last decade, people who work with the latest gadgets and languages are, as a group, younger than the rest of us. Terry contrasted the technological comfort of his children with his own, and I'm in the same situation. I can get by, but my son Craig is a whiz! While I know many very, very good technologists in their fifties, sixties, and older, it is true that the majority of the professionals in this area are not yet forty. With that youth come attitudes and capabilities born of the times in which they were brought up. In many ways, dealing with these professionals is like doing business in another country, and a delightful one at that.

On the edge of technology there is a pioneering spirit that is hard to find in other departments in a company. There is also an appreciation for the work of others as it relates to their own. Every project has unique pieces, but all projects have to fit together, so I suspect it is much easier for them to see their own work as part of a whole, and to respect and help those who are also working to the same technical end, albeit on another piece. This cooperation can often extend outside the company, to others working on similar problems.

As an example, I think of what happened in 1998 and 1999 as the concern about Y2K was taking technological center stage in our business. Naturally, we were concerned about potential glitches in the systems, and the legal folks were concerned about liability. During one particular period, it seemed that every company in the United States was writing to its suppliers asking them to guarantee that they were Y2K compliant. In essence, everyone was looking for someone to be ultimately responsible for any losses that might occur as a result of non-compliant systems.

Well, the suppliers had lawyers too, so naturally, they were writing back saying, in essence, "We're doing the best we can, but no guarantees."

In that environment, it was vital that all people in the industry cooperated, and yet some business leaders were reluctant to share details of their strategies and plans. In the midst of this liability discussion one day, a senior technologist spoke up and said, "Why don't you just leave it to the technologists? We talk to one another, and we'll work it out." That is a very different attitude than we are used to as we struggle to gain competitive advantage.

This new brand of technologist I've described is really the second generation of on-line specialist. The earliest on-line, real-time technology professionals started working in the 1970s and early 1980s and they are different still from their newly minted counterparts. They cut their teeth inside a business, in the "basement," doing traditional business applications, and they are closer, as a result, to the people who now run those same applications in different ways.

They have many of the same traits as their younger counterparts, but they have a perspective that allows them to appreciate and harness the exuberance that goes with working in this marvelous and exciting world.

Appreciate the Differences—and Benefit

Every business needs some of both of these groups, the experienced and the new. Our own business depends on the seasoned professionals who know the history of our systems and know the bridges to the new. We also need a host of new, leading-edge technologists who can take us boldly into the future of the Internet.

I hope I am conveying my deep respect for technology and the people who specialize in its development and application. I sing their praises every chance I get, and frequently and truthfully tell the world that we are "a technology company in the financial services business." I know of the difficulty and absolute necessity of integrating technology into the kind of business that we have, one that puts the customer experience first. I know that all of us need to use technology to increase our own productivity, and we need to understand the implications of technology on our future and the future of our customers. Not everyone does, as the next example illustrates.

In 1997, when on-line trading was just beginning to become popular and efficient, I was speaking to a conference of business analysts about our strategy. The speaker before me was the CEO of one of our competitors. When asked about technology, he remarked that it had a "choke-hold" on the business. I couldn't help but think of what the technologists in his company must have thought of that remark. At one time, I might have felt that way. When I was working in data processing at Citibank, information technology was strictly an internal function, and I'm sure that operators saw the immense expenditures as merely a necessary evil, one that they could not control because they didn't have the necessary knowledge to question it. But now, information technology affects everything, both internally and externally. It drives the customers' experience of our company and is, accordingly, the lifeblood of our ability to compete. I'm sure this gentleman would not have characterized expenditures for customer service as having a "choke-hold" on his business. The remark showed a lack of understanding of the impact of technology on his business, and a lack of empathy for those who would build it and make it work.

Get On-Line Yourself

Chuck Schwab was our company's first on-line investor. He could see the potential of the Web because he could feel it in his own accounts, and he was deeply respected for it. This is just fundamental—it is a price of credibility. If you can't operate a PC, you will be snickered at and appropriately criticized for elitism. How do you learn? If you are senior enough, you might do what I did. In 1995, when I realized it was time that I became PC literate, I had a technical tutor come to my office to teach me. If you can't yet attract that level of personal attention, then go back to school. I'm dead serious. I consider an understanding of technology to be one of the core competencies for business leadership in the next decade. I'm making sure that every succession plan in the company includes a component that addresses this aspect of management knowledge, especially for aspiring executives. To me, it's as important as knowing their native language.

LEARN THE LANGUAGE OF BUILDING SYSTEMS

Technology is now so integral to business that a leader simply must be smart about the key elements and tradeoffs. Although it may be impractical for seasoned executives to take one- or two-year assignments in technology management, it is not so for aspiring executives. We simply have to learn the jargon and the concepts behind the jargon to be effective. While it isn't necessary to be able to program in C, merely being able to respond to e-mail is not enough. Basics that any executive should know include elements of a successful project, fundamental systems concepts, and project evaluation criteria.

Elements of a Successful Project

The business leader has to understand the project plan and what happens at each step, including the feasibility study, design (which includes user, functional, program, and systems' specifications), the actual programming, testing (unit, program, and system), acceptance testing, parallel testing, and implementation. The leader has to know and be able to ask questions about the critical elements for each step of this process.

In our company we try to define those elements very precisely, and we're getting better at it. For example, one of our success criteria is a close and trusted business and technology partnership. Without that relationship in place, we feel our chance of optimizing the system is nil. That means that the executive has to be involved and competent—not an easy set of criteria to fill. These "people" requirements yield a clear and agreed-on vision for the project.

Fundamental Systems Concepts

A business manager can't evaluate or manage technology without a fundamental grasp of some details. She has to know fundamentals, including:

- The difference between operating systems and applications systems.
- How networks move data around between computers.
- The differences in mainframe, server, and router capability, and the advantages and disadvantages of each.
- Basic strategies for systems backup, their cost trade-offs and their advantages and disadvantages.
- The different ways of testing programs and systems and the relative risks of each.
- What words like "UNIX," "Windows NT," "HTML," and "Java" refer to.

I could go on, but this is a good list to start.

Knowledge of these fundamentals will accomplish two things. It will make you much more effective in evaluating and bringing greater perspective to projects, both in the proposal and implementation phases. More important, it will signal the technology group that you are interested and competent in their realm. You will become a partner rather than a patient, and the possibilities for success will be substantially enhanced.

Project Evaluation Criteria

In 1999, I was visited by Warren McFarlan, a professor from Harvard who wanted to do a case study on Schwab. I recognized him from my days at Citibank, when I had attended his course for executives on data processing in 1979. Although he didn't recognize me (I obviously didn't distinguish myself in his course!), I remembered his model for managing technology projects, and I have used it ever since.[1] Based on his teaching, I look at a project's risk, and therefore its feasibility, in terms of five criteria:

- *The size of the expenditure:* How big is it, both in absolute dollars and in dollars relative to the return?
- *The project's duration:* Anything longer than one year needs to be broken into interim deliverables and plans. The risk of keeping the team intact over time goes up dramatically with multiyear projects.
- *The technical reach in the project:* Are we familiar with the technology, or does it go beyond our current capability?
- *The structural aspects of the project:* How many divisions of the company are affected? Does this require a major change in hardware? How clear are the objectives?
- *The skill of the people required to do it:* Do we have the expertise in house, or will we have to depend on vendors and consultants?

I ask us to evaluate all these criteria and use this mix to mitigate risk. The riskier the project, the higher the payback has to be. As with understanding fundamental systems' concepts, asking questions around this model accomplishes two things. First, it helps the technologists connect the proposal to the strategy and operation of the business. Second, it demonstrates your knowledge and interest in a way that reinforces the sense of partnership with technology, rather than setting it aside as merely a necessary function, a part of the business that has a "choke-hold" on the operation.

Between my own questions and those of the technologists, we can use these criteria (and others) to mitigate the risk of the best projects. An expensive, long-term project that affects all parts of the business, one that we have to do primarily with consultants because it is a large technical leap from our current way of doing things, is not a good bet to be successful. But if we can chop it into shorter time frames, with operational deliverables along the way, we might be able to incrementally build our own expertise, learn as we go, and get value at each of the checkpoints even if the entire project hits a major bump.

How it Works

We started a massive project in 1990 to fundamentally revamp the way we did information technology. At first, we saw it as the end of mainframes and older legacy systems. We planned to replace all the mainframes with client-server technology, and we knew that it would take seven to eight years to complete. As projects go, this one was risky. We had to build the in-house expertise, it was going to cost $250 million (expensive by our standards), and it was long range. It would ultimately affect every aspect of the company.

Knowing the risk, we began by breaking the project into measurable pieces. We worked on the new easy things first. We built a few new applications so we could have some success and build our internal expertise. Then we took on the bigger, more complicated conversions when we had people who understood the technology as well as the business. There was a huge amount of business involvement with all of the things we had to do.

Of course, you can't build new systems in a vacuum. The business continued to change even as we were working on the original plan. As we got into the project, we realized that we could be more flexible. We could live with some of the old code. We learned as we developed that mainframes were not going to go away, and Dawn redefined the systems goals. Our real systems goals were not replacement of the old systems and hardware, but building throughput, reliability, and flexibility into our systems. This shift allowed us to use new technology as it came along and to keep any old technology that fit the criteria. Our fundamental view of the world changed as we were building, and because we remained flexible, technology emerged as a significant competitive advantage to our company. As of this writing, we are nine years from the inception of the project, and what we have seen is a migration rather than a replacement. It's been quite a success.

I hope what I've demonstrated here is the necessity for a leader of a company, or any organization, to understand technology and be able to speak and ask questions that are meaningful and relevant. It helps, too, if you can make a suggestion once in a while that will "make some lights go on" for the technologists. When you can, you have an excellent opportunity to build business sensitivity into the technology arm of the company.

Dawn also believes in this partnership approach, and as a result, she has an excellent record of promoting technologists into roles as general managers. As of this writing, two of our business enterprises, one in electronic brokerage and one in Europe, are run by former technologists. I expect that there will be more.

GAINING LOYALTY TO THE BUSINESS

I've devoted a separate chapter to technology because of its growing importance to any business. The Internet has changed the standard for systems excellence. Customers want to be assured that their Internet link to your business is as "reliable as a dial tone." Because every company has to manage its own reliability, and because mistakes are now immediately obvious to customers, technology management has become a critical skill for a business leader. We want to manage our system so that anytime the system goes down, there isn't even a flicker on the customers' display. To do that will require real alignment of purpose.

So far, I've spoken about the formalities: learning the language of technology, understanding the models for success, and knowing the differences in the skills and attitudes of technologists. None of these would be adequate to build real passion unless the business leader really engages the technologists themselves. In reality, these principles of operation point the way for the business leader to show empathy and respect for the people who are performing a critical function for the company. They are all ways of building trust, of enlisting the support and partnership of those critical to the business. None of the principles will be effective unless they are used in that spirit.

Ultimately, I don't have any trouble in making sure that the technologists at Schwab know about the importance of their contribution, because I believe in it so deeply. Young or older, experienced or new to the company, working on maintenance projects or working on the leading edge, they are as valuable as the very best branch manager, portfolio manager, or equity trader—or the CEO. Everyone plays a part in the larger purpose of our company. It is my job, through learning, asking questions, and acknowledgment, to make that obvious.

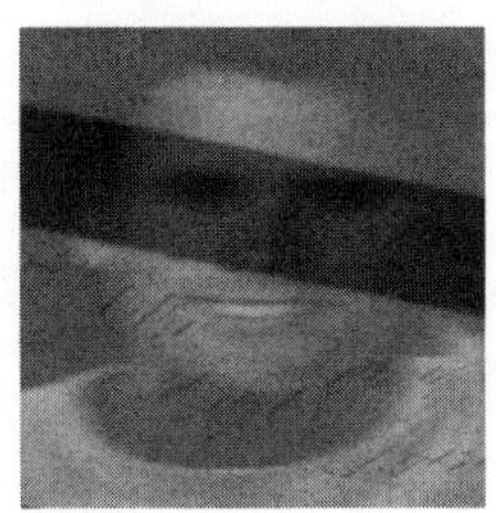

FROM UNDERSTANDING TECHNOLOGY TO MARKETING

Dave devoted the preceding chapter to a discussion of technology and developing a partnership with those who build that technology. What does a partnership between business and technology, an engagement between the two groups, require? Inclusion. The business leader has to go to technology meetings, sometimes just to listen, and she has to invite technologists to marketing and operations meetings as well. She has to speak to the technology groups about the greater goals of their combined efforts, talk about the application of what they are doing together that makes a difference in peoples' lives. And she has to be able to speak the languages that technologists understand.

In Schwab (and probably in other companies), Mr. Spock of *Star Trek* is frequently mentioned by technologists as their role model. Spock, the Vulcan, is the ultimate logical and objective being, basing all of his decisions on his mind and its conclusions. But in this long-running and popular series, we are most interested and connected with Spock when his Vulcan nature is suddenly and surprisingly invaded by emotion and caring, when he shows his "human" side. Acknowledging both sides is important. The business leader has to realize that Spock the technologist thinks logically and interprets literally. Further, the business leader has to understand that, at the core, Spock the technologist is a human being with different skills and capabilities, a human being who wants to know that he is contributing to something greater than himself.

To achieve the synergy between business and technology, the leader must acknowledge and appreciate the differences in age and attitude. She has to get on-line, literally and figuratively. She has to study and become reasonably fluent in the language and rules of the technologist. At minimum, these include elements of a successful project, fundamental systems concepts, and project evaluation criteria. More important, the leader has to acknowledge that those who build technology are full partners. Without this synergy, the challenges and opportunities of the Internet world will be out of reach.

In the opening chapter, we proposed "the promise of service to others" as a core component of a passion-driven culture. We further suggested that the customer experience is the ultimate benchmark of success in such a culture. These propositions assume that people actually want to serve others, want to make a difference to others, and that business can provide those opportunities as a first priority.

I feel the breath of Milton Friedman on my neck.

When I was studying business and religious philosophy in college, friends often remarked about the apparent paradox in pursuing these fields at the same time. I couldn't articulate a reconciliation until much later. I only knew that my own spiritual convictions sprang from experience rather than doctrine, that true expression of my convictions required action, and that most action seemed to be in the worlds of business and politics.

Today, I often remind students that business was invented by humans. There was no McDonald's on the beach when we crawled out of the ocean. I suspect, although it certainly can't be proved logically, that the business of trade began with the impulse to help one another. It is clear that barter itself, the human connection and exchange of talent, was the first enterprise. From there, the invention of money to symbolize value was a natural step, as the complexity of needs outgrew our ability to find the person who needed specifically what we had. It was easier to shop for goods than to shop for customers. Without going through the entire anthropological history, let's just say we've come a long way, and we are many times removed from that original personal transaction model, with its exchange of gratitude and gratification. Certainly, our impulse is to come back to it, and technology just might be providing that opportunity. Fundamentally, companies need to communicate what they have to offer, and then provide it. The next two chapters are about those fundamentals: marketing, advertising, and providing the customer experience.

These are Dave's favorite parts of the business, so he will be writing about the details, giving some great advice on execution. He looks at operational questions: What kind of marketing is the most efficient? What really makes a great advertisement? What is essential to provide to customers and what is extraneous? How do we balance resources to provide the right expectation, and the right experience, without overpromising or underdelivering? I love the practical nature of his commentary, and I love the way the people of his company execute on it. When we discuss those direct questions, it's important to remember the greater context of marketing and advertising, the role they play in the greater scheme of the business, and especially the role they play in generating the commitment of people inside the company to keep the promise to the customer. Marketing and advertising never create success on their own. These functions are communication sciences, and the very best practitioners are asking, "What are the promises of our business?" and, "How can I communicate our promises to customers in a way that inspires them to at least try our products or services?" It's up to leaders to make sure that the people *in* the business feel these questions as personal ones, so that in reality, marketing and advertising represents them as individuals as well as the company as a whole.

Some promises are specific statements about what the company will do for its customers. These are time-specific offers, requiring timely and flawless execution. When a company makes an offer and the people in the company don't have the resources to deliver to the customer, each employee should feel it directly, as a personal failure.

This kind of emotional involvement and sense of personal responsibility will ultimately make the company more responsive and productive, exactly the environment we are trying to create.

Other promises are more general, brand advertising. These marketing and advertising messages communicate the sum of who the company is. They imply or state explicitly the purpose, character, and values of the company, and by implication, the purpose, character, and values of the people who make up the company. Nike rarely mentions specific products in its advertising, instead Nike presents a symbol for all people to be active and to live up to their dreams. The brand also means "being competitive." Even the Nike logo suggests that idea, and the Nike campus near Portland provides the opportunity for all the company's employees to be active, to train, and to be physically fit and competitive. Saturn declares itself a "different kind of company"—and lets us know about its community. The slogan "Intel Inside" means a standard of quality for a computer. Brand is, in essence, the family name, and it conveys the intangible qualities that underlay product and service offerings.

The Internet has magnified the importance of brand in two significant ways. First, for customers, brand provides a broader measuring screen for their judgments. Because of the Internet and the spread of other mass media, brand is now vital as a basis for confidence. There is a cacophony from new firms, some with little or no track record, getting louder and more confusing. Each one declares, with Web site banners and buttons, that it can perform a service or offer a product better than others. This new freedom to communicate is the blessing and curse of the Internet. It is possible, with this inexpensive and ubiquitous channel, for any company, anywhere on the globe, to create the *image* of a reliable brand at relatively little cost. It is marvelous for a customer to have so many choices, but the customer is left to discover whether the brand is real or illusory by testing the more specific offers of the company.

Second, for a company, brand integrity provides an opportunity to build company loyalty rather than mere transaction satisfaction.

There is a chance to build *community* with brand, and in an Internet world otherwise dominated by the attractiveness of the most recent offer, brand loyalty is a valuable competitive advantage. This idea is consistent with my own experience. IBM is a company built on principles that were clear. Those principles, "the pursuit of excellence, respect for the individual, and the finest customer service in the world," defined the brand, and as such, set the standard for every customer and employee of the company. To be associated with IBM was to be associated with those traits. In a business that places a premium on reliability and consistency, IBM became a dominant brand in the 1960s and 1970s. Many customers were so loyal that they would not only put up with IBM's foibles, they would help the company fix whatever problems arose. Working for that company during that time meant wearing a badge of honor and accomplishment. Those of us employed by IBM might as well have had a sign on the backs of our conservative attire that said "IBM Means Service."

Of course, today, employees actually do wear clothes that proclaim "Hewlett-Packard" or "Schwab" because they like to be associated with the values and reputations of their firms. Such clothes proclaim that they belong to a desirable community. People enjoy being stopped by others and asked, "Oh, do you work for Schwab? Let me tell you about the wonderful experience that I had with your company last week." When employees of these companies see their advertising on television, they are not cynical, they are proud of it—they are passionate about it.

Now the consultant in me has to make a commentary. In the introduction to this section, I commented on the value of reengineering, how this new framework of thinking encouraged us to look at functions in their entirety, front to back, rather than in disconnected pieces. This was an extremely valuable shift, especially for the financial and product parts of the business. Systems thinking makes it more obvious that people are contributing and responsible for the final result.

Ironically, one aspect of the business that was overlooked in the reengineering movement was communication itself. A front-to-back approach to communication would provide recognition that every message, from the internal memo to the television advertisement, carries with it the DNA of the company. Every communication is linked, from the employee interview or the initial customer contact to the customer satisfaction survey and the career development plan of every employee. This kind of alignment and consistency builds loyalty and passion in employees and customers alike.

Few businesses, however, realize the alignment potential from marketing. Despite the fact that all messages are now heard by employees, external messages are managed by different groups who are "more artistic." Marketing and advertising are separated from internal communication as though they operate in a vacuum. Yet, clearly, in the age of the Internet, chat rooms, and forums, as well as other mass communication media, employees and customers alike have an unprecedented opportunity to hear and compare all of it, internal and external to the company. The Web has created an open environment, whether the company culture and the marketing department embrace it or not.

Because these communication functions continue to be kept artificially separate, and because the channels are so much broader and louder, inconsistencies in messages are noticed more than ever. Employees know when they are capable of keeping the promise of their company's marketing message, and they know when they can't, or worse, when the company doesn't intend to. Employees also know when the brand image being portrayed in advertising bears no resemblance to the actual values of the company or its executives. Conversely, they know when there is sincerity and execution behind the major marketing and advertising messages, and they are generally proud to make those messages come true.

Marketing and advertising are effective only when they are consistent with what the company can actually deliver. If the right message is delivered in a compelling way, and is followed by a consistent customer experience, a company has demonstrated the character and capability that make it a magnet for all potential stakeholders.

When we crawled out of the ocean and started trading value, we began this process of building businesses. Today, passion is built by revisiting those basic principles—by making good promises, making good on those promises, and giving people a chance to collectively and individually respond to their impulse to serve, to make a difference for others.

That's enough of the doctrine. Let's hear some real experience.

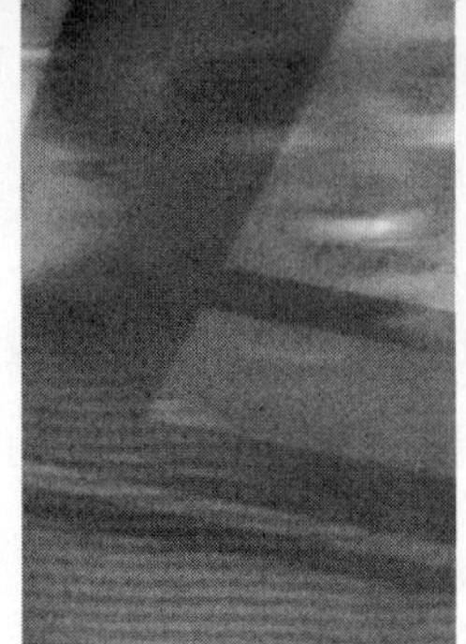

NINE

MARKETING: YOUR COMPANY'S VOICE, YOUR PEOPLE'S PROMISES

From the time of the barter system to the time of the Internet, the field of marketing has transformed into a science by itself. As Terry mentioned, this transformation has sometimes been to the detriment of companies just trying to pay attention to basics. Although the field has become specialized, many who are not actually operating in that field still use the terms *sales, marketing,* and *advertising* as if they were one thing. In the interest of clarity, I want to use the term *marketing* as inclusive of advertising and suggest that it drives sales—the actual transaction between a company and its clients.

Marketing is a conversation between a company, its employees, and its customers. The conversation can be about many things, including what customers want and need, what companies offer to those customers, and how employees intend to make good on the offers that their companies make. Marketing includes long-term strategy that builds brand and cements customer loyalty, and short-term advertising tactics that revolve around launching new products or reinforcing current offerings, with the intent of acquiring customers or selling product. Today, the beginning and renewing of this conversation happens not with talking, but with listening—listening to employees and customers, first for ideas on developing and refining products, then to determine if the customer finds enough value to support the offering of the product or service, and finally, to measure how well you've delivered. Marketing also includes the messages that grow from that listening, messages that reflect what your company is offering and messages about the character of your enterprise and the people in it.

This idea of marketing is only complicated because of the size of business and because the field has been thoroughly studied and documented. Sometimes, analysis can obscure the basics. If you or I started a new company, we would know that the conversation that we have with customers (our marketing) would have to be focused on their needs, and closely tied to both our central purpose and the offering that our company was making.

But as our company grew, we might hire functional professionals, either as employees or consultants, to help us with our offerings and brand advertising. These people would be good at the art of what they do, but would not necessarily be as knowledgeable or passionate about our company's uniqueness as we are. The larger we grew, the more risk we would have that marketing would get disjointed from the core of the company and would be run strictly by professional marketers, more interested in the message cosmetics than in the individual customer or the character of our company. That scenario is frequently played out as companies grow enough to decentralize the marketing function. In fact, we saw this same scenario in the field of marketing as a whole, as our economy matured from barter to mass production.

CONVERSATION IN THE MARKETPLACE: ONE-TO-ONE OR ONE-TO-MANY

Terry's barterers literally went to market. In the primitive village, there was a stall for every trade. Villagers and farmers who didn't make their own candles went to the candle-maker to have the candles they needed made to order. Generally there was only one candle-maker: that was all that was needed. Even if there was no choice of vendor, there was a choice of product, and there was a relationship. People met face-to-face to exchange value, sometimes money, sometimes goods. The vendor spent very little time hawking wares, and a lot of time listening and satisfying each individual customer. As life grew more complex, more and more people chose to purchase goods rather than make their own, and more and more vendors assembled to meet the need for each craft—all dealing with their customers one by one.

With the Industrial Revolution, we changed focus from customers to products. We entered a mass-production environment that shifted the market from intimate customization to mass standardization. The assembly line and the middleman arrived. Distribution channels were established between manufacturer and consumer; efficiency became king—price, and therefore cost, were the primary competitive differences. With mass production came mass merchandizing, mass marketing, and mass advertising. The idea was to get the simplest message to the most people ("Tide Gets Clothes Clean!") We spent most of our time and money shouting the message. Conformity was accepted and even coveted. You could get your Model T Ford in any color you wanted, as long as it was black. In this phase of our national growth, marketing was not about conversation, it was about telling.

Since the 1960s, however, we've seen a trend back toward one-to-one marketing. It began with market segmentation and media fragmentation, each more specialized and targeted. The census and the advent of ZIP codes, area codes, and regional radio and television, and most of all, credit cards, made it possible to target specific audiences with products they would be more likely to want. Data collection became a profession, as every transaction from gasoline purchases to doctor visits helped classify and further segment markets. Then the World Wide Web became the worldwide switchboard, allowing people to talk to one another one-to-one again, in a virtual town square. In fact, some of the most popular Web sites are barter sites, where buyers and sellers "meet" and engage in an offer-and-ask ritual—the auction.

It happened very quickly; the shift is roughly complete. We have come nearly full circle . . . back to that candle-maker and his intimate understanding of his clients. We can once again "speak" to individuals. The Internet offers a route back to intimacy and customization. Ironic, isn't it, that the technology that can beget isolation can also lead us back to personal relationships with customers?

Just as the rules of barter didn't work in a mass-production environment, the rules of mass marketing won't work now. Internet customers have a lot more power. As Lester Wunderman of the Wunderman Cato Johnson advertising agency says, "The chant of the Industrial Revolution was that of the manufacturer who said, 'This is what I make, won't you please buy it?' The call of the Information Age is the consumer asking, 'This is what I want, won't you please make it?' "[1]

INCLUDING EMPLOYEES IN THE CONVERSATION

When you consider this change from mass merchandising to personal marketing from the standpoint of the employees of a company, it is even more profound. Merely making and pushing product is different from satisfying customers' needs. One requires only efficiency, the other requires relationship skills. Employees, once excluded by marketing professionals, now must be included again in the conversation.

For years, at Schwab, we refused to use what we called the "S word" (sell!) because it carried with it the baggage of the old-style broker who pushed the securities that were the most profitable to him, whether the customer needed them or not. We have always wanted to be known as a *service* brokerage, not a *selling* brokerage, and we have defined the difference between service and selling as relevance. If we call a customer who doesn't have any kids to announce a "college-saver" account, it is selling. If we call only people who have kids, parents who want to know about new ways to finance their children's college education—and who might have even asked us to call—then the call is service. This difference makes the call a relevant offer to the second customer, not to the first. Servicing customers' needs is consistent with the vision of the firm: "to provide the most useful and ethical financial services in the world." It is also consistent with our values of responsiveness and being worthy of our customers' trust. The difference between selling and servicing makes it possible for us to offer customers what they want, and to provide employees with a chance to serve.

True service requires a true conversation. The start of that conversation comes down to listening. It's something the leader must do, short term and long term, for the organization, for the employees—and for the benefit of the customer.

THE LEADER AS LISTENER

An important function of any leader, including the CEO, is to listen. This aspect of the job, that of chief listening officer, is not one to delegate completely. Philip Kotler, Northwestern University's dean of international marketing, makes the case that for a number of reasons particular to today's business atmosphere (segmentation and the Internet supplanting mass marketing, employee commitment becoming vital to success), and with most of the traditional experts stuck in ten-year-old technique, the CEO has to be the chief marketing officer.[2] I agree. Chuck is intimately involved in marketing for Schwab, and so am I. In fact, the leader of any business that includes marketing must be personally involved.

In the world of specialists, perspective is rare, and it takes a broad perspective to see multiple possibilities. My travels and contacts generally give me greater exposure to the changes in the field and the impact of new technology, and I know that marketing is the primary way that a company grows its franchise. Marketing direction clearly falls into that category I mentioned in the very first chapter . . . the critical role of the CEO includes involvement in the strategic decisions. A leader can't let strategic marketing decisions be made strictly by marketers, who can be blinded by their old habits, bad science, or their own insularity. Some professionals don't appreciate the interference of a generalist; consequently, in recent years, I've tried to teach rather than interfere. I have learned to apply some very specific principles to help bring us together. They are about how to listen, what to listen for, and who to listen to—about product, about price, and about the nature of the offers you make.

Listen to the Customer Through the Clatter

Each of us, whatever our professional role, hears the clamor of the consumer marketplace. Every day we're bombarded with thousands of messages created by professionals, each one designed to cut through the racket and to "target" our particular "sliver" of "demographic." We as consumers judge these messages, consider their merits, and sometimes take action. Most of us are pretty tough targets. We are on overload, we've seen it all, have become somewhat insulated from the noise, and we simply tune out. Many companies don't have the chance to even attract our attention.

So what do we buy? First, we buy what we need. Then, we buy what we *think* we need. Then, we buy what we want. Then, we buy what we *think* we want.

Remember, customers actually drive innovation and new product development. Any company that can discover what the customer really needs, create it quickly, and then let customers know about it effectively is going to be successful in the marketplace. But hearing what is needed is not as easy as it seems. Unfortunately, customers won't just walk up to the listening post and tell someone about the next blockbuster product or service. You have to help them get it out.

Listen for Frustrations and Dreams

A great paradox in marketing (and one of the most difficult skills to develop) is how you learn to listen to customers, to hear what they can't say directly, and then selectively choose what to believe and act on. I sometimes teach this skill as "selective listening." It's a way of listening and not listening at the same time. It is a very subtle ability . . . and I don't recommend you try it at home!

First, I ask customers about their experience with services like ours. Then I try to listen, beyond what they say, for frustrations and dreams. I almost pretend I'm on a hunt to hear what they *would* say if they had the necessary experience.

Most breakthrough products are the result of this kind of creative interpretation. Before the microwave was invented, a customer couldn't dream of saying, "Gee, wouldn't it be great if you could make an oven that excited the water molecules in food so fast that it cooked a whole meal in four minutes?" Instead, they'd say, "I'm so tired and hungry when I come home from work I can't wait forty-five minutes for the Stouffer's to cook in the oven. Wouldn't it be great if I could come home to a hot dinner?" They might cast about for a solution—ovens that turn on before they get home, local and reasonable catering services that deliver, and others. But with some greater understanding of what is possible, the inventive marketer can listen to what they want—a quick hot dinner—and come up with the solution that works.

So I love to ask customers to dream. In the process they'll tell me, "I wish it could be like this." They don't design the product—but they describe their problem and their ideal world where the problem disappears. It's up to the marketer to listen and to create something to overcome those frustrations, those disappointments, those objections of the customer.

We've had many successes, and avoided many disasters, from this kind of selective listening at Schwab. In fact, whenever we do market research—and we've been doing this for fifteen years—we ask people, "How important is having a local branch office?" It actually scores fairly low, maybe seventh or eighth on a customer's typical wish list. Yet every time we open a local office we double the new business we get in that community. As of this writing, we have more than three hundred such offices, and we are planning more, despite the customers' lukewarm direct response in a market-research setting.

Our success with local offices particularly flies in the face of conventional Internet wisdom. This wisdom suggests that price is king—we should minimize fixed costs and have no respect for any distribution channel other than electronic. Interestingly enough, even as we are doing 80 percent of our transactions electronically, we are opening 70 percent of our new accounts face to face in branch offices.

Why would branches still be important? Well, when you ask people, "How important is service?" or "What are your biggest frustrations?" they'll talk about Web sites that are confusing or don't work, or about dealing with people over an 800 number. They'll talk about their fear of having a problem and nobody to resolve it, and that they don't really know who they're doing business with. In many ways the customer doesn't even understand, the local office becomes a security blanket to obviate these concerns. They can't or won't articulate these needs, and the words "branch office" don't trigger the response. Nonetheless, that local human presence is important to many people. If we only listened to the words, we would never open local offices. It's when we listen to fears and frustrations that the need becomes obvious.

The mini-van, the hottest-selling category of new cars in three decades, followed a similar route. It was turned down by Ford, because no one ever said directly, "I want a van that drives like a car." But the designer heard the frustration of many soccer moms, who complained about the dirt in their sedans, who needed more room, and who didn't want to drive what felt like a truck, and Chrysler listened to the designer.

Listen to the Data: Intuition Meets Science

Even when the customers' message is clear, it doesn't point directly to breakthrough products. How could it? It's impossible to ask questions directly about something that hasn't been invented. The product has to come from using intuition on the data, not the data itself. So marketers who skew questions in a focus group, asking a predetermined audience about a preconceived product, will learn very little. The best answers are not available only from the science of market research. The science has to be interpreted by a human being in the real world.

Years ago, I wanted to develop a product that would offer a higher rate of interest to Schwab customers if they left more money in their account. It was sort of a premier version of a product we had, called the Schwab-One Account—and I wanted to call it Schwab-One Gold. I had marketers who didn't think that this was a very good idea, but finally they agreed to do some market research and see the reactions of customers. They came back to report to me that customers said they would *not* bring us significantly more money if we offered a .25 or even .40 percentage point higher rate of return.

I just knew that could not be true. I asked to see the market research notes, and saw that focus group criteria specified people who had at least $10,000 portfolios. Set a minimum of $10,000, and what kind of people do you get? You typically get a roomful of people with right around $10,000. It's easier to get people with less money to participate in a focus group because there are more of them, and the $100 honorarium they receive motivates them to show up. Result: the room gets filled up close to the minimum standard. I knew this was not really the target market for the product I had in mind, so I swallowed hard, applied my intuition, and went forward.

We did create a higher-yielding money market fund, which did pay a .40 percent higher rate, required a $25,000 minimum investment in the fund, and guess what happened? It's been the fastest-growing money-market fund at our company. Within several years, we had more than $10 billion in that fund. In many ways, the decision to go ahead was like the decision on the mini-van. I knew that this idea would work in spite of the fact that we had failed to prove it with the science. Occasionally, intuition has to override the conclusion of the data.

Listen to Each Person: Make a Few People Ecstatic

In the generation of mass merchandising, ideas had to be right for a very large audience, or the product failed. (Edsel, anyone?) But today's manufacturing systems are much more flexible, and for information products, the Web gives nearly infinite flexibility. Offers can be changed overnight and customized for individual delivery. Accordingly, in virtually any research project, I'd rather have 10 percent of the population rate a product idea as "fantastic" than have 50 percent of the population rate a product idea as "good." After all, there's so much clutter and competition out there that if a lot of people think you're pretty good—who cares? It's better that a small segment thinks you're great, because now, in this environment, you have a good chance to reach and dominate a series of sliver markets.

Unfortunately, the real world of market research is still skewed toward the mass market. Too often, as with the Schwab-One Gold offer, the research company can't fill a room or a survey sample with the ideal demographic or psychographic, and a relatively mediocre sample population is gathered for the research. Ideas are presented. Two out of ten participants love the ideas but the other eight are uninspired. The product concept is tossed based on those eight.

Ten years ago, that would make absolute sense, but today, we have to treat those two excited people as a very good sign. We would ask, "It's a great idea for those two people, so what's different about those two?" Maybe they are the only two who are wealthy, or maybe they alone have very old parents or very young children, or kids in college. Or maybe they're the two in the room who are worried about losing their jobs, and thinking, "Boy, that IRA rollover, that pension rollover—I'm going to have to live on that." We have to recognize that there are two people in the room that really love this product and find out why. That little extra research will create a profitable segment.

Naturally, the Internet makes it easier to find those niches, as we can discover preferences in virtual segments around the world. The critical factor is our willingness to respond to small segments rather than to continue to expect mass market to respond to what we have. When Bob Lutz, president of Chrysler, decided it was time to redesign the Dodge Ram truck line, he told his research team, "I want something radical. Something exciting. We have three percent of the truck market now, so I don't care if you come up with something that ninety-five percent of the people absolutely hate, as long as five percent absolutely love it. Build me something that elicits a strong reaction and we'll increase market share."[3] This is why you see Dodge Rams (and competitors' copies) on the road today that reflect the big-rig look of Peterbilts and Kenworths. Dodge tripled its truck market share in ten years. A focus group or survey mentality that looks for averages rather than spikes will filter out the exciting opportunities around the edges, the super-successful niches like this one, that made *Dodge Truck* mean something again.

Listen for the Right Price: Balance Research and Reality

Even before the advent of e-commerce, pricing presented the most difficult and the most important part of marketing. Now, at least in this interim, the road rules of e-commerce suggest that "free" is the right opening price for products and services being marketed on the Internet. The notion is that the Web can lead to geometric growth rates and "he who has the market share will win" when the dust settles and the inevitable shakeout comes. This rationale has turned all the conventions upside down. In our industry, we see public companies pricing at rates that continue to yield losses at the bottom line, and it is tempting to follow their example, to try to gain market share with the blunt instrument of low price. Fortunately, in the longer run people expect to pay for value. Bizrate.com, a Los Angeles company, tracks customer satisfaction in e-commerce. For the first quarter of 1999, the level and quality of customer service was the top factor in determining whether a customer returned to a particular merchant, beating out on-time delivery and, yes, price.[4]

Unfortunately, research in a laboratory environment will not determine what people will actually pay for a product. There are no processes, short of actual testing, that will even present the question that the customer actually faces at the time of his decision to buy or not to buy. When the facilitator asks, "What is this worth?" respondents tend to have notions of fairness or reasonableness. If the facilitator asks, "Is this worth $10?" a respondent might say, "Yes." If the question is, "Would you buy this for $10?" the response might again be, "Yes." But put that same respondent in a store, walking down the aisle with $50 in his pocket, not being asked direct questions, trying to compare the marginal utility of alternative purchases. Now ask him, "Would you buy this product?" The question now isn't, "Is it worth

$10?" It becomes, "Is this worth more to you than that other thing that costs $10?" I haven't learned any way to discover the right answer except to see how real people behave when they make real choices. Simulations and other predictive models can point us in the correct direction and be quite useful, but there's no substitute for market testing.

For the same reasons, I believe in testing at different levels at the same time. The single thing that has surprised me most in my fifteen years at Schwab has been the extent of elasticity of demand for our services. It's amazing how often thoughtfully and carefully reducing price can yield faster growth, greater profits, and happier customers. Not constantly testing for price is a missed opportunity in business.

So these are ways that I've learned to listen, critically and openly, to what people are saying and not saying. I've learned that people's dreams are more valuable than their experience, and their frustrations are more important than their current satisfaction. I've learned that although analysis is valuable, intuition makes the difference between marginal success and a spectacular offer. I've learned that people will pay for value that they perceive in the real world of choices, not in the laboratory of artificial questions. Finally, I've learned that surveys and focus groups are no substitutes for the human ear attached to a human body with a brain and the wonderful sense of intuition that hears intention rather than mere words. Personal preferences are still discovered primarily with personal involvement.

Knowing that we apply these rules of listening gives everyone in the company a great deal of confidence that we are trying to improve their chances of serving customers better. It also lets them know, once again, that what they hear from customers is valuable, what they solicit from customers can be used. By listening so carefully, we are saying to employees, "We want to do the best thing for those we serve by *their* standards, not by the standards of a marketing company." By pricing for value, we are offering our customers more service per dollar than they can get anywhere else. These methods build on our joint commitment to serve, and reinforce our cultural promises of fairness and responsiveness.

With good execution, our methods tell us what the customer needs from us, and our testing allows us to build these products and price them to deliver on our promise. The next challenge is to communicate the offer to everyone, employees and customers, in a way that is compelling. How?

STRATEGIC MARKETING: CONGRUENCE OF MESSAGE, VALUES, AND SERVICE DELIVERY

"Offer customers what they want" is substantially different from the definition of marketing that I first learned on the job. That first definition appeared to be "do creative things so that people notice you." It took a few years of experience, some bad, some good, to broaden my perspective. I was not a marketing student in business school, so I came to the practice of marketing unburdened, as they say, by facts. I learned my own lessons through extensively reading the works of recognized experts, by trial and error, and then through applying some relatively simple disciplines.

I first came to marketing during my days at Citibank, kind of "graduating" from the quantitative side of finance and operations. I immediately felt totally out of my element; in fact, I was mystified. I would go home at night and think, "I never saw a field so full of hot air." We hired consultants with highfalutin concepts and campaigns, and we'd get excited and spend money and never get measured! This was remarkable to me. I came from production, where people measured everything and gave me minimal budgets; where I saved and squeezed every dollar to try to create a positive result. And here was marketing—a world of $30,000 photographs, a world of "we're going to go on this shoot, we're going to print this four-color brochure."

This was quite an education, and I just kept reading and studying and observing in order to learn more. I kept quiet, observing and following instructions of the marketing experts at the bank. I was told often that I shouldn't worry, that sooner or later I would get it. This admonition was especially loud when I asked the sort of innocent questions that an operating officer would typically ask:

- Why were we spending so much money on expensive production of disposable literature?
- Why were our advertising headlines cute and obscure?
- Why were our name and phone number buried in the ads?

These questions came from my operating discipline and my reading. Even today my marketing heroes remain John Caples and the late David Ogilvy—tough, old-world practitioners who respected the creative but demanded measurable results. Almost the day I started at Schwab as head of marketing, Chuck handed me Caples's classic *Tested Advertising Methods* and said, "Read this. It is my bible on advertising." I knew I was in the right place.

One of my favorite passages on marketing comes from Caples: "The most difficult things to discover in the study of selling are facts." His advice: "Test everything. Doubt everything. Be interested in theories, but don't spend a large sum of money on a theory without spending a little money to test it first."[5] And to paraphrase Ogilvy: The whole point of marketing is to bring in customers. So no matter how pretty or clever, it ain't creative if it doesn't do that.[6] These two comments net to *Test your theories in the field, and measure their accuracy only by results.*

Given this bias for measurement and results, I wasn't too tolerant at Citi and Shearson when I heard the answers to my impertinent questions, or rather the *lack* of answers, and I formed an opinion that while there was a specific science to marketing, very few professional marketers really wanted to spend time in the science. Many of them wanted to spend time doing what they enjoyed, which was largely creative or theoretical. I became rather jaded about most of the outside marketing consulting I bought and paid for. I formed my own ideas about what was important.

After a few months, I found myself advocating that marketing was not just a creative sales nicety but a central strategic concern—a discipline that could and must be measured. I've seen this idea become increasingly important until today, in our Internet-driven age, it is arguably the central strategic concern, not just outside the company, but within. That's because of the need for alignment and integration of the following:

- Product offerings with customer desires
- Product offerings with employee capability to deliver
- Product offerings with brand attributes
- Advertised brand attributes with practiced values of the company (and of the employees)
- Brand attributes with customer experience
- Internal messages with external messages

Congruence among these elements supports the integrity of the company, and thereby enhances its ability to build satisfaction and loyalty, inside and out. Effective marketing strategy and execution are fundamental to this alignment. To be successful in today's environment of customer power, marketing cannot be measured only by budget, creativity, and reach. It has to be measured by its effectiveness in actually bringing in and keeping individual customers, and by its effectiveness in representing the employees' desire to serve rather than sell. We have to measure our success by the extent to which it helped us accomplish all of these alignments in today's world, a world that is, without doubt, being shaped by the Internet.

In just about any business, I believe that the Internet will be a great channel of marketing—for those who insist on fundamental congruence of messages and action with customers and employees alike. I'll try to offer some specific recommendations, keeping three questions in mind:

- How can we make sure that our messages to the customers also inspire employees?
- How do we make our offers match what the customers want?
- What messages are effective to convey those offers in a way that brings customers in?

INSPIRING EMPLOYEES WITH MARKETING

At Schwab we pay a lot of attention to how employees feel about every offer we make. While headquarters experts might think the offer makes absolute fiscal and market sense and that it fits with our values, we only know for sure when employees on the front line of our company hear the feedback directly from customers. We have cardinal rules about what we sell, and most of these measurements have to do with the way we feel personally about the offer.

We ask some tough questions: Would we buy this ourselves? Do we believe in this product? Would we recommend this product to our family? Would we recommend this product to our neighbors (not at a special price, but at the price we sell it to the public)? Are we proud of what we offer? Is it a good offer in the marketplace given what our competitors are offering or might offer?

In Chapter Five, I talked about altering a decision on account fees because some of the employees could not answer some of these questions in the affirmative. In fact, many of our innovations have come because the industry as a whole has not asked these questions on a regular basis. We were one of the first firms to offer "price improvement" for orders—to attempt to find prices better than those currently quoted. Now the industry does this as a matter of regulation. Our offer of the "No-annual-fee IRA" was stimulated by a complaint that charging a fee to open an account was "like a restaurant charging a fee for sitting down, even before the customer saw a menu." We entered the term life insurance business because we felt there was an opportunity to offer customers substantially better rates than the standards in the industry. We are constantly looking for opportunities like these, in parts of our industry where traditional firms are, through the habit of incumbency, taking advantage of customers. We see these opportunities because we are looking for offers that express our values as a company.

The result of this discipline is clarity to employees that we intend to serve, not sell. They reflect that spirit in their own work . . . just the result we want. So the content of the offer is critical. The way in which we offer it also reflects our values. The standard media invite prospects to read or listen. As we all know, outbound cold calling can be intrusive at best and absolutely offensive at worst. We just don't do it. Instead, we now can use a magnificent tool for directing an offer: the Internet itself.

WHAT CUSTOMERS WANT: SPEAKING TO AN AUDIENCE OF ONE

E-mail is a marketer's dream. It provides an opportunity to send out an immediately deliverable, almost infinitely customizable, targeted message that costs next to nothing. It is like being able to write a full-page ad in each customer's favorite newspaper, aimed only at them. Better still, to respond, a customer doesn't have to pick up a phone or mail a letter. They merely have to click on the URL. It doesn't get any better than that.

It would seem ideal—especially for the service aspect of the business. The customer can read the e-mail message at will; the sender doesn't have to worry about interrupting dinner with a phone call. Best of all, the e-mail is personalized, and by assimilating the data from direct response, we know exactly, or at least have a reasonable approximation as to what this customer wants or needs. This type of targeted e-mail is a service, not a sell.

As always, with the dream comes the nightmare. The problem with e-mail is rooted in its benefits. Because it's such an easy channel to use, marketers use its mass marketing ability rather than its customization ability by inundating e-mail in-boxes with "spam"—messages that are not targeted very well and are therefore irrelevant in many cases and unwelcome in most. This may not cost much in dollars but in sending mass mail, a company makes *all* its messages, relevant or not, unwelcome. At worst, this practice infuriates customers, invites government regulation of the channel, and may ultimately result in the legitimate and service-oriented messages being lost in the clutter or rejected by customers.

Success in e-mail marketing will be forged from the right combination of data mining, segmentation, and customization. In the course of sorting out this remarkable channel, public policymakers will surely devise ways of letting consumers refuse messages. Companies that remember the distinction between sales and service will no doubt be more welcome than those who don't. E-mail needs to be used in combination with other channels, and it needs to answer the same basic questions that a marketer always faces. What's for sale, and who is selling it?

MARKETING WITH MEANING—BRINGING IN CUSTOMERS

Recently, *Business Week* ran a story called, "Great Ad! What's It For?"[7] That headline pretty much sums up my early opinion of the field. Most ads just don't work, literally!

On any given day, pick up the *New York Times* or the *Wall Street Journal* and read the ads with a critical eye. How many make it hard to find the name of the company being promoted? The fact is, 95 percent of readers look only at the headline, so to determine what is a good ad, just ask yourself if the headlines stand alone and communicate a compelling message. "Schwab Makes It Easy to Buy Mutual Funds" is clear, simple, not terribly arresting, and certainly not cute. But it makes a point for those who are considering a mutual fund, and gives them a reason to read on. If, by the time they're done, they've skimmed the sub-headlines, looked at the chart, and considered the call to action, this ad has done its job. If the ad's well-constructed, the reader believes Schwab is offering a "unique selling proposition" (a package of benefits they could not get anywhere else) that suggests we're the best place on earth to buy funds, and the reader should respond right now by calling our 800 number, visiting our Web site, or going to a branch office for a face-to-face meeting.

Still, most ad agencies and almost all ad agency executives I know hate working on ads like this: They're boring, but they work because of the attention to advertising disciplines and the inclusion of the unique selling proposition—the USP. This concept, as old as the first marketing book ever written, is still the guidepost for an effective ad. The USP makes it clear to everyone, employees included, why the customer should respond to the ad. While terribly creative ads that have whimsical meaning might be stimulating to professionals, they are boring to potential customers. Customers need the USP to move them to action.

Creative content can be wonderful, and certainly there are many vocal champions for it (including most of the industry awards). My own voice will speak much more in defense of the science of advertising and marketing rather than the creative side. That's why at Schwab we have maintained a rigorous intellectual honesty about our marketing, from our first focus group to product development to advertising. We want the customers to tell us what they want (as much as they can), we want to develop whatever that is, and then we want to communicate it to them clearly, so that they know exactly what they are getting.

Because offer advertising is an area full of snake oil, and because I like cute and ineffective advertising as well as the next person (it can be wildly entertaining), I've made a top-ten list of rules of good advertising that I've included in Appendix C. I apply these ten rules when I'm evaluating our own offer advertising or someone else's. Some are specifically print and some TV, some apply to both. Many apply to the Internet. They are simple, sure, effective, and largely ignored by others. They may not help you win creative awards but you can comfort yourself with sales increases. I include them, knowing they are detailed, but hoping that if you see them in the context of this broader topic, they may save you some time and effort learning them through experience.

NAME VERSUS BRAND, HYPE VERSUS EXECUTION

There is no question that established companies have to leverage the Internet. But the questions for those of us in established businesses have to do with the rules of performance, marketing, and advertising in this new Internet climate. Will offers, messages, brands, and the traditional disciplines of strategic marketing fall to a new set of axioms in the new economy . . . axioms based only on banners and buttons in cyberspace? Or will the Internet serve as a super tool to apply the established rules, and a penalizer for those who don't practice with discipline or who fail to build the culture and infrastructure to assure they can meet the expectations created by the cleverly crafted mass messages of their marketing staffs and consultants? I believe it is the latter.

Shopping.com is a case in point. This company opened its virtual doors as a discounter in 1998, and got a rush of orders at Christmas. It could not handle the volume, and in the words of one reporter, "The results were quick and harsh."[8] So harsh that the local Better Business Bureau received nearly three hundred complaints.

Compaq Computer bought the fledgling company after Christmas, and immediately offered $250 gift certificates to anyone who had filed a complaint, instituting a program that made it clear to customers that service was the primary goal. Compaq later sold the unit after restoring some credibility to it. This experience, and several hundred like it, shows that "customers lured online with low prices and one-click ordering still demand the same level of service as they do in the real world."[9]

The experience of Shopping.com suggests that marketing has to be practiced, more than ever, as part of a system of listening, building, and delivery. It requires the application of some fundamentals that have nothing to do with the medium itself, but because of its relatively low cost and flexibility, the Internet will reward the good practitioner even more richly than did the media of the past.

Now comes the hardest and most rewarding part of passion-driven growth: *delivering* on the offer. As we do, we are building our reputation one experience at a time. We can eventually convert that reputation into a promise that is broader than any one offer. It is the brand, the family name. This broad guarantee of character is not made just to the customer, any more than a wedding vow is made only to the wedding guests. The promise is made to ourselves and to one another. The way we keep it ultimately determines our fate—and our legacy.

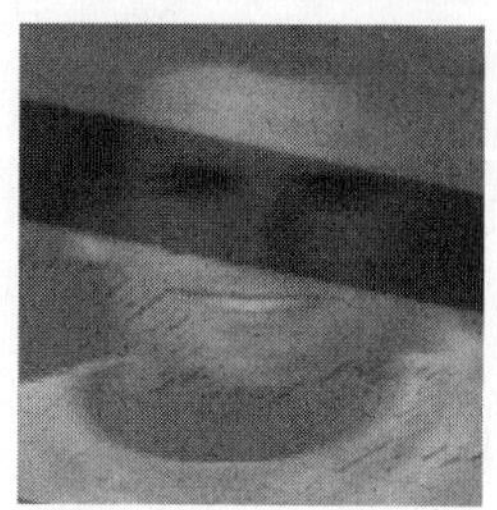

FROM MARKETING TO BRAND AND CUSTOMER EXPERIENCE

As Dave emphasized, marketing is conversation, and for the leader, that conversation is mostly listening to both customers and employees. It is listening to what is said—and what is not said—to filter through the hubbub and find what is needed. If we do that right, then creating the products and services that people really need and that fit with the values of the firm follows naturally. Then we can communicate our offer in a way that is clear to customers and that conveys the pride of employees. Thanks to the changes that the Internet has brought, we can target the message with astounding accuracy to ensure its relevance. Used in this way, as a virtual town marketplace, the Internet can be enormously useful for business and consumer alike. But it's new—and there is much to learn about what using it well really means. For now, we can strategically add e-mail to our mix of direct mail, print, television, and radio to reach just the right audience at the just the right time.

In addition to enhancing our listening ability, the Internet has produced a climate where small newcomers can compete with huge established firms in another dimension of marketing and advertising—the volume of messages. At the beginning of the Internet growth curve, Amazon.com outspent Barnes & Noble for two years, E*Trade spent more than Merrill Lynch or Smith Barney, and Priceline.com outspent American Express Travel. These new companies believed that name recognition would be critical to lure the second wave of Internet users, those who were not as technologically savvy and who might be wary of doing business electronically with unknown companies. In fact, a few of these companies went public in part to take advantage of the buzz around their stock—yet another way to push their name into the public's awareness.

Barriers to entry had never been lower, so a name-recognition war was inevitable. Because the brokerage business enjoys so much Internet-driven leverage, it was a natural to lead the way in this dynamic. Indeed, at this writing, a multitude of firms are going like crazy in the evolving on-line brokerage market. I suspect that other industries will evolve in a similar fashion. But volume of message and name recognition is not enough to assure success. The key is brand building.

A company's brand is the symbol of promises and expectations. Dave has made the distinction between building name recognition through "shouting," and building *brand* through providing service over time consistent with the company's promises. He has also frequently made the distinction between words and music, show and substance, advertised and actual—the image and the authentic of the business world. We have tried to stress the importance of values as the basis for a company's treatment of everyone, not just customers, but every stakeholder in the enterprise. We both feel that it is impossible to separate what happens for the customer from what happens for everyone else. Any enterprise that exploits employees to run after every customer whim will implode. Likewise, companies that lose their focus on serving customer needs will become irrelevant. How then can we keep everyone focused on providing the best experience in the most efficient way?

"Customer service," "the customer experience," "customer-focus," "customer-driven"—all these phrases describe the most important driver of business success. Indeed, starting out, any business is based on a perceived customer need. After all, that's what creates the opportunity to open the doors and start marketing. Filling that need is the first imperative for the enterprise and for those in it.

After thirty years of giving advice on this subject and offering services through my own business, I am still left with some central questions. Just what is the experience that the customer is after? What is it that we find most valuable? What is symbol and what is real? Without critical thinking we could continue blindly down a conventional path. In filling the customers' need, we will be rewarded with money and in some cases stock in the company. We could then easily decide that these symbols, which we ultimately exchange for other material goods and nonmaterial pleasures, are the desired result of the whole process of business. This is conventional wisdom, questioned only by philosophers.

Certainly, business has evolved in a way that the idea of customer service has been a tactic, not a purpose. Customer service is not considered the reason for the existence of a profit-making business, and only a softheaded tree-hugging spiritual junkie would suggest that customer service is the only aspect of a business that has meaning in itself. We assume that making money is the purpose of commerce, and customer service is the way we get it.

Surely, we can't stay in business without making a profit; without offering some service that the customer is willing to exchange value for. But is the money the desired result—or symbolic of the desired result? I think it is the latter, and from time to time, I am reminded of the force of this point.

Just recently, I was struck by a story told in a documentary about the life of Jalaluddin Rumi, a thirteenth-century Persian poet. To illustrate the power of Rumi's life, one of the narrators allegorically told of a winner of the Nobel prize who was accepting the coveted award for his life's work and was told by the presenter that the prize was a million dollars. The winner said, "Oh, that's very nice, but I was hoping for love." I laughed out loud until I thought about it. It was, as they say, "too true to be funny."

The very next day, I was sent a story by someone at Schwab, a story that the sender said reminded him of the ethic of the company.

> Let your imagination put you in a grandstand at the Seattle version of the Special Olympics. There are nine contestants, all physically or mentally disabled, assembled at the starting line for the 100-yard dash. At the gun, they all start out, not exactly in a dash, but with a relish to run the race to the finish and win. All, that is, except one boy who stumbles on the asphalt, tumbles over a couple of times, and begins to cry. The other eight hear the boy cry. They slow down and look back. They all turn around and go back . . . every one of them. As you watch, one girl with Down's syndrome bends down and kisses him. You hear her say, "This will make it better." All nine link arms and walk across the finish line together. Everyone in the stadium, including you, stands up, and the cheering goes on for several minutes.
>
> People who were actually there are still telling the story, four years later. Why? Because deep down we know this one thing: what matters in this life is more than winning for ourselves. What truly matters in this life is helping others win, even if it means changing our own course.

For any but the most cynical, this story is inspiring. This is a context where only service counts. Love speaks loudly here as the sole motivator . . . so loudly that it can't be ignored, it has to be cheered. Giving and receiving this kind of selfless service has to be acknowledged as fundamental to what we want.

Whenever I reflect on the most important times of my life, the most rewarding events, the times when I was most moved, the most valuable times, I invariably focus on the instances when I could most completely express gratitude and its other name, love. These were also times when I was in the greatest service to others, without regard to my own welfare.

OK, enough stories, let's get down to sheer opinion. I don't think that loyalty of customers or employees is dead, as many pundits are claiming, and I think there are companies out here that prove that it isn't dead. Throughout this book, Dave and I have offered stories of extraordinary service to customers, of decisions taken that support values, of defining moments that show businesses as expressions of what really matters. Of all the organizations I have served in thirty years of business, Schwab is clearly the most service-driven. Customer service is Chuck Schwab's passion, indisputably so. When others are worried about competitors' actions, he is focused on what Schwab can do that is in the customers' best interest. When others fret about regulations, he is foursquare behind changes in the industry that can benefit consumers, even when it means that the company has to change the way it does business.

Dave is a fifteen-year disciple of this frame of mind, although he practiced it for many years before. Most of the people who work in the organization develop this mind-set or they leave. Lest you conclude that the frame of mind only works in large-margin businesses in raging bull stock markets, consider Home Depot and Wal-Mart, Whole Foods and Gap. They have it too. In these companies, that attitude of service extends not just to customers, but in large part, to their colleagues in the company as well.

This is not an accident. We began by describing the importance of culture building, and defined the elements of culture as a language, a shared purpose, a set of values, and the actions that make the values real. Everything else we described or argued for supports the importance of that foundation of values expressed through action. If the culture is the foundation, then the pinnacle is the experience of the customer and the employee when they benefit from the culture. Yes, the customer *and* the employee. The customer experience *is* the employee experience. It can be no different. We know that—that's why we smile on the telephone even when no one can see us. We transmit our passion in subtle ways every time we relate to someone else.

And the subtleties are important. There were many upsets during the filming of the movie classic *Gone With the Wind*, but none more legendary than the flap created over the expenditures for the great ballroom scene. The film was already over budget when the producer, David Selznick, got a bill authorized for payment by director Victor Fleming for thousands of dollars' worth of silk petticoats for the ballroom scene. Familiar with the shooting angles, Selznick was reportedly furious, and went ranting to Fleming. "Silk petticoats!" he screamed, "The audience won't even be able to see the petticoats. All of the shots are above the waist!"

"Yes, the shots are above the waist," admitted Fleming, "But the audience will see the silk in the eyes of the dancers."

He was right. For the purposes of the camera, the petticoats could well have been cotton. But not for the purposes of the customer experience. Watch the movie and you'll see that the radiance of dancing in silk shines out of the dancers' eyes, through the lens, and into the audience's imagination and heart.

So it is with any business in this new world of commitment, service, and innovation. We want to spend our money on things that the customer can see, but many times, spending on the deliverer of the service, the employee, creates the spark that makes a big difference in what the customer actually experiences. The customer experience is not just the product or service, and it isn't limited to the expertise of the company's employees. The customer experience is also the look in the eyes, the sound of the voice, the dedication in the action of every single person that they come into contact with. The customer experience is the whole gestalt, the objective and the subjective. The sum of that experience is the sum of a business's brand.

Name recognition is grounded in media. Brand building is grounded in the day-to-day work of people who care. Building brand is a step-by-step, moment-by-moment process of service. In this rapidly accelerating environment, if a company ignores the technology of speed, it may well lose a great deal to those who wish to use the Net's power to extend possibilities and convenience. But I believe if a company limits itself to the Internet, it will surely limit the experience of its own employees and its customers; they will be at least once-removed from one another.

If the premise of this book is correct, then filling a need is not just the way to make money, it is the way to create commitment to any organization that has such a purpose. If we are correct, then the desire to serve others is a greater motivator than the desire to beat the competitor. And if these two ideas are right, then playing collaboratively on a team, helping others be as good as they can be, is a more desirable state to most people than competing with others within the organization for position and power. That slight shift in thinking can make the difference between a passionate group of people, working together to build a collective brand and accomplish something greater than any one of them could, and a group of individuals out for themselves, touting "Brand Me" only as a way of selling themselves to the highest bidder.

Giving people what they want and letting them know about it. That's what builds brand, and that's what builds loyalty. Let's see how it works.

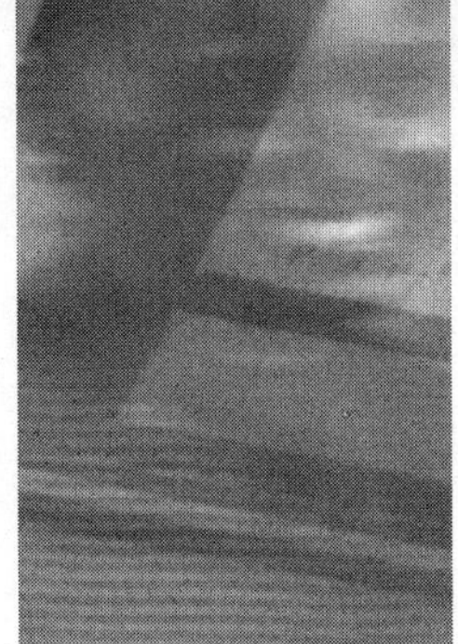

TEN

BRAND AND CUSTOMER EXPERIENCE: THE HEART OF A PASSION-DRIVEN BUSINESS

The ultimate goal of marketing is to make sales through compelling offers, but when specific offers are wrapped in a brand, their success is not dependent only on a single transaction. The brand is a tangible trust that transcends and often outlives any particular product. Just as offspring of a reputable family are assumed trustworthy until proven otherwise, offers from a trusted brand are assumed to carry the attributes of the brand. We all know what to expect from Starbucks or Tiffany, because we have experienced the quality and service over time. If either of these stores offered a new product, we would assume the same quality and attributes that we had experienced before. Brand assures some level of consistency. It is, as Terry suggests, a shorthand statement of expectation and promise.

In the last chapter, I discussed how specific offers have to be consistent with the values of the firm and the conviction of the people who are going to make the offers real to the public. The unique selling proposition also has to be clear, so that prospects and customers can make a clear choice. This is a winning formula for specific offers, and it was the only way that Schwab advertised until we began to recognize the value of the brand itself in the late 1980s and early 1990s.

BUILDING THE BRAND

Once we had mastered the skills of transaction processing and had lost a bit of our "rebel" status, we began to realize the real potential of our company. The customer experience in the old world of investing was often so bad that small improvements made a big difference. Now we began to realize that we could offer many more services under the same umbrella of trust and integrity. The customer experience was actually different at Schwab, not just because customers had to make decisions for themselves, but because there was a real commitment to what we used to call "the three No's": no conflict of interest, no sales pressure, and no overpromising. Some would say these are the bases of treating customers with respect. We felt so and still do.

In this chapter, I'd like to look at what brand really is, and try to differentiate it from well-recognized names and trademarks. Then I'd like to suggest some new thoughts about the customer experience of Internet companies, and show how a company can integrate the Internet, using its capability to build loyalty in all its stakeholders.

First, some history. In the first ten years of its existence, Schwab established itself, through its individual offers and its skill at transaction processing, as a company that was focused on providing fast, accurate transactions and quotes to customers. Those skills would have been enough to grow a healthy company for some time, but there was more to Schwab than fast and accurate transactions. Chuck was very public about his desire to provide access to markets to everyone, not just the privileged few, so customers trusted him for a fair deal. Employees, too, were cognizant of the boss's intention, to provide not just a volume of services, but "useful and ethical services."

Chuck had appeared in our print ads since the 1970s. Then, in the mid-1980s, after more than fifteen years of being in business, we decided to feature Chuck on TV and we began to advertise who we were as well as what we did. It was time to start leveraging the attributes of the company itself, attributes that were more than just talk, more than product offerings, and more than skill, although all three of these were important components. As I've come to see over time, brand serves three distinct functions relating to culture, family name, and focus—each of them important.

Brand as a Symbol of the Culture

In Chapter Two, I spoke of the importance of image in sustaining culture. A brand—the mark itself—is vested with the values of the community it represents, such that it is a shorthand for the expectations of behavior within that community. The American flag is a brand; people know that it represents freedom and democracy, and when we display the flag and hear the national anthem, we often actually experience the feelings that those values represent. When immigrants come to the United States, they have expectations about how they will be treated and what opportunity they will enjoy, all based on the brand.

Companies, likewise, try to endow their brand symbol with the cultural attributes that will inspire the loyalty of all of their constituents. Lexus immediately comes to mind as a company whose brand of quality service has been built more by the firm's culture than by advertising.

Brand as the Family Name

From the employees' point of view, the brand is also the symbol of their own psychic investment in the company . . . it is the family name. The following e-mail message to me is typical: "Dave: I was in France for a short vacation last week and was asked by several people if Charles Schwab was going to open any offices in France. (They seem eager to have us.) Then on the plane back, a charming retired school teacher from Manchester, UK, told me how much she loves us. I guess my Schwab shirt is a giveaway!"

IBM employees are "IBMers," PeopleSoft employees are "People-People." The people at our company refer to themselves as "Schwabies," like a very close-knit and focused family. There is an informal social structure and a camaraderie that offer the same sense of sanctuary as a house full of happy relatives. The brand identifies acceptable and unacceptable behavior, both in dealing with one another and in dealing with other stakeholders.

Brand as the Primary Focus of the Firm

Brand as the focus is the most important aspect of brand and one that is frequently misunderstood. I know, because I have experienced firsthand the difficulties of getting it right. It is just too easy to define the focus of a company as the product or service that the company offers. People don't expect Sears to sell BMWs, and they don't expect BMW to sell lawnmowers. So brands can create limits to the product or service line.

This limitation can be a blessing and a curse. By the mid-1990s, the Schwab brand was the second best known in our industry behind Merrill Lynch. In fact, when a random sampling of investors were asked in a research study where they would open an account if they were going to move their assets to a different firm, Schwab was mentioned more often than any other company. In other words, our prospects knew the brand, they liked what we stood for, but they also still thought of us as "America's Largest Discount Broker." At the same time, our customers were growing their assets with us, and because they too thought of us simply as a "discount broker," many of them were moving at least part of their money to other companies that had a "full-service" reputation for providing services that we offered, but that they assumed would not be available from a "discounter." For example, our research showed that these customers felt they needed more advice and help in deciding how to invest their money. I spoke briefly about this in Chapter Six, as we had to reexamine the entire basis for our refusal to give advice. We realized that we had not offered advice because we had equated it with the kind of self-serving, conflict-ridden practice that has been so prevalent within our industry. It wasn't until our customers started to move some of their assets that we realized that they would *like* us to give advice as well—advice without conflict, advice with integrity.

By then, however, we had a well-established brand that meant, in part, "transactions-only." (You, the investor, make the decision, and we will help you execute it.) We had to redefine the brand from "no advice and no help at Schwab" to "no conflict of interest and a lot of help at Schwab" and at the same time, infuse our own employees with the idea that we are the only company capable of reinventing full-service brokerage into something closer to what customers want. We had to communicate this both externally and internally in a way that defeated the old confines of the brand and empowered the new attributes of the brand.

As of this writing, we have achieved more success internally than externally in communicating this new message. We are just beginning to be known externally for who we are becoming as we have to overcome the past perceptions people have of discount brokers as a whole, and Schwab in particular. VisionQuest was enormously helpful internally, and a strong public relations and advertising campaign helped with customers and prospects. We are increasingly being seen as a high-integrity investment services company that can and will provide objective help and advice and a full range of investment services to help customers get the best access possible to markets. This is really hard work and the progress is slower than we would like, but we know that the brand is built, not merely advertised. As we perform, the brand will strengthen and shift until the old meaning is replaced.

Here's the point: *When a company confuses brand attributes with company products, it misses the essence of the brand.* It fails to identify the substance and instead promotes the symbol. We want the essence of our brand to be trustworthiness and the promise of a good experience for the customer. Similarly, IBM, for years, advertised with just the brand and the subtitle, "IBM Means Service." Then the company's practice made the brand mean "IBM Means Mainframes." (Great in the 1970s, not so great in the early 1990s.) If Cadillac means "luxury gas-guzzler," then Cadillac is out of business during an oil crisis, or whenever consumer attitudes turn toward more economy in driving. If Nike means "running shoes," then other sports would go wanting for the spirit of the swoosh, and there would be no hats, watches, or shirts to symbolize potential customers' interest in being fit and competitive. Conversely, when a company is able to build the brand around its dedication to the customer rather than its dedication to its product, it will last for a good long time. We have learned that lesson at Schwab, and even though we have many messages to deliver in our advertising, the primary focus of the firm continues to be the essence of the brand. The customer experience—or as Terry said, really giving the customers what they want—is central.

When an organization forgets the essence of the brand, it makes a tragic mistake, and in my view, takes a risk of losing what makes the brand a brand and not a slogan. Look at our current, at best confused, interpretation of the Olympic Rings. The Olympic Rings had been vested with meaning throughout their history: the best competition, for the love of the game, in the spirit of international peace and cooperation. We had expectations of the Olympic games based on that brand's being built over time. But recently, the brand was redefined as the product, and the product was "the best athletes in the world," rather than the "purity of competition without personal gain." Once big-money professional basketball, hockey, and tennis players were involved, the "product" may have improved—but the brand was at risk. Given the modern violations of ethics, I doubt that the Olympic Rings will ever again stand for the values that made the games unique and special within the entire spectrum of athletic competition.

Procter & Gamble was a dominating brand in American consumerism for decades. But recently, the president of P&G's North American operation acknowledged that his company had forgotten that fundamental of brand management. "We lost focus," he said, "and drifted like everyone else, into practices which not only did not reinforce brand loyalty—they created disloyalty. We confused customers with endless line [product] extensions and ended up trying to buy the loyalty of brand switchers with promotions and complicated trade deals. We forgot rule one: Focus only on the consumer—not on competitors, and certainly not on senior management."[1]

These examples and Terry's commentary really put the discussion on the right level. In his story of the Special Olympics, he makes the case that we all have the very human impulse to serve. But when "us" becomes a profit-based company and "them" becomes a customer needing help, the opportunity to serve seems less compelling. Oftentimes, customers can be seen as the problem. ("They are so darned demanding! Don't they know how hard our job is?") It is up to leadership to make the customers' needs apparent and to cast them in a broad enough light that everyone can be inspired by those needs. Despite the complexity of a business with customers, the need is still there, and the opportunity for service is just as real as it was in that stadium in Seattle. Getting twenty thousand people to take action every day in that spirit is indeed a different challenge. We are constantly communicating with our staff to help them see the bigger meaning of what we do. My guess is that we still don't do it enough. We describe the customer need and our role in filling it as being "the custodians of our customers' dreams." We simply know that we must strive to serve them with more responsiveness and integrity than anyone else in the business.

THE CUSTOMER EXPERIENCE: WHAT DO THEY WANT?

The simple answer is, customers want value. Part of that value is the product or service, part of it is everything around the product or service—including the brand, the customers' impression of the trustworthiness and competence of the company. Leonard Berry, my own personal favorite authority on customer service, discusses this one idea thoroughly in *Discovering the Soul of Service.*[2]

To buy a simple, utilitarian product, say a garden implement, one knowledgeable but frugal customer might pick something out of an Internet auction site, wait the three days for shipping, and feel like she got value. Another might be in a hurry, walk to the local drug store sidewalk sale, and pay a bit more to be able to walk away with the implement that very day. She too, got value. A third person will go to the upscale garden store on the corner, chat with the owner about the weather and its impact on the growing season, find out the best plant to go into that shady corner against the fence, buy the same implement as our Internet and sidewalk shoppers for three times the price and still feel like she got value.

Passionate Growth Means Expansion of Value

Any business that wants to grow will find the array of ancillary services that are most valuable to the customer, expand to include them at a fair price, communicate their availability with good advertising, and figure out how to distribute them conveniently and reliably to customers. In other words, business growth is about expanding the combination of products, services, and brand that clients find valuable, not to just whittle away at the cost and possibly the quality of what you already provide. Why? Because to maintain passion in the business, to keep employees interested, we simply have to provide opportunities for growth in their ability to serve. To do otherwise is to get caught in a downward spiral of prices, one that inevitably ends in a simple emporium of products, inadequate resources to really make a difference to employees, and a customer who finds little difference between you and the sidewalk vendor.

Since today's hyper-competitive markets leave little room to expand price, and indeed the Internet model is bringing prices *down* for many products, the only way to maintain profits and growth is to really focus on reducing costs—costs that don't reduce service quality. We have to be relentless in driving costs down in order to reinvest the savings in places that the customer will notice.

Watching for the Zone of Indifference

In Chapter Nine, I described the very difficult job of finding out what customers really want. Although the "what" is important, there is another dimension that will ultimately determine our ability to provide it—"how much is enough?" We know, for example, that most of our customers expect us to answer the phone in less than a minute. So we define sixty seconds as "minimally acceptable." We also know that if the phone is answered in less than twenty seconds by a person who is known to the customer, someone who may even recognize her voice and greet her by name with her latest account activity in front of her, then that customer is duly impressed—this service is the equivalent of "wow!" She will tell her friends and become an evangelist for Schwab. But between sixty seconds and roughly twenty seconds, there is a large zone that really makes no difference to the customer. While ninety seconds may feel too long, forty-five seconds feels the same as sixty. The cost to reduce the average answer time from sixty to forty-five seconds is significant, and if customers don't greatly value the difference, then this is not a place to spend our money. Deciding what to offer entails considering how to spend the right amount of money for the right things—first to make sure we are always above minimum standard, and then to get to "wow!" on the factors that make the most difference to the customer. The traps are failing to spend enough on the things that count, or spending too much on something that makes no difference to the customer at all. Len Berry calls this space between minimally acceptable and "wow" the "zone of indifference." He believes, and I concur, that if you can't get to "wow," then incremental improvement is probably not cost-justified.

Getting to "wow" and staying there can be an ongoing pursuit. Competitive actions and the rising expectations of customers can keep raising the bar. For example, we discovered in the early 1990s that part of becoming one of the world's largest marketplaces for mutual funds was to offer some device to our customers that helped them make their fund selections. (There are now more than eight thousand mutual funds available.) We formulated a report called the Select List, which used Morningstar data to rate funds' performance. We listed domestic stock and bond funds that had a five-year history (international funds are evaluated on a shorter time frame), and immediately got rave reviews from the industry. The Schwab Select List became a standard in the industry. It was "wow!"

Soon, of course, others started to announce their own funds supermarkets, and along with them, other ways of selecting mutual funds. Some were even predictive. We decided that mutual funds research was going to grow in importance to our customers, so we hired a talented team and created the Schwab Center for Investment Research. This group developed some analytics that not only showed past performance of funds but adjusted that performance for the risk that the fund manager took in getting the performance and the consistency of that performance over the years. The report shows the customer how to balance that risk-adjusted rating to her own tolerance for risk, and addresses other factors to help in creating a mutual fund portfolio. We have also created information on the right time to buy and sell funds.

Have we taken our mutual funds advisory products back to "wow"? It's too soon to tell. Customers have to know the importance of the products, build a habit of using them, and we need to see the positive indicators of repeat purchases and increasing share before we really feel confident that we've arrived again at "wow" . . . for now.

Making Relationship Possible: Segmenting the Market

Market segmentation is a clinical name for one of the richest opportunities that new technology has afforded us. We are able to gather information on customers and actually determine more about what they want. This allows us to increasingly delight the customer, and it also gives employees opportunities to target offers that are relevant, thereby increasing the feeling of service and reducing the sense of selling.

We know that our wealthiest and most active customers expect and need services that are not expected or needed by our less affluent and younger group of customers. An individual just starting out needs some advice on asset allocation, some encouragement to invest on a regular basis and an occasional check-up. A wealthier and more active customer will need substantially more service, a more knowledgeable broker, and perhaps specialized services that are created just for her. This kind of segmentation gives everyone a chance to build a relationship based on customer need rather than on a particular product offering.

INTERNET AND THE CUSTOMER: PUTTING "CLICKS AND MORTAR" TO WORK

After the hype dies down, I believe we will see the Internet for what it is: a new technology enabling new models of information distribution, product ordering, and client relationship. It will enable us to develop cost structures, resultant prices, and service models that were unimaginable in the pre-Web world. However, I don't believe the new models will replace the retail store, and most certainly the Internet will not replace the local coffee shop or the church or synagogue.

As of this writing, a key question haunting business leaders throughout the world is, How does an established company integrate the Internet and use it to competitive advantage? As Martha Rogers put it in her research on e-business:

> The single most difficult task preventing an existing company from setting up a successful e-business is resolving the conflicts that exist between the cyber-world and the real world. The cyber-world of direct-to-consumer deliveries threatens most companies' real-world channel structures, and the self-help customer service offered online is often inadequate unless it can be linked with service calls or repair scheduling. Resolving these conflicts, by using real-world strengths to leverage an online presence, has proved overwhelmingly difficult for many firms. Barnesandnoble.com, for example, has never been able to leverage its hundreds of bricks-and-mortar bookstores to pull an end-run around Amazon.[3]

Rogers goes on to suggest possible scenarios, and give Schwab credit for being one of a handful of firms to figure it out. Truthfully, we were the first established financial services firm to really grasp the enormous potential of the Net to reinvent our business model from top to bottom. Nevertheless, the process of reinventing ourselves was wrenching and it is far from over.

Right now, on-line grocers are grabbing headlines with fresh products, home delivery, and great service. Why have we not heard from the likes of Whole Foods, Safeway, and other premium brands? Barnes & Noble appeared to be totally surprised by the genius of Jeff Bezos and Amazon.com. Let's look at that case more closely, looking particularly at the opportunities to build brand and create employee passion, both ways to directly improve the customer experience.

THE BOOKSELLER'S WAR: NEW MEDIA, OLD PRINCIPLES

As of this writing, Amazon.com is a terrific example of a company that is building name recognition on the Internet. It *began* as an Internet company. It has made no profits but is instead investing the proceeds from the venture capital money and stock sales in expansion and advertising.

Barnes & Noble has an established brand. It is a spectacular and well-established physical retailer of books, and is faced with serious competition from Amazon.com. While Barnes & Noble has established a Web site, the company is coming in late and with far less experience in electronic commerce than its new nemesis.

How will this competitive battle shape up?

Jeff Bezos, Amazon's founder and CEO, knows his challenge. In July 1999, he was interviewed about this issue by a reporter for the *Wall Street Journal Almanac.* In my view, he showed his complete understanding of the challenge when he responded to a question about how he spent his marketing budget.

"In the old world, customers didn't have the Internet as a megaphone to tell each other what they really believed. The right thing was to spend 30 percent of your time building a great customer experience, and 70 percent of your time shouting about it. But because word-of-mouth is so amplified today on the Web, you want to invert that. Spend 70 percent of your time building a great customer experience, and 30 percent of your time shouting about it. We figured that out early."[4]

He goes on:

"To have someone be an evangelist, you have to create something 10 times better than what they're used to. You can't just make something marginally better. That will make them happy, but it won't make them an evangelist."[5]

This sounds great, but the proof is in the performance. Again, Bezos knows what it takes. When asked about his competitive advantage, he didn't go on about Web designers or distribution channels. He said:

"The most important thing we have that's hard to duplicate is our culture of customer obsession. It pervades [everything]. . . . Cultures are impossible to copy . . . either you have them or you don't. A company culture is like quick-drying cement. You can't just send someone to a customer-focus class for six weeks and expect results."[6]

So Bezos knows that he is building a real brand, not just garnering name recognition. It is in the customer experience that the brand lives, not in the "shouting." And the customer experience is built transaction by transaction by the people in the company, operating in a culture that is obsessive about the customer experience. He hopes to be able to use the brand attributes to get customers to his other Web options—toys, auctions, and eventually, I suspect, general shopping.

But does this doom Barnes & Noble? Hardly. It is, in many regards, like Schwab. Amazon is an "e-commerce only" company, while Barnes & Noble has the advantage of a number of very successful physical stores, in wonderful neighborhoods around the world. Its employees are smart about books. They *love* books, and they love telling people about them. This is considered by some to be the "old mode" of bookselling. But in the past, new modes of commerce did not often simply replace old modes, they forced them to sharpen their focus. Despite dire predictions, television didn't replace radio, but it did force radio to focus more on specific segments (talk radio, sports radio, light rock, and so on). Video players did not eliminate movie theaters, but they did force theaters to become more of a destination, an entertainment experience with popcorn that far exceeds what comes out of your microwave, great sound systems, comfortable seats, and multiplexes with many more movie choices than before. The Web won't kill stores, it will force them to vastly improve the customer's experience. They will have to provide a reason to visit the store that is more compelling than merely "picking out merchandise." Those that don't are likely to perish.

Now's the time for me to try my own hand at consulting. What should Barnes & Noble do in response to Amazon's threat? (This is terribly presumptuous of me, but consultants have to be presumptuous, they can't bill enough to find out the facts!) Here goes.

First, it should not even try to "out-Amazon" Amazon. Rather, it should try to employ its physical assets to offer something different and substantially better than Amazon. It could sharpen its focus, using the Web to identify segments and individuals and giving spectacular and broad service as a result. For example, it could offer on-line ordering and same-day delivery from the store, or on-line ordering and next-day store pickup. If you didn't have time to come into the store, you could pick up the order at curbside without ever getting out of your car. It could offer coupons for ordering on-line, good for a free or discounted latte at the in-store restaurant. It could also directly advertise the local store readings, lectures, signings and concerts, just by accessing your physical location from your inquiry. It could poll you on the types of activities you enjoy most in the stores, it could feature reviews by its own local workers. In other words, it could make the Web work as an extension of the Barnes & Noble community. It could use the Web presence to reaffirm and extend the "brand" as the local experience that it is.

Here is the key: Amazon.com will probably never have a store. It is far too expensive to go from electronic space to physical brick and mortar. So to the extent that people need and want to interact with real people, see others, have a physical place to go, Barnes & Noble will enjoy an insurmountable competitive advantage. But it has to exploit that advantage.

By the time this is published, I'll probably know if I could have charged a fee for this advice. For now, it serves as an example of how traditional firms can use the Internet as a tool to apply the principles of listening to customers, inspiring employees and building brand. The Internet changes how things look, it changes the experience, it changes the pace. The principles, the heart behind the action, remain.

FROM BRAND AND CUSTOMER EXPERIENCE TO THE FUTURE

In the process of writing this book, Dave and I were sharing our recent experiences at Target. I related that when I had wanted to buy a set of place mats, I made the trip to the store. I got in my car, went to the shopping center, found the mats, bought them, and returned home. "Next time, I'll do it on the Web," I said. "I was in no hurry, the selection would be just as good or better, and I wouldn't have to get in my car, fight the traffic, and wander around the store." Place mat shopping is not my idea of an especially fun leisure activity, nor are the mats especially important to me. But Dave's experience was different.

Just the week before, he had been "invited" by his daughter Stephanie to help her shop for things for her new apartment. She didn't know everything that she would need, so they got in the car and went to Target. They shopped and talked, bought things that they both would have forgotten that she would need. As Dave tells it, they had fun together browsing the store and debating which set of Teflon-coated pans looked the best and were worth the money. Had she simply made a list and shopped on the Web, the two of them would have missed a valuable experience together.

Some stores are creating this. "Supersports" stores are springing up, not only stocked with a variety of merchandise but built around small basketball courts and climbing walls, so that people who shop there can actually experience using the equipment themselves. The one near my house has a net-covered driving range. I could not get that experience on the Internet. Disney, Nike, Sony, and others are creating the same kind of experience emporiums. Even L. L. Bean, a pioneer in shop-by-mail, is not only providing on-line shopping but has expanded its one outlet in Maine to include nature displays, places to test mountain bikes, and films and lectures on a variety of outdoor adventure possibilities. It is becoming an attraction rather than merely an outlet.

Dave told me that Levi Strauss is experimenting with water-filled vats and dryers to allow customers to "shrink-to-fit" their Levi's right in the store. This is a little much for me, but I have some very close relatives who would love it—and who would count it as a major reason to buy Levi's over the competitors. Imagine, too, the commitment of the people who shepherd rookies up a climbing wall at Bean, help golfers try out clubs, or operate the "dunker" at the Levi Strauss retail store. These are enjoyable and rewarding jobs. Whether you actually do these things, or help make them available in some other way, you are involved in something besides stocking and displaying merchandise.

It really all comes down to providing the experience that the customer needs at the moment. Providing that kind of service is what inspires people to continue to serve. We are entering an era in business when the competition will not be for just excellence of product. It will increasingly be for excellence of service, of customer caring, of brand building, of relationship. The Internet will make ordering merchandise or doing transactions simple. The company, then, will have to focus on the intangibles to make a difference. And the company will have to focus on developing the kind of people who will want to deliver that kind of customer care.

Building brand by giving the customers what they want. Simple, difficult, profound, the future. The future. It makes us catch our breath. What will it hold? Will our principles prepare us?

To round out the book, we'll see what others have to say about that future, about what the Internet and the changing world might bring. And what we should be working on now to prepare.

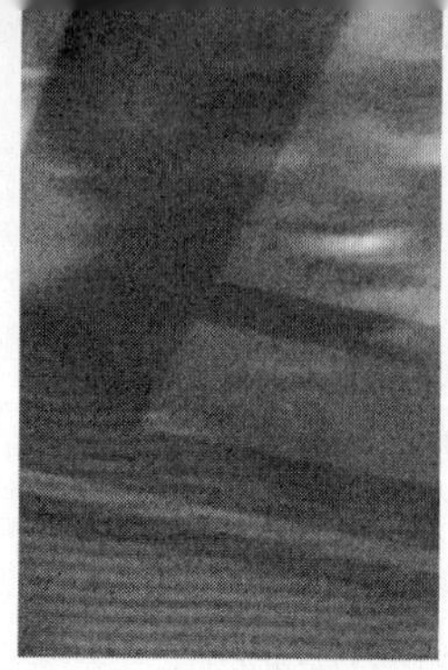

DIALOGUE ON THE FUTURE

We used to have debates in undergraduate religion classes about whether prophets predict the future or create it. I came down on the side of creation because I had seen the impact of declaration on the action of others. "All men are created equal" was not fact until Jefferson and others said that it was so. When it was established by declaration, everyone who wanted it to be true took action to make it real, and those who didn't want it to be true took counteraction. So to me it seemed reasonable that declaration was an act of creation, not an act of clairvoyance.

In that spirit, Dave and I asked eight extremely well-respected people from the worlds of academia, business operations, venture capital, and consulting to join us in a dialogue about the future, one that we hoped would put some rhetorical stakes in the ground, helping to create the future of the world of commerce. The participants were:

- Steve Ballmer: President, Microsoft Corporation.
- Leonard Berry: Distinguished Professor of Marketing, Lowry Mays College and Graduate School of Business, Texas A & M University. Author, *Discovering the Soul of Service,* Free Press, 1999.

Affiliations given are those as of the time of the discussion. Steve Ballmer is currently CEO and President, Microsoft Corporation; Lew Platt is now CEO of Kendall Jackson Wines; Condoleezza Rice is National Security Adviser for President George W. Bush.

- Tom Gerrity: Professor of Management, Director of the Electronic Commerce Forum, and former Dean, The Wharton School, University of Pennsylvania.
- Bill Harris: Former President and CEO, Intuit, Inc.
- Lew Platt: Chairman, Hewlett-Packard Corporation.
- Condoleezza Rice: Former Provost, Stanford University.
- Eric Schmidt: Chairman and CEO, Novell, Inc.
- Ann Winblad: Co-founding Partner of Hummer Winblad Venture Partners.

To get the dialogue started we asked these questions:

Looking ahead ten to twenty years: Other than technology and change management, what factors will most affect organizations' ability to thrive?

It is often said, "employee and customer loyalty are dead." To the extent that this is true, what is driving this perception? How do we reverse it? Do we need to?

The Internet is certainly driving enormous price competition. What beyond price will matter to consumers and what will be valued most? How will companies differentiate themselves in an Internet-driven world?

Is the new technology like the telephone or the assembly line that will transform business, or is it the beginning of a revolution that will have an impact on every area of our lives?

Of course, it was nearly impossible to coordinate everyone's schedule, so in the spirit of our theme, the conversation was a virtual one. Let's listen to what was said.

❋ ❋ ❋

Dave Pottruck: First of all, thank you all for participating. I feel as though we should be around a fireplace somewhere in Vermont, but given our respective commitments this cozy virtual room will have to do. I want to start by affirming the necessity for a business to produce outstanding financial results. The business proposition is a carefully engineered exchange of value. People are still in business expecting to make a profit, and people still go to work to take care of their families. But in this new world of the Internet, the model to produce the best results has changed substantially.

Everything Terry and I have written about in *Clicks and Mortar*—building and sustaining culture, practicing more inclusive and inspirational leadership, and modifying business practices themselves—these all wind up in financial results for the stakeholders of the business. To understand the elements we've written about is really to understand a business model that generates revenue and controls expenses.

We all know the importance of technology and change management in this kind of world, but other than those elements, what's important to maintain success in this new environment?

Leonard Berry: Given the environment, I think it is vital for companies to keep good people. You hit on the key factors for that in your first couple of chapters. A clear, compelling corporate value system rooted in respect, excellence, innovation, integrity, teamwork, joy, and social profit power . . . this is the foundation for companies that will still be thriving in 2010 and 2020. Strong humane values are an organization's lifeblood; they pump energy, vitality, ambition, and commitment into the "human machine" we call a company.

The more the world changes around us, the more critical it is to have a central core philosophy that doesn't change. Human beings require guiding ideals to embrace amid swirling, nonstop change.

Great companies are in a constant state of innovation to improve the value proposition that you just spoke of, Dave. But the innovation is channeled and purposeful only when it revolves around strong values. It's really a wonderful circle. The right kind of corporate values lead to the right kind of customer value. Values inspire people, and inspired people do great things. When they do, they find ways to produce value for customers, and that improves either cost or revenue or both.

Terry Pearce: Obviously, we believe that values are central to success, but we watch our own kids, all Gen-Xers, and we hear them most interested in stock options or the ability to play on the Internet, or to be employed in the field of their choice. They find their "rootedness" in family and the community of friends that they develop in their work, even in the project they are working on, but not necessarily in the company itself.

Len: You guys should be talking to your kids more! When I wrote *Discovering the Soul of Service,* I studied fourteen companies with strong values, which included, by the way, the encouragement to have a high quality of life on the job, not just off. All of them had unusual employee loyalty (including the technologists). Indeed, these companies function in many ways like extended families and practice open communication, trust, sharing of resources—values that research shows fit many of the so-called Gen-Xers and Gen-Yers. Undoubtedly, life in a company isn't for everyone, but community itself seems to be desirable. There is no reason why a company can't provide that as well as a group of friends outside of corporate walls. Companies that do have a good chance to maintain the loyalty of really good people.

Bill Harris: I really agree with Len. An explicit value system keeps people in the company, and more important, it keeps them happy. We are in a time when the things that are valued are less tangible, more intangible, less physical and more intellectual. It's fair to say that the tangible stuff was owned by the company, but intangible property is owned by the employees. They can decide to contribute or not to contribute. You have to have a strong culture that values people and their ability to contribute, otherwise they will leave.

New companies, founded in the Internet world, are more and more virtual—people can work from any place in any time that they choose. That's both good and bad news. It provides tremendous flexibility to an organization, but it can also breed fragmentation. Since we can't depend on buildings and time clocks to bind people together, we have to have a culture that will do that. Culture crosses time and space boundaries easily. I would guess this virtualization is a real challenge for companies that started out as more traditional.

Lew Platt: It has been for Hewlett-Packard. It wasn't that long ago that we were fundamentally one company. Now we are many companies, and I'm not just referring to the spin-off of Agilent Technologies. Our suppliers and strategic partners are part of our company too, even though their paychecks don't say "HP" on them. We have thousands of contractors that we depend on and who might never see the inside of a Hewlett-Packard facility. They all contribute to what the customer sees in the end. It has taken major organizational and attitudinal changes to move from real facilities to virtual facilities.

Bill: When you think about it, electronic communities on the Web are held together only by common interest, and there is tremendous loyalty there. Defining that common interest, that mission that is compelling, is one way to hold people together.

Dave: That really brings us to the next question. It is often said that employee loyalty and customer loyalty are dead. Are they? And if so, what can we do about it, or should we even worry about it?

Ann Winblad: I think loyalty is being resuscitated by companies that really integrate the new technology. In fact, all companies have seen an evolution in the number of contact points between customers and their company. Lew alluded to it when he talked about HP becoming more virtual.

Historically, in the technology world, it was challenging for software developers to connect with the customer. The number of employees who interfaced with the actual consumer of the product was small. Frequently the interface was to the distribution channel; no one in the developing company interfaced with the customer at the point of sale. Although the channel itself was the "customer," the feedback loop was often not directed at the product itself. The customer was invisible. The product engineering group waited a long time for the actual feedback loop to be completed . . . and sometimes even a long time for the product sales to materialize. The only consumer feedback was in customer support, and of course product errors were the grist for the early calls. The fruits of everyone's labor seemed hard to quantify and hard to use as a motivator, let alone to build an employee-customer bond. In those days, employee-customer loyalty was close to dead.

The Internet has made a remarkable difference in employee-customer loyalty health and in the health of companies themselves.

One of our young CEOs called me last Friday as I was walking out the door for a three-day weekend. Rivals.com is a multifaceted sports site, and in its first month had tens of millions of page views. The fifty people in the company had worked incredible hours to launch the site and that Friday, they brought up "team sports commerce" for five teams. The feature helps fans buy paraphernalia that represents their favorite teams, sometimes from shops right in the home-team geography. All the employees were dog-tired, but were watching the fans order team sports gear rather than going home for the holiday. They loved the fact that they had made it possible for a Michigan fan to buy directly from "Moe's" in Michigan, directly off their site.

Dave: You're suggesting that the Net makes it possible for more employees to touch the customer directly, and that builds loyalty. I know in our own company, it was difficult at first to deal with the fact that customers no longer had to go through the traditional branch channel to do business with us. It put some strain on our branch bonus structure. But in the end, because we didn't pay commission to employees anyway, the channels of distribution could be modified fairly easily. Now, of course, more and more of our people, especially technologists, touch customers directly, and it does, certainly, give more people a sense of contribution. It's as though we are tearing down and remodeling the distribution channels to get right there with the customers.

Ann: Yes. The shortening of the distance between product and customer has created an immediate feedback loop for all employees—the fruits of labor appear instantly. It has also made strategy more team-oriented. The sales and marketing versus development and support conflict is disappearing. Everyone knows the customer bats last, and can see the customer up at the plate. New positions are being created at companies: "customer retention manager," "customer loyalty manager." More and more technology is appearing to encourage the customer to communicate with the company. "Reach" and "stickiness" are the new metrics for success.

The old model of design, build, ship, wait for customers to complain, and rebuild is gone with the Internet. Employees talk in terms of the product or service the customer wants now, not just in terms of the product they could possibly build. That closeness, that chance to make a difference every day for someone else, builds loyalty.

Tom Gerrity: Ann raises a great point about the tightening of the feedback loop. I do think that customer loyalty is under growing pressure with the Internet's greater ease of price and function comparison. There are just more alternatives for the customers, and it has raised consciousness among suppliers who are getting faster and faster market reactions, positive or negative, to their latest move. So the market is powerfully raising the stakes for excellence in customer awareness, focus, understanding, and even good old-fashioned human factoring.

That being said, to the degree that customer loyalty of the past was partly a product of habit, ignorance of alternatives, perceived high switching costs, and the like, loyalty will still be under greater and greater pressure. This is not a bad thing at all, since a heightened value will be placed on quality customer service, understanding, with a real premium on adaptability, responsiveness, clarity, and 100 percent dependability.

I don't think employee loyalty is dead either. Although this period of rapid expansion in technology utilization brings with it a dramatic increase in the pace of change and its associated feelings of rootlessness and disorientation for some people, I believe that it is actually heralding an era where healthy human and humane values in organizations may be even more important than ever before. Certainly with the increased mobility of employees that Bill talked about, those companies with the most compelling shared vision, values, and principles will command higher loyalty and higher attraction. They are likely to be more nimble as well.

The technology itself adds to a real sense of community. I've seen this clearly here at the school. I'm struck by how the links of voicemail, e-mail, and the Internet support a stronger and stronger sense of team and personal connection in our increasingly distributed global activities which could otherwise pull us further apart. The technology enables a better base of "shared learning" as well, which is a real advantage in this environment of rapid change.

Terry: You mentioned the power of the Web to make it easy for customers to find the best deal. What is it beyond price that will matter to consumers, and what will be valued most? How will companies differentiate themselves if price is both leveled and lowered by this technology?

Lew: There is no question that price has been leveled. If someone sells a printer for a lower price on the Net, then that is the new price. Companies have to differentiate in new ways to be successful.

My wife and I recently bought a new car. She was pretty sure about the make and model she wanted, and there was a good dealer in town. I suggested that before we went to the dealership, we should at least find out what price we could buy it for over the Internet. I admit that I have not liked the experience of car shopping in the past. The "dance" of offering and counter-offering that I was used to was not something that I looked forward to. I had also learned that there was a good automobile broker in town who would deliver the car to our driveway and take care of all of the details for under $100—pretty compelling.

We went to the dealer, and the salesman was bright and responsible . . . not at all my old experience. But when it came time to actually do the deal, I looked at him and said, "Now, I have shopped this car over the Internet, and here is the price I got. Your price will have to be something very close to that, or we will buy it on the Internet."

He looked me straight in the eye and said, "That's the price."

I said, "That's amazing. You guys are in real trouble. How are you going to survive?"

He took me outside and showed me a row of low-rise buildings under construction on his site. He said, "These are the new additions to our dealership, and they are all service bays. We know that the margins are going to get thinner on all products, but we believe there is a great business in customer service. We want to provide your car, but we also want to provide your service. That's the future of the car business."

There isn't any business that won't be affected in the same way.

Eric Schmidt: I agree. The early phases of the Internet's growth were all about connecting people and businesses. The Internet's next wave is all about managing relationships. It's a company's ability to develop personal relationships on the Internet that will matter most to consumers. Businesses will differentiate themselves by offering more personalized relationships based on an understanding of the customer's preferences and habits.

Dave: Certainly, when we used to interact only in person, we had to make notes on what we learned and then transcribe them. Even a telephone conversation requires some documentation. But the computer never forgets; questions and preferences are recorded. This technology builds a profile. Is that what you mean?

Eric: Partly. On the Net, better relationships start with smarter technology. New directory technology, for example, enables profile marketing, aimed at a party of one. That respects relationships and provides custom content to the user. You used the example of the book retailer. . . . Amazon.com or Barnes & Noble tells you when the latest John Grisham becomes available and offers you a special discount based on your past affinity for that particular author. A travel service gives you a nonsmoking room or books you an aisle seat. These are just primitive examples of what can be achieved with technology able to recognize your identity. Consumers, especially at the high end of every market, will seek out the kind of personal service you expect from a familiar waiter at a favorite restaurant.

Condoleezza Rice: This ability to customize is certainly a compelling aspect of the new technology, but since that ability is only based on my own expressed preferences, it doesn't apply to some critical fields. I use the Internet for all kinds of information, but I am constantly nervous that the information may not be correct. For example, when I have a medical question for my doctor (say before my yearly exam), I do go to the Internet to see what the latest articles are saying. This is not just a matter of price and selection. I want to be sure that the information is the best I can get.

I use old-fashioned authentication. If I find what I need at the National Institutes of Health, I am confident. The American Medical Association has been selling its name so much that I am more cautious but still relatively comfortable there. If information comes through a university that I know well, I am also pretty confident. Beyond that, I assume the information may or may not be right.

But what about the user who isn't quite as capable of differentiation? That is the issue for those who will use the Internet to sell a product or communicate with customers. "Brand Name" and probably a zero tolerance for mistakes will mean a lot.

Eric: There is no question that this new capability puts more responsibility on our companies. Authentication of information that consumers rely on is a critical issue. So is privacy. The trail of data that you leave behind when you use the Internet—what some call your "digital fingerprint"—is a rich source of information about your habits, your preferences, and the company you keep. Today, when you visit a Web site, the Web site is actually visiting you. How would you feel, for example, if, as a result of one of your health inquiries, you started to get unsolicited e-mail about vitamins and supplements?

The challenge for Web businesses is to provide an Internet relationship that puts the user back in the driver's seat. Here too, technology can offer solutions in the form of digital identification tools that allow the users to control what personal information they share on the Internet and what businesses they share it with. By providing these tools as part of their services, Web businesses establish themselves as brands that you can trust. Ultimately, it's your ability to support trusting relationships that will determine your success or failure on the Web.

Dave: You two have broached the issue of trust, and this is something that concerns me a great deal, particularly in our field of financial services. It just won't do for people to be getting unsolicited e-mail about various schemes to "invest" their money. As you said, Eric, building a profile doesn't necessarily build trust. Knowing a customer's wants and needs doesn't equate to having his best interest in mind. But such information can become the basis for such a relationship.

Condi: There may be a generational split here. For those of us over forty, the Internet augments other sources of information and commerce. We tend to be more aware of the pitfalls and dangers. For students born into this age, it is the primary vehicle. They seem to take it for granted.

Ann: You may be right. I look at my e-mail as a delicious box of chocolates. I have adjusted to the fact that 24 by 7 by 365 by all time zones in the world creates a situation whereby I can't possibly read them all immediately. Most of my mail is about business ideas and résumés and interaction between a network of people I want to have access to me. I actually get very little junk mail. (Although there is varying quality to the business plans I receive!) With very lightweight technology, I set my screening preferences on my e-mail so that messages from my partners are always up front, as is e-mail from the companies we have invested in.

The junk mail is easy to spot and evaporates in a click. It isn't unlike sorting your "real" mail over the garbage can, which I'm sure most of us do. I assume the reason I don't get a lot of junk mail in the four hundred to nine hundred messages I get a day is that I interact with sites that are top-notch businesses and know that abusing e-mail drives customer loyalty away. I do like that my personal data is used to help me on the Net. I like technology that determines what I am likely to enjoy or when I am likely to run out of yogurt. This is frequently built into the site as a "recommendation" button. None of my personal information is unveiled, just used to help me. I recently tested a Web site that said it would remove me from the solicitation calls and junk mail I receive at home. So far results on that front have been dismal.

Condi: I wish I had the "box of chocolates" perspective. I remember when my father gave my mother and me those Valentine-shaped boxes of candy. I hated those chewy nut centers and always resented having to bite into four or five before I got something I liked. That is a little like junk mail and the Internet. I do think it's a problem and for those of us (like me—your ordinary customer) who don't know how to screen, the junk mail is really annoying. I think it's a problem for serious companies wanting to make the Internet responsible.

Eric: This is obviously a critical issue. The solution for personalized marketing is to guarantee consumer privacy. I believe we will be treated very harshly, and companies that violate privacy will be shunned. The spammers will be shut down by their service providers and by community pressure.

The overall message about privacy and communication is that people will demand privacy protection and limitations on reuse of their personal information. In many cases, people will demand that their permission be given explicitly before information given by them is used. There may eventually need to be regulation in this area.

Bill: Agreed. Some regulation may eventually be valuable, but the marketplace is rapidly taking steps toward self-regulation right now. Already, the vast majority of sites are trustworthy and certified, and the technology is available to let people protect their privacy. And to put the privacy challenge into perspective, let's remember the security challenge that preceded it. Only a short time ago, the vast majority of Web users did not believe the Internet was secure—so much so that they wouldn't even put their credit cards on the Net. I think the large majority of Web users now feel secure using their credit cards on the Net. And they do so with the knowledge that—though not perfect—the security of an electronic transaction is almost always better than the security of the paper-based transaction that it replaces.

Does commerce on the Net need regulation and oversight? Of course. All of commerce—whether electronic or traditional—needs regulation and oversight. We need protection for privacy, for contracts, for intellectual property . . . the whole free-market system depends upon our underlying system of laws. The Internet is no exception.

Dave: That really brings us to the last question. Is the new technology like the telephone or the assembly line that will transform business, or is it the beginning of a revolution that will have an impact on every area of our lives?

Steve Ballmer: I'm coming in late here, but I've been listening to the discussion, and I think the Internet has *already* transformed the business world, and will continue to do so through new and improved forms of communication, information flow, commerce, productivity, pricing, and customization of products—all of which are generating new business models and choices for consumers. Equally important, it has created a new platform on which new businesses have been built. As you and Lew have pointed out, Dave, traditional businesses have had to adapt rapidly. As you recall, we took dramatic steps at Microsoft to move our business in that direction in a hurry.

We are just at the beginning of what those businesses and industries will mean, not just to consumers, but to society, culture, and economics.

Tom: I'm on the "revolution" end of the spectrum. The new technology will certainly transform business, but its impact on society will be even greater. The very essence of the Internet is vastly expanded communication and available information (and then knowledge, and perhaps even ultimately wisdom) and its impact on human experience and possibility will be dramatically greater than we can now imagine.

Steve: It's the changes that we can't possibly foresee that will have the greatest impact on us. So far, the Internet's growth has been focused on connectivity, information presentation, and access. The next important technological phase is about the Web becoming programmable, where Web applications and Web services are there for developers to use to customize and change things. This will be an incredibly important phase that involves how we think about Web sites and what they do for us. During this period, the Internet will evolve very, very dramatically. For sure, as the PC and new devices enable people to be connected to the Internet anytime, anywhere, it will fundamentally change the way our society works.

Lew: Yes, regardless of the direction that technology changes it, the most powerful continuing influence of the Internet is its ability to give people power that they didn't have before. When some entity—a company, a country, or a person—is public with values, it puts real pressure on integrity. The louder that values are voiced, the more certain it is that someone will notice behavior that is inconsistent with those values. In the same way that a culture will hold your integrity to the fire, the Internet holds your brand to the fire.

Bill: We look at this with a good perspective right now. We might see it as revolutionary. But others, particularly our children, see it as ordinary. It's not like the invention of the airplane, when so much time had to pass for us to realize the benefits.

I was listening to a very popular Internet author tell an experience about his own perspective being challenged. One of the networks asked him to do a live thirty-minute television show, surfing on the Web. He did it—he was nervous, but it was successful.

Later, he was telling his kids, ages thirteen and nine, about his experience. Their reaction? Incredulity. Why would anyone be interested in someone surfing the Web? They said, "Gee, Dad, that's great. Maybe next time they could do thirty minutes on you changing the television channels or looking in the refrigerator."

I think it is revolutionary, and like most revolutions, the next generation will take it for granted.

Terry: I agree—it's revolutionary, perhaps well beyond what we can now imagine. In fact, I like to compare the Internet to the beginning of space travel in its impact on our consciousness; the shift it may engender is much more dramatic than that of the telephone or any other tool. In the same way that the picture of the Earth from space made us somewhat more experientially aware of our place in the universe, the Internet makes us aware of our interconnectedness. In looking at it in that way, I have great hopes for the technology, that it will actually transform our relationships with one another, both individually and internationally.

Dave: I share Terry's hopes, and I think one major road to realizing the kind of impact he describes is through our respective businesses and activities.

In truth, this whole discussion has inspired me. It's not hard to imagine the future that we have discussed—one in which the Internet gives customers the power to cut through false advertising and inaccurate claims, one in which responsible people and companies with integrity will thrive—because companies that don't display such integrity are immediately found out. And it is particularly inspiring to imagine a world where practiced values are the most important ingredient in determining the loyalty of those who do business with you, as employees, customers, suppliers, partners, or stockholders.

Thanks to all of you for the discussion. You will all, of course, have a hand in creating this Internet world, and the task couldn't be in better hands.

⁂ ⁂ ⁂

Dave: Well, Terry, It seems appropriate, somehow, to end the book with this discussion. It may sound simplistic, but what was actually said by our eight guests was that in the world of nearly runaway technology, success, more than ever, depends on people—what they want as customers, what they crave in their work, what they invest in as stockholders. The technology is just a tool—a magnificent tool—for people to learn what they want to learn, do the work they want to do, and get whatever material and nonmaterial things they want and need.

Terry: It's always been that way, of course. The companies that really thrived had the best people.

Dave: But it hasn't always been so obviously necessary. In the past, when the products were more tangible and there was no easy way to change overnight, incumbents had great advantages. They had scale, brand, distribution, technology, and access to capital. Now, those advantages can actually be detriments. Today it takes flexibility and creativity to attract capital, not just inventory. And those attributes take a special kind of team, a special kind of people, and a spirit that just wasn't necessary before.

Terry: That's why culture, leadership, and other tools for building passion need to be improved at the same pace as the technology. People want to connect with others in ways that go beyond the Internet. . . . That's why people with coffee-makers still go to Starbucks. That's why *Cheers* was the longest-running TV show ever. That's why there are only a few thousand honest-to-god hermits in the world. Most of us want to be with others who know our name, doing something that will make the world different because we were here. It seems to me that the "com" in "dot com" has to stand for "community" as well as "commerce."

Dave: Absolutely. I think most people, in their heart of hearts, want to have the kind of power that the Internet provides. Every single person can be an author, every person can have access to most information; the technology provides the means for more self-responsibility and more self-development than any technology in history. There are immeasurable opportunities for individual creativity and innovation. Any company that wants to thrive has to create an atmosphere where those new ideas can be expressed.

But business growth doesn't just come from generating new ideas, it comes from using creativity for the good of others . . . in service. Technology itself interests us, but it's what technology can help us do for others that *inspires* us, whether it's opening cybercafés, servicing cars better, providing medical counseling, making it possible for fans to buy a Michigan football jersey, or helping people make their financial dreams come true. Without the technology, these tasks would be harder, but without the passion of caring people, these tasks simply wouldn't get done.

Ultimately, the Internet and its cousins make it possible for each of us to become more powerful and more responsible, to contribute in ways we could not have without it. It makes individual and collective "passion-driven growth" more likely.

What a dazzling prospect and inspiring vision for our time.

APPENDIX A

TIMELINE OF SCHWAB'S GROWTH

Schwab's Major Milestones and Service Innovations—High Tech and High Touch

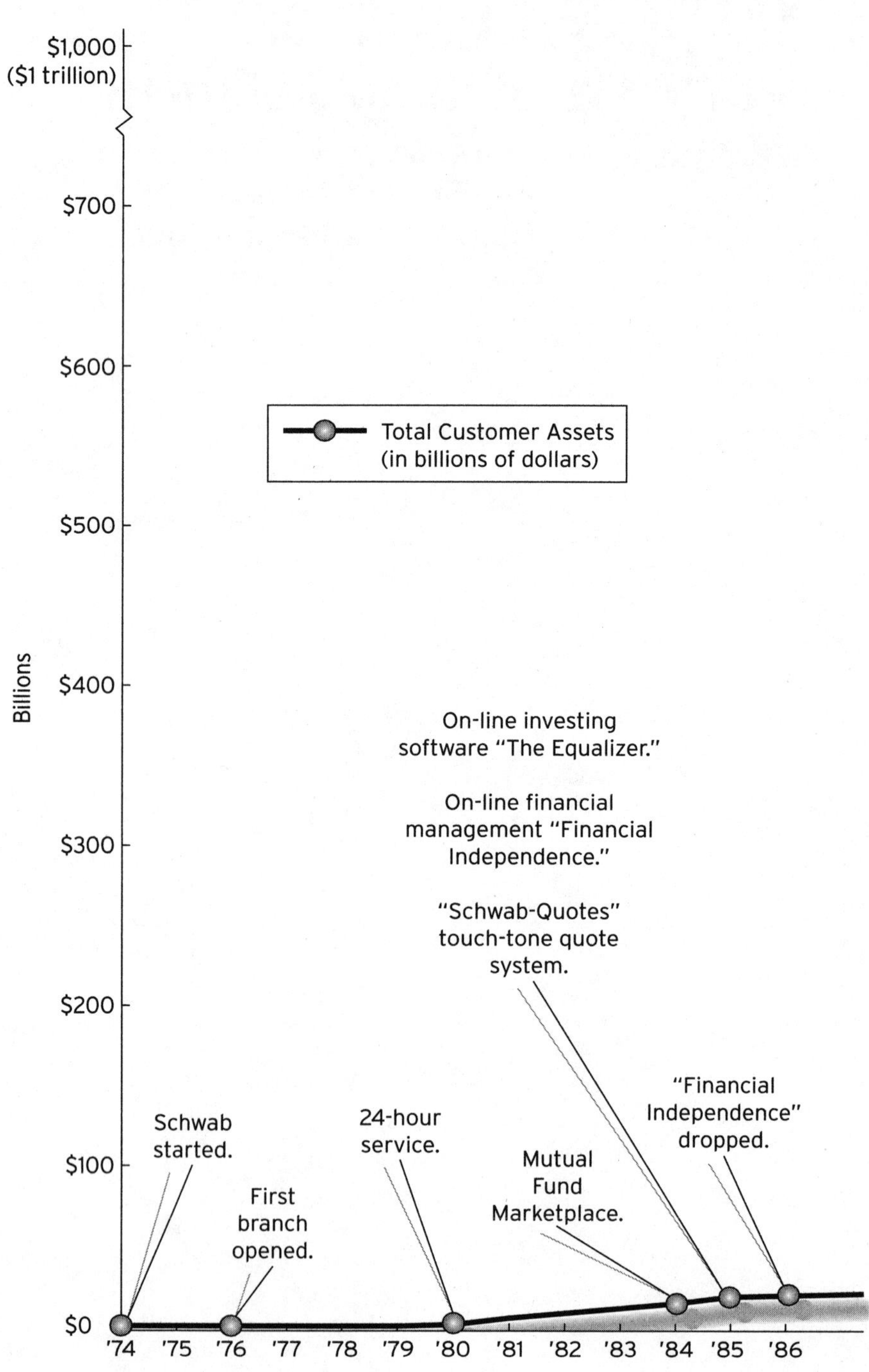

$1,000
($1 trillion)
$700
$600
$500
$400
$300
$200
$100
$0
Billions
Total Customer Assets
(in billions of dollars)
On-line investing
software "The Equalizer."
On-line financial
management "Financial
Independence."
"Schwab-Quotes"
touch-tone quote
system.
"Financial
Independence"
dropped.
Schwab
started.
24-hour
service.
Mutual
Fund
Marketplace.
First
branch
opened.
'74
'75
'76
'77
'78
'79
'80
'81
'82
'83
'84
'85
'86

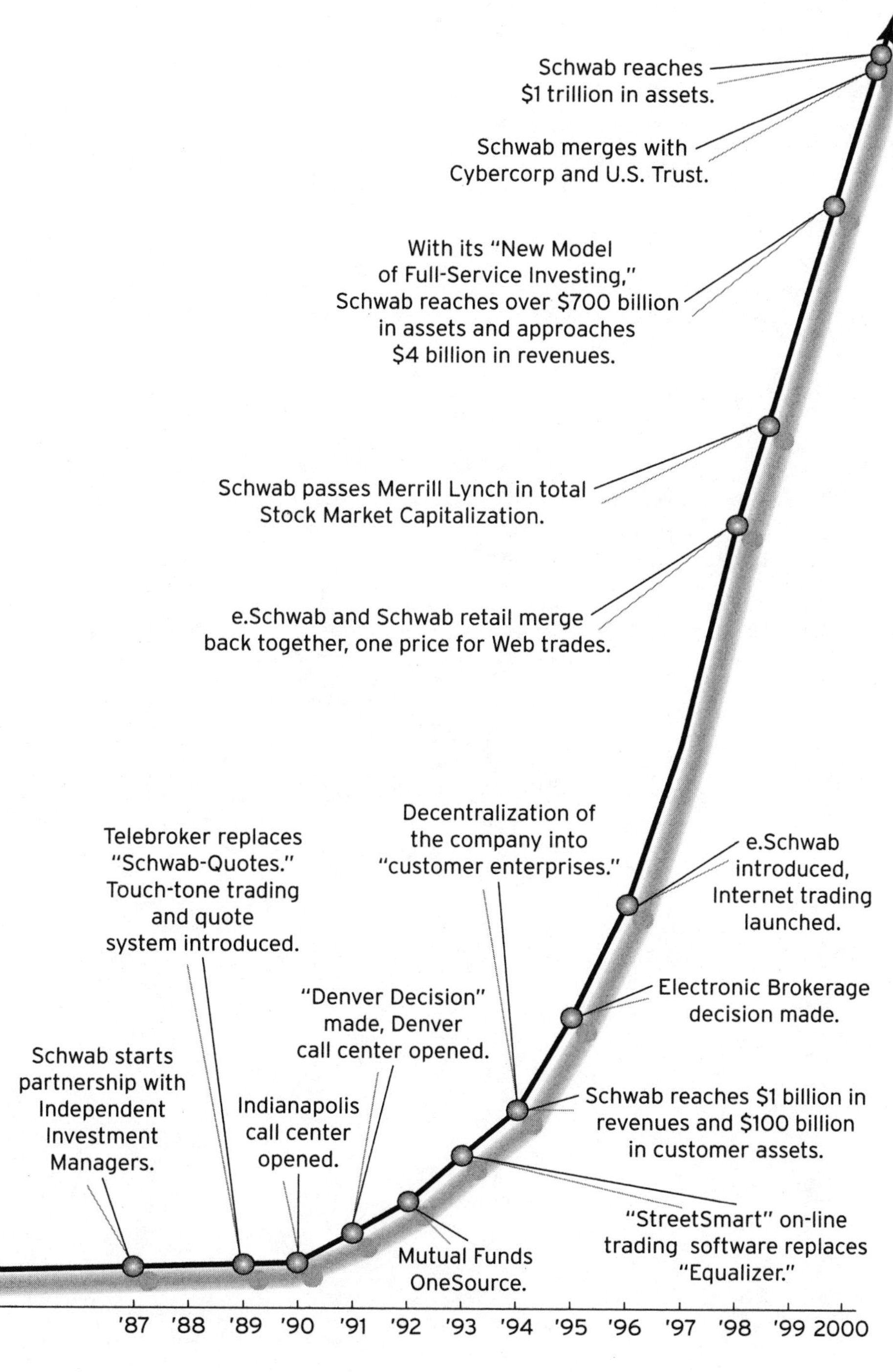

Schwab reaches $1 trillion in assets.
Schwab merges with Cybercorp and U.S. Trust.
With its "New Model of Full-Service Investing," Schwab reaches over $700 billion in assets and approaches $4 billion in revenues.
Schwab passes Merrill Lynch in total Stock Market Capitalization.
e.Schwab and Schwab retail merge back together, one price for Web trades.
Telebroker replaces "Schwab-Quotes." Touch-tone trading and quote system introduced.
Decentralization of the company into "customer enterprises."
e.Schwab introduced, Internet trading launched.
Electronic Brokerage decision made.
"Denver Decision" made, Denver call center opened.
Schwab starts partnership with Independent Investment Managers.
Indianapolis call center opened.
Schwab reaches $1 billion in revenues and $100 billion in customer assets.
"StreetSmart" on-line trading software replaces "Equalizer."
Mutual Funds OneSource.
'87
'88
'89
'90
'91
'92
'93
'94
'95
'96
'97
'98
'99
2000

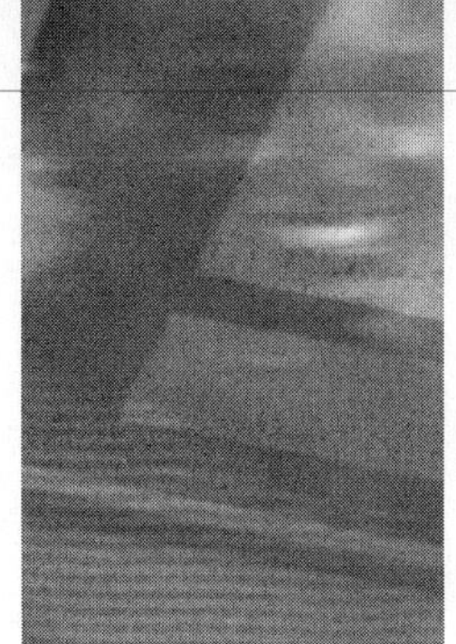

APPENDIX B

SCHWAB'S VISION, VALUES, AND STRATEGIC PRIORITIES

In this appendix we reproduce portions of the Founder's Edition of the vision statement created by the senior management team of the Charles Schwab Corporation in September 1995. We also include, in brief, the ten strategic priorities that the team created.

OUR COMPANY'S VISION AND VALUES

In the early seventies, we started our company with a simple idea: "to provide investors with the most useful and ethical brokerage services in America."

During our first twenty years, we defined this vision as transactional brokerage and custody services. The changing needs of our customers demand that we continuously strengthen our existing services and broaden and extend our vision. Beyond transaction and custody, we must now also develop relationships offering a more extensive range of help and guidance and an expanding array of financial services.

A new generation of investors needs help in making better, more-informed investment decisions. For these customers, as well as our more experienced investors, we will develop new tools, new services and new products to help them monitor and ultimately improve their investment outcomes. For those customers who want help in selecting qualified independent money managers, we will provide referral services.

We will help companies provide employee retirement plan services for the millions of individuals who work for corporations. For those customers who can benefit from electronic investing and global investing, we will be leaders in these emerging customer trends, both domestically and internationally. We will play a major role in increasing the efficiency and reducing the cost of capital markets transactions on behalf of customers. Finally, we will expand our brand of ethical, value-driven financial services to all customers as the regulations and boundaries that separate brokerage firms and other financial institutions continue to dissolve.

Recognizing these changes in our customers' needs, we have expanded our vision to: "provide customers with the most useful and ethical financial services in the world."

We will apply the same straightforward values that have been our foundation for twenty years:

- Be fair, empathetic, and responsive in serving our customers,
- Respect and reinforce our fellow employees and the power of teamwork,
- Strive relentlessly to improve what we do and how we do it,
- Always earn and be worthy of our customers' trust.

By applying our values to a broader range of services, I expect that Schwab will serve ten million households and custody over one trillion dollars within the next ten years. Staying focused on the interests of those we serve will ensure that we have no limits in pursuit of our vision.

Charles R. Schwab
September, 1995

WHY CHANGE WHEN WE ARE SO SUCCESSFUL?

This is a question only asked by great companies. Others wait until performance wanes, and by then their customers and competitors have built momentum toward new frontiers. For more than twenty years, we have led a transformation in our industry on behalf of our customers. We have boldly envisioned and created new possibilities for investors—and for ourselves.

Chuck founded the company to serve independent investors and establish a new standard for accurate and timely transactions, at the lowest possible price. We dominated this niche because the combination of service and price that we offered was unparalleled. As our reputation for ethical and useful service spread, more and more customers—some with less experience than our traditional clientele—wanted to do business with Schwab.

The 1980s saw investment speculation grow. The decade also saw declining public trust in Wall Street, as a number of well-known brokerages featured in scandals over unethical dealing. The substantial market correction in the fall of 1987 was the final precursor to the emergence of a more cautious investor.

At the same time, a broader spectrum of America was beginning to invest, increasing the need for objective help in making investment decisions. As mutual funds made diversification easy, the industry exploded, creating even more need for tools to help investors navigate and make choices.

As our company grew, we also saw the need to differentiate Schwab through the use of leading-edge technology. At first this technology was focused solely on guaranteeing the best possible transactional efficiencies. But before long it became clear that we must also offer technological advantages directly to customers. Now, of course, access to global networks and the broad availability of computers make it possible to deliver customized products and services to more customers than ever before.

In recent years, as our industry has grown and transformed, competition has intensified and, in fact, changed in its very character. Our traditional competitors have copied our offerings and mimicked our advertising. Full-commission firms, discounters, and mutual fund companies have begun to offer "Schwab-like" services like our no-fee IRAs, TeleBroker, Mutual Fund OneSource, and services for fee-based advisers. At the same time, deep discounters have continued to lure active traders with low prices.

With deregulation, other financial institutions have begun to offer some brokerage services through their extensive branch networks. And the advent of electronic commerce has brought new competitors to our industry who have substantial resources and strong brand identification. Software builders, network providers, and telecommunication giants are entering the field of online financial services.

Schwab's unprecedented growth is rooted in our customers' trust. Our values are translated into products and services that fundamentally help people help themselves. As other brokerage firms have faltered, we have continued to thrive because of our unswerving dedication to high-value, ethical state-of-the-art offerings. To continue this legacy in the face of changing customer needs and increasingly intense competition, we have to constantly reexamine everything we do, how we do it, and why.

We have to be able to manage change better than our competitors. We have to listen to more customers more effectively, and we have to anticipate needs and respond to what we hear more rapidly than ever before. We have to offer much more help proactively. And we have to become more active in supporting not only our customers' choices but their investing outcomes as well.

Through the years we have often chosen radically new directions when we were at the top of our game. We have understood the desirability and the necessity of embracing change from a position of strength. Now—while we are strong—we need to again change some of our behaviors, build important new skills, and shift our structure and processes.

If we have the courage to be led by our vision, we can truly make a difference in our customers' lives. We can serve others, serve the community, and be proud of our profession and our company.

The following ten priorities will guide our progress.

Why change when we are so successful? To give our customers and ourselves the very best of what will be needed tomorrow.

I look forward to being with you on the journey.

David S. Pottruck

SCHWAB'S STRATEGIC PRIORITIES

I. Providing Spectacular Customer Service: Exceeding Expectations
II. Developing and Empowering People: Moving Decisions Closer to the Customer
III. Fostering Innovation: Increasing the Pace of New Products and Processes to the Point Where Competitors Cannot Keep Up
IV. Providing "Schwab-Style" Help and Advice: A New Standard for the Industry
V. Expanding Our Offerings: Growing into Related, Complementary Lines of Business and into International Markets
VI. Developing Electronic Financial Services: Taking Technology Beyond Our Walls
VII. Taigeting Different Customer Segments
VIII. Extending the Reach and Meaning of the "Charles Schwab" Brand
IX. Continuously Improving Our Processes: Achieving World-Class Standards in Order to Be the Low-Cost Provider
X. Maintaining Superior Technology: Serving Employees and Customers, and Fueling Our Competitive Advantage

Before adding their individual signatures to these strategic priorities, the senior management team stated as follows:

> IN CONCLUSION, these priorities are meant as focal points for our efforts as we take the next step toward our vision. As our customers' needs change, and as we continue to evolve as a company, the specific tactics currently suggested by these priorities may also change. What will not change are the values Schwab was founded on. These fundamentals of integrity, and their enduring importance, are unquestioned.
>
> We commit ourselves to maintaining that vision of "providing the most useful and ethical financial services in the world" by consistently applying our values and by supporting each other in making it possible for our customers to realize their financial dreams.

APPENDIX C

DAVE'S TOP TEN RULES OF ADVERTISING

1. *Tell your story in gulps.* If the headline doesn't tell a powerful story, you've missed your biggest opportunity. Get the "unique selling proposition" (USP) into the headline—or if you are on the Web, into your banner. Your name is not enough.
2. *Identify yourself clearly.* If your readers can't find the name of the company because the art director buried the name and logo, they will turn the page—or click past your banner—immediately. Make an impression even if you don't make a sale today. A headline or banner that includes a USP tied to your name ("Schwab saves you money.") can make an impression filed away for later reference.
3. *Use pictures.* People love to look at pictures, and will read captions under the pictures. Use the opportunity the caption offers to create exactly the context, exactly the take-away you want to create.
4. *Don't sacrifice USP for art.* Cuteness is tempting. It gets your ad to stand out in the clutter. But what's the point if it isn't compelling someone to act? We ran an ad recently whose headline read, "How do you decide to buy, sell or hold a Mutual Fund in your portfolio?" The subhead immediately under this offered, "With Schwab's new Mutual Fund Report Card you can follow these simple steps to begin to evaluate your mutual funds." In the top left-hand corner was a small icon that read, "Now available exclusively for Schwab customers at Schwab.com." Will this ever

win advertising awards? Absolutely not. Is it a little wordy? Perhaps. Does it get results? Spectacular results. The same principles apply with banner ads—especially because the graphics are so tempting. But the objective should be *message*, not getting good site rating. People can ignore you or link to you in a fraction of a second.

5. *Avoid emotional attachment to the ad.* It's easy for those close to the creative process to get engaged with the creativity, not the result. This is especially true of Web banners because of the possibilities created by graphics and streaming video or audio. Try to keep the copywriter and art director focused on the point—the offer or the brand, or both. A general manager has to have some detachment from the art. You may not understand the images, but you have to understand the fundamentals well enough to make independent judgments. Don't tire of an ad too soon and don't stay with a tired ad too long. On the Web, banners are expected, seen often, and therefore often missed after the first couple of visits.
6. *Test, test, test.* Many publications and Web sites will allow what publications have always called an A/B split. You can run two ads or banners to the same audience at the same time, and measure which one is more effective. Advertising is expensive, so testing is an extremely important discipline.
7. *Feature the brand.* One of my favorite tests is the number of times the brand appears without appearing contrived. In a typical Schwab TV ad, as a person walks into our branch, the camera zooms in on the Schwab logo on the door. The person walks up, shakes hands with the Schwab representative, and the Schwab representative hands over something to read. The camera zooms over the person's shoulder to the brochure, and reveals the Schwab name at the top. There are several opportunities to get the Schwab brand in front of the viewer during the course of the ad in ways that don't look at all artificial. Good companies do that. This is like finding the rabbits in the picture maze. Try it. You'll be amazed at how many red cans of Coke appear over and over in Coca-Cola advertising.

8. *Turn off the volume.* People remember visuals much more than they remember spoken words. If you watch the ad on television without sound and come away with the essence of the message, the ad has the makings of greatness.
9. *Make your message uniquely you.* Ask yourself: "Could our competitors have run the same ad or Web banner by just putting their name at the end?" And if in fact they could, you need to reevaluate your USP. The qualities of the offer have to represent the uniqueness of the company that is advertising.
10. *Choose your media—and cascade them.* Priced correctly, the Web can be a reasonable medium for building brand awareness and click-throughs—yet it's not much for building brand attributes. The most successful Web players have learned that building brand equity is done with off-Web advertising. If you want to build a really powerful Web brand you have got to advertise in multiple media. Traditionally, and still in the Internet Age, television is a *hot* medium—one that emotionally opens up your audience to be receptive to targeted selling messages from other media. A great campaign begins with tilling emotional soil with television, then follows up with print or banner advertising that communicates the specific offers and compels response "now!" by explaining benefits and making an offer. TV is an emotional, demonstrative medium; print and the Web are the workhorses, the selling media. They work together beautifully if orchestrated effectively.

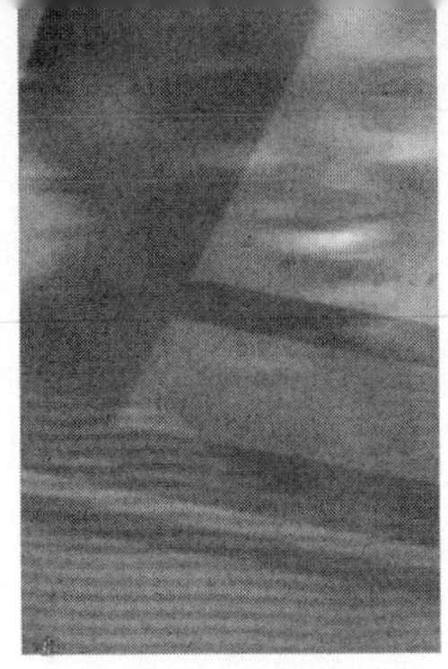

NOTES

PART ONE

1. James Taylor and Watts Wacker, *The 500-Year Delta* (New York: HarperBusiness, 1997), pp. 207–208.
2. James M. Kouzes and Barry Z. Posner, *The Leadership Challenge: How to Keep Getting Extraordinary Things Done in Organizations,* 2nd ed. (San Francisco, Jossey-Bass, 1995), p. 218.
3. Michael Ray and Rochele Myers, *Creativity in Business* (New York: Doubleday, 1986), p. 182.

CHAPTER ONE

1. "High-Tech Talent Search," *PC Magazine,* November 18, 1997, p. 9.
2. See James Collins and Jerry Porras, *Built to Last* (New York: HarperBusiness, 1994), p. 224.
3. J. Tarrant, *Drucker: The Man Who Invented the Corporate Society* (New York: Warner Books, 1976), p. 244.
4. G. Silverman and L. Nathan Spiro, "Is This Marriage Working?" *Business Week,* June 7, 1999, p. 134.
5. R.B.L., "Selling the Sizzle," *Fortune,* June 23, 1997, p. 80.

CHAPTER TWO

1. Peter Senge, *The Fifth Discipline: The Art and Practice of the Learning Organization,* 1st ed. (New York: Doubleday, 1990), p. 17.
2. I. Berlin, *Against the Current: Essays in the History of Ideas* (New York: Viking Press, 1980), p. 284.

3. Howard Gardner, *Leading Minds: An Anatomy of Leadership* (New York: Basic Books, 1995), p. 144.
4. Noel M. Tichy, *The Leadership Engine* (New York: HarperBusiness, 1997), p. 180.
5. James M. Kouzes and Barry Z. Posner, *Encouraging the Heart: A Leader's Guide to Rewarding and Recognizing Others* (Jossey-Bass, 1999), p. 105.
6. R. K. Cooper and A. Sawaf, *Executive EQ* (New York: Grosset/Putnam, 1997), p. 188.
7. R. Buckman, "Schwab Becomes a Symbol for Internet Bullishness," *Wall Street Journal*, April 7, 1999, p. C2.
8. S. Branch, "The 100 Best Companies to Work For in America," *Fortune*, January 11, 1999, p. 126.
9. L. Smith, "The Future of Technology in Teaching," *USA Today*, March 2, 1999, p. 26

FROM SUSTAINING CULTURE TO CULTIVATING COMMITMENT THROUGH DIVERSITY

1. For a complete discussion, see David Armstrong, *Managing by Storying Around*, (New York: Doubleday Currency, 1992), p. 7.
2. William Sonnenschein, *Diversity Toolkit*, (Chicago: Contemporary Books, 1999), pp. 4–5.
3. David Shenk, *Data Smog* (New York: HarperCollins, 1998), p. 112.

CHAPTER THREE

1. Geoffrey Colvin, "The 50 Best Companies for Asians, Blacks, and Hispanics," *Fortune*, July 19, 1999, p. 70.
2. Petzinger, T., "The Front Lines," *Wall Street Journal*, May 25, 1999, p. B1.
3. Colvin, "The 50 Best Companies for Asians, Blacks, and Hispanics," p. 54.
4. R. Crockett, "A Web That Looks Like the World," *Business Week E. Biz.*, March 22, 1999.
5. James Traub, "The Class of Prop 209," *New York Times Magazine*, May 2, 1999, p. 45.

PART TWO

1. James Collins and Jerry Porras, *Built to Last* (New York: HarperBusiness, 1994), p. 234.

2. John Naisbitt, *Megatrends 2000* (New York: Morrow, 1990), p. 12.
3. D. Donahue, "Happiness by the Book," *USA Today*, February 11, 1999, p. 1D.
4. John L. Locke, *The De-Voicing of Society* (New York: Simon & Schuster, 1998), p. 196.
5. Robert Bruce Shaw, *Trust in the Balance: Building Successful Organizations on Results, Integrity, and Concern* (San Francisco: Jossey-Bass, 1997), p. 20.

CHAPTER FOUR

1. Q. Hardy, "A Software Star Sees Its 'Family' Culture Turn Dysfunctional," *Wall Street Journal*, May 5, 1999, p. A1.
2. Aldous Huxley, *Brave New World* (New York: Harper & Row, 1946), p. 167.
3. S. Levine and M. Crom, *The Leader in You: How to Win Friends, Influence People, and Succeed in a Changing World* (New York: Simon & Schuster, 1993), p. 27.
4. R. K. Cooper and A. Sawaf, *Executive EQ* (New York: Grosset/Putnam, 1997), p. 59.
5. James M. Kouzes and Barry Z. Posner, *The Leadership Challenge: How to Keep Getting Extraordinary Things Done in Organizations*, 2nd ed. (San Francisco: Jossey-Bass, 1995), p. 260.
6. Warren Bennis, "The Leadership Advantage," *Leader to Leader*, no. 12, Spring 1999, p. 19.
7. A. Shultz, "Surprises in the Aisles, No Services, Right? Why the Loads?" *New York Times*, January 17, 1999, Business Section, p. 9.
8. William Miller, *Quantum Quality* (New York: Quality Resources, 1993), p. 24.

FROM LIVING LEADERSHIP TO LEADERSHIP COMMUNICATION

1. James M. Kouzes and Barry Z. Posner, *The Leadership Challenge: How to Keep Getting Extraordinary Things Done in Organizations*, 2nd ed. (San Francisco: Jossey-Bass, 1995), p. 21.
2. Stevens W. Anderson (ed.), *The Great American Bathroom Book*, vol. 1 (Salt Lake City, Utah: Compact Classics, 1992), Section 3, p. A-4.

3. Terry Pearce, *Leading Out Loud: The Authentic Speaker, the Credible Leader* (San Francisco: Jossey-Bass, 1995), p. 130.

CHAPTER FIVE

1. Seth Shostak, "You Call This Progress," *Newsweek,* January 18, 1999, p. 16.
2. Edward M. Hallowell, "The Human Moment at Work," *Harvard Business Review,* January/February 1999, p. 58.
3. Hallowell, "The Human Moment at Work," p. 59.
4. Noel M. Tichy, *The Leadership Engine* (New York: HarperBusiness, 1997), p. 172.
5. Colin Powell, *My American Journey* (New York: Random House, 1995), p. 52.
6. Abraham H. Maslow, *Motivation and Personality* (New York: Harper & Row, 1954), pp. 89–91.

FROM LEADERSHIP COMMUNICATION TO GENERATING INNOVATION

1. Peter F. Drucker, "Knowledge-Worker Productivity," *California Management Review,* 1999, *41*(2), 79.
2. Karen Stephenson, "Who's Mentoring Whom?" *Forbes,* May 19, 1997.
3. Ikujiro Nonaka and N. Konno, "The Concept of 'Ba': Building a Foundation for Knowledge Creation," *California Management Review,* Spring 1998, *40*(3), 40.
4. Gary Hamel and Jim Scholes, "Strategic Innovation in the Quest for New Wealth," in Frances Hesselbein and Paul M. Cohen (eds.), *Leader to Leader: Enduring Insights on Leadership from the Drucker Foundation's Award-Winning Journal* (San Francisco: Jossey-Bass, 1999), pp. 81–94.

CHAPTER SIX

1. Clayton M. Christensen, *The Innovator's Dilemma* (Boston: Harvard Business Press, 1999), p. 162.
2. A. Kearney, "Dialogue: CEOs Face Up to the Innovation Imperative," *Executive Agenda,* March 1998, p. 32.
3. Christensen, *The Innovator's Dilemma,* p. 160.

4. Nick Imparato and Oren Harari, *Jumping the Curve: Innovation and Strategic Choice in an Age of Transition* (San Francisco: Jossey-Bass, 1994), p. 81.
5. M. Treacy and F. Wiersema, *The Discipline of Market Leaders: Choose Your Customers, Narrow Your Focus, Dominate Your Market* (Reading, Mass.: Addison-Wesley, 1995), p. 159.
6. James Collins and Jerry Porras, *Built to Last* (New York: HarperBusiness, 1994), p. 44.
7. Christensen, *The Innovator's Dilemma*, p. 173.
8. Christensen, *The Innovator's Dilemma*, pp. 161, 175.

FROM INNOVATION TO MANAGEMENT PRACTICES FOR THE INTERNET WORLD

1. See www.swatch.com, www.4time.com, and www.4watches.com.
2. Gordon MacKenzie, *Orbiting the Giant Hairball* (New York: Viking, 1998), p. 21.

PART THREE

1. N. Munk, "How Levis Trashed a Great American Brand," *Fortune*, April 12, 1999, p. 89.
2. Paul Hawken, *Growing a Business* (Don Mills, Ontario: Collins, 1987), p. 21.

CHAPTER SEVEN

1. Thomas Petzinger Jr., "The Front Lines," *Wall Street Journal*, May 25, 1999, p. B1.
2. Ester Dyson. *Release 2.0: A Design for Living in the Digital Age* (New York: Broadway Books, 1997), p. 69.
3. Chris Argyris, *Teaching Smart People How to Learn* (Cambridge, Mass.: Harvard Business School Press, 1998), p. 95.
4. Argyris, *Teaching Smart People How to Learn*, p. 92.

CHAPTER EIGHT

1. F. Warren McFarlan, "Problems in Planning the Information System," *Harvard Business Review*, March–April 1971, p. 82.

CHAPTER NINE

1. Lester Wunderman, *Being Direct: Making Advertising Pay* (New York: Random House, 1996), p. 279.
2. Philip Kotler, "The Marketing of Leadership," *Leader to Leader*, no. 11, Winter 1999, pp. 22–23.
3. Robert Lutz, *Guts: The 7 Laws of Business That Made Chrysler the World's Hottest Car Company* (New York: Wiley, 1998).
4. See *Consumer Online Report, Q1*, 1999, published on-line by bizrate.com.
5. John Caples, *Tested Advertising Methods*, 4th ed. (Englewood Cliffs, N.J.: Prentice-Hall, 1974), p. 254.
6. David Ogilvy, *Ogilvy on Advertising*, 1st American ed. (New York: Crown, 1983), p. 7.
7. E. Neuborne, "Great Ad! What's It For?" *Business Week*, July 20, 1998, Marketing, p. 118.
8. Timothy Hanrahan, "Special Report on E-commerce," *Wall Street Journal Interactive*, July 12, 1999, p. 1
9. Hanrahan, "Special Report on E-commerce," p. 1.

CHAPTER TEN

1. Morgan Anderson White Paper, "How Marketers Are Refocusing to Protect and Enhance Their Companies' Brand Assets," No. 5, 1997, p. 1.
2. Leonard Berry, *Discovering the Soul of Service: The Nine Drivers of Sustainable Business Success* (New York: Free Press, 1999), p. 210.
3. Martha Rogers, "'Clicks-and-Mortar' Initiative," *Inside Itol, Peppers and Rogers Group*, August 12, 1999, p. 1.
4. George Anders, "The View from the Top," *Wall Street Journal Almanac, Special Report on E-commerce*, July 12, 1999, p. 8.
5. Anders, "The View from the Top," p. 8.
6. Anders, "The View from the Top," p. 7.

INDEX

D

E

F

Q

R

S